LINKING, ALLIANCES, AND SHARED SPACE

THE INTERNATIONAL PSYCHOANALYSIS LIBRARY

General Editor: Leticia Glocer Fiorini

IPA Publications Committee

Leticia Glocer Fiorini (Argentina), Chair; Salman Akhtar (Philadelphia); Thierry Bokanowski (Paris); Alessandra Lemma (London); Sergio Lewkowicz (Porto Alegre); Mary Kay O'Neil (Montreal); Piers Pendred (London), Ex-officio as Director General; Cesare Sacerdoti (London), Ex-officio as Publications Director

Violence or Dialogue? Psychoanalytic Insights on Terror and Terrorism
    edited by Sverre Varvin & Vamik D. Volkan

Pluralism and Unity? Methods of Research in Psychoanalysis
    edited by Marianne Leuzinger-Bohleber, Anna Ursula Dreher, & Jorge Canestri

Truth, Reality, and the Psychoanalyst: Latin American Contributions to Psychoanalysis
    edited by Sergio Lewkowicz & Silvia Flechner

Verdad, realidad y el psicoanalista: Contribuciones Latinoamericanas al Psicoanálisis
    edited by Sergio Lewkowicz & Silvia Flechner

Resonance of Suffering: Countertransference in Non-neurotic Structures
    edited by André Green

The Geography of Meanings:
Psychoanalytic Perspectives on Place, Space, Land, and Dislocation
    edited by Maria Teresa Savio Hooke & Salman Akhtar

LINKING, ALLIANCES, AND SHARED SPACE
Groups and the Psychoanalyst

René Kaës

Foreword by
Lewis A. Kirshner

translated by
Andrew Weller

The International Psychoanalysis Library

**International
Psychoanalytical
Association**

LONDON

First published in 2007 by
The International Psychoanalytical Association
Broomhills
Woodside Lane
London N12 8UD
United Kingdom

British Library Cataloguing in Publication Data

A C.I.P. for this book is available from the British Library

ISBN: 978-1-905888-04-7

10 9 8 7 6 5 4 3 2 1

Produced for the IPA by Communication Crafts

Printed in Great Britain

www.ipa.org.uk

CONTENTS

THE INTERNATIONAL PSYCHOANALYSIS LIBRARY
IPA Publications Committee   vii

ABOUT THE AUTHOR   ix

PREFACE   xi

FOREWORD
Lewis A. Kirshner   xiii

Introduction   1

1   How the question of the group
        was posed in psychoanalysis   17

2   The epistemological problem
        of the group in psychoanalysis   37

3   The group as a psychoanalytic situation   53

4   Clinical psychoanalytic work in the group situation   69

v

5 The group as an intrapsychic formation:
       psychic groupality and internal groups   93

6 Forms and processes of group psychic reality:
       the group psychic apparatus   109

7 Associative processes in groups   135

8 Phoric functions:
       speech-bearer, symptom-bearer, dream-bearer   157

9 The common and shared dream space:
       dream polyphony   179

10 Unconscious alliances   205

11 The subject of the unconscious,
       the subject of linking   231

Epilogue   245

REFERENCES AND BIBLIOGRAPHY   249

INDEX   257

THE INTERNATIONAL PSYCHOANALYSIS LIBRARY

IPA Publications Committee

The International Psychoanalysis Library, published under the aegis of the International Psychoanalytical Association, is the product of the editorial policy of the IPA Publications Committee: to serve the interests of the membership and increase the awareness of the relevance of the discipline in related professional and academic circles, and to do so through a continuity of publications so that the benefits of psychoanalytic research can be shared across a wide audience.

The focus of the Library is on the scientific developments of today throughout the IPA, with an emphasis within the discipline on clinical, technical, and theoretical advances; empirical, conceptual, and historical research projects; the outcome of investigations conducted by IPA committees and working parties; selected material arising from conferences and meetings; and investigations at the interface with social and cultural expressions.

We are very grateful to René Kaës for his generosity in giving us the opportunity to publish this volume, a landmark of his work. It is a fitting tribute to him that simultaneous to our original English version, editions in Italian and French are also published. The previous Publications Committee's commissioning of this work is acknowledged, and we are glad to have completed this project.

Leticia Glocer Fiorini
Series Editor

ABOUT THE AUTHOR

René Kaës, Doctor of Psychology (PhD) and Arts and Human Sciences (Doctorat d'Etat en Lettres et Sciences humaines), is Professor Emeritus of the Université Lumière Lyon 2; a psychoanalyst; past President of the Cercle d'Etudes Françaises pour la Formation et la Recherche: Approche Psychanalytique du groupe, du psychodrame, de l'institution (CEFFRAP); Member holder of the International Association of Group Psychotherapy and of the French Society of Group of Psychoanalytical Psychotherapy; Member founder of the European Association of Group Transcultural Analyse; Member of various French and other scientific societies; and Scientific director of the Collection *Inconscient et Culture* (Paris: Dunod). He is the author of more than 16 books, including, most recently, *Les théories psychanalytiques du groupe* (1999); *Le psychodrame psychanalytique dans les groupes* (1999); *La polyphonie du rêve* (2002), with C. Chabert, J. Lanouzière, & A. Schniewind; *Figures de la dépression* (2004); *Os espaços psíquicos communs e partilhados. Transmisão e negatividade* (2005).

PREFACE

The IPA Publications Committee suggested that I write this book with the idea that my research could contribute to a sensitive debate in the domain of contemporary psychoanalysis, whose frontiers are now more open. I accepted this proposition with gratitude.

The question that was put to me attests to this openness: "How does the psychoanalytic approach to groups concern psychoanalysts?" The whole question amounts, in fact, to understanding how the individual subject—that is, the one we are dealing with on the couch—is also a subject whose unconscious is held and shaped by the intersubjective links or ties of which he is a member, by the unconscious alliances that precede him and that he enters into for his own benefit, and by the common psychic spaces that he shares with others. The psychoanalytic approach to the group is one of the ways of posing this question and of finding some sort of answer to it. But in order to do this, one must first understand how a group functions and, furthermore, how, within the unconscious alliances that are contracted in it, its own specific psychic reality is formed.

The book is thus addressed to a wider audience of readers than that of practising group analysts. After a few introductory chapters, I have chosen to organize my exposition around a *first* clinical situation. Its numerous facets allow for different levels of reading and contribute material that is favourable for the analysis of certain fundamental processes, from the standpoint of both the common and the shared psychic reality that specifies this group, and from that which is proper to each subject.

Given that my research is anchored in a rather typically European cultural and epistemological context, I felt it was appropriate to provide the reader with some indications as to the issues and concepts that are a source of debate within the psychoanalytic community, and on which the psychoanalytic approach to groups can shed new light: in particular, the question of subjectivation and intersubjectivity.

This book could not have been written without the support and encouragement of Emma Piccioli and Cesare Sacerdoti, both of whom I wish to thank warmly. I am equally grateful to Christine Anzieu, André Missenard, and Jean Henriet for having given my first drafts a close reading.

I would also like to thank Andrew Weller warmly for his remarkable work of translation: his pertinent questions and suggestions have contributed to improving my text.

FOREWORD

Lewis A. Kirshner

The publication of René Kaës's monograph, *Linking, Alliances, and Shared Space: The Psychoanalytic Approach to Groups and the Psychoanalyst,* addresses a dual gap between English-speaking and French psychoanalysis. First, as is well known, writings by many influential French authors have not been translated, even at present, and important concepts remain unfamiliar to analysts within each tradition. But, perhaps more important, the development of theory and practice has diverged in important respects in the two spheres. In particular, French psychoanalysts have made extensive studies of group phenomena, including the clinical use of psychodrama and theories of transgenerational transmission, neither of which has made an equivalent impact on psychoanalytic practice in many countries. In this new distillation of his lifetime in research on groups and families,

Lewis A. Kirshner is a training and supervising analyst at the Boston Psychoanalytic Society and Institute and Associate Clinical Professor of Psychiatry at Harvard Medical School, Boston, Massachusetts. For many years he served as Affiliate Professor in the Department of Psychology at Université Lumière, Lyon 2. He is the author of "Intersubjective Transmission: Families, Groups, and Culture: The Work of Rene Kaës" (*Journal of the American Psychoanalytic Association,* Autumn 2006), as well as several articles dealing with intersubjectivity in psychoanalytic theory and practice.

René Kaës shows how concepts deriving from this work address
important issues in contemporary psychoanalysis, notably the problems posed by the theoretical perspective of intersubjectivity and its
therapeutic applications.

Kaës speaks of the false opposition between the individual and
the group in psychoanalysis as part of its history and self-definition.
"It is thus not surprising", he writes, "that this critical tension, which
has given rhythm to the entire history of psychoanalysis and kept it
alive, was renewed when psychoanalytic practices were extended to
the treatment of parent–child relationships, couples, families, and
group relations." Although many authors have attempted to develop
models that could bridge this divide—for example, in the area of psychoanalytic family therapy—very few institutes include this material
in their curricula. This omission deprives candidates and teachers of
an important source of data in learning and revising psychoanalytic
models.

One important aspect of Kaës's approach concerns the dual
origins of subjectivity in an individual unconscious drawing both
from somatic sources and intersubjective links to the group. His
work suggests alternatives to the current polarization in psychoanalytic thought that opposes an intrapsychic, drive-oriented model of
mental functioning to a relational, interactive one. The notion that
psychoanalytic theory has as its object the functioning of a "mental
apparatus", drawing on biological forces within the organism and
mediating between pleasure-seeking drives and survival instincts,
seems to locate the truth of the human subject in a deep stratum
where soma and psyche have their interface. Of course, this formulation is in some sense inescapable, since the underpinnings of psychic
life depend on the hardware of the human brain. At the same time,
as Freud reminded us in "On Narcissism" (1914c), human existence
draws upon two sources: the biological products of an evolutionary
process based on reproduction and survival and its subjective position as a link between generations. The nature of this dual inscription is Kaës's focus: how can we understand the human psyche as
deriving simultaneously from individual somatic roots and from the
social world into which the human is born as the carrier of specific
unconscious meanings?

Kaës sees his work as taking up Freud's suggestions about group
psychology through a systematic application of psychoanalytic theory
to settings involving a plurality of participants. "The problem", he

states, "is one of constructing a new psychoanalytic object using an adequate methodology." In this inquiry, Kaës follows in the tradition of Didier Anzieu, Foulkes, and Bion, among many others. His research has involved psychotherapy and training exercises in small groups and clinical work with families. Individuals seem to carry an almost universal motivation to participate in groups, he observes, in part to affirm a unique sense of identity and selfhood, even as the subject is inevitably threatened by the possibility of non-acceptance or disconfirmation by the group. This fundamental insight, taken from Hegelian phenomenology, has been succinctly summarized by Arnold Modell (1984), who wrote that man's narcissistic dilemma is his need for recognition by others, but that the encounter with the other can also shatter the self. Kaës explores how this basic dilemma relates to intersubjectivity: the insight that we depend on others in every conceivable way for the creation and establishment of our subjectivity, but at the same time we require elaborate defensive compromises to withstand the disruptive gaze of others.

The philosophically derived term, "intersubjectivity" has come into vogue in American psychoanalysis in recent years, but its usage too often seems to lack a deeper conceptualization of the subject as more than a monadic relational self-functioning within a social field. In particular, the current interpersonalized version of intersubjectivity bypasses the elaboration of Freud's insight that the subject is a link in a chain, a human chain of transgenerational narratives and inscriptions. The diverse transferences generated within group and family therapy situations, Kaës argues, commonly restage these basic conditions of subjectivation in the shared unconscious space of the collectivity. In his clinical examples from psychoanalytic groups, he shows how the individual participant deploys transference objects transmitted and received in his intersubjective history through what he calls "diffraction–distribution" of transferences between members and leaders. Analytically oriented work with families likewise discloses such shared fantasy structures, which may be repeated in several generations.

The phenomenon of shared transference objects in a group is a dramatic illustration of the mechanism of interpsychic transmission, found only in a partial form in individual analyses. For Kaës, the group represents a privileged site—a kind of clinical laboratory— where profound questions concerning Laplanche and Pontalis's primal phantasies about origins, sexuality, and gender are regularly raised. While Laplanche emphasized enigmatic signifiers implanted by parents, Kaës seems to go further in developing the Lacanian insight (built, of course, on Freud's most speculative writings) of specific inscriptions and symbolic debt carried across the generations. Kaës provides many rich descriptions of how members of a group tap the same sources in playing out these unconscious legacies through their mutual identifications and shared phantasies. He has further elaborated this notion in his description of the double umbilicus of the dream, drawing on both "mycelia" of the individual's "private" unconscious and the intersubjective field of the groups to which he belongs.

There is without a doubt a mysterious quality to the phenomenology of shared unconscious space in the examples offered by Kaës. The mechanisms behind the metaphors and symbols revealed in the discourse of the group are unclear, and perhaps we still lack the requisite concepts for them.[1] His theorizing from clinical phenomenology runs counter in many ways to the contemporary discomfort with highly abstract psychoanalytic concepts in favour of a neurological reductionism that seeks to naturalize subjective experience in terms of simple physical–chemical processes. Kaës understands that psychoanalysis needs to pay closer attention to intersubjective phenomena as they unfold in group and family contexts to support its unique perspective. The complexity of the human subject involves more than the products of neurochemical mechanisms in his head (the subject is not the brain). Psychoanalysis, we are coming to understand, has as its unique object the field of intersubjective functioning and the complex interaction of transpersonal meanings and signs, even as science attempts to work out the physical mechanisms and underpinnings. If it is to have an important conceptual and therapeutic contribution to make at this moment in its history, it may well be in pursuing the research inaugurated and cogently summarized in this volume by René Kaës.

NOTE

1. The work by neuroscience researchers on the "mirror neuron" systems of the brain may offer some answers to this question, a problem for psychoanalysts since Freud first spoke about unconscious communication in *The Ego and the Id* (1923b) (see, for example, the comprehensive review by Gallese, Eagle, & Migone, 2007).

LINKING, ALLIANCES, AND SHARED SPACE

Introduction

The research that I am presenting in this book is shot through with a constant process of questioning that forms the leading thread: I have tried to discover how the psyche of the individual subject is formed, transformed, or alienated through the various modalities of the intersubjective links that precede him, which he establishes, and which finally constitute him, in a decisive manner, as subject of the unconscious. The unconscious alliances that are formed between the subjects of a linking configuration (a couple, a family, a group, etc.) are, from this point of view, powerful interfaces between the psychic reality of the link and that of each subject considered in his singularity.

These researches are most certainly not foreign to the preoccupations of Freud, who, in a speculative mode, outlined several of their directions. But the method of the couch did not allow him to develop them satisfactorily, insofar as it does not give direct access to the formations and psychic processes proper to the configurations of intersubjective links or ties, even though the formation of unconscious alliances is not foreign to the psychoanalytic experience of the treatment. Nonetheless, the transference–countertransferential field cannot be reduced to such a configuration, and though it gives a glimpse of it, it is limited to registering certain effects of it in a subject considered in his singularity, under conditions in which the psychoanalyst presents himself to the analysand not as a set of other realities, but as an imaginary or symbolic representative of his objects and internal characters.

Different from the individual treatment setting [*dispositif*] are those settings in which several subjects encounter one another in the presence of a psychoanalyst within a precise frame [*cadre*], governed by the psychoanalytic method. Since the second half of the nineteenth century, psychoanalytic work in groups and with groups has made it possible to characterize what I designate as the unconscious psychic reality specific to plurisubjective configurations such as groups, families, and couples. An important work of theorization has been carried out on the basis of these configurations, and most of these constructions have been centred on the description of the formations and processes of the psychic reality proper to these configurations. Pichon-Rivière, Bion, Foulkes, Anzieu, and a few others have each conceived a group theory by considering it as a specific entity.

My work has been to try to articulate the psychic reality of the group and that of the individual subject in an attempt to account for the role played by the former in the formation of the latter, and for the way in which the subject is formed in intersubjectivity as subject of the unconscious.

Thus stated, what is at stake in this research goes beyond the objective of a psychoanalysis applied to groups. Although clinical work has an important place in this book, I have not written a treatise on group psychoanalytic psychotherapy. The group psychoanalytic method is undoubtedly of great therapeutic interest, but it is also a path of access to a fundamental problem: namely, the unconscious consistency of intersubjective linking, that of the subject's unconscious functioning in linking, and that of the subject of the unconscious inasmuch as he is a subject of linking. A certain conception of the unconscious emerges from the study of the relations between these three spaces of psychic reality.

This is an ambitious and complex programme, involving postulates, presuppositions, and hypotheses that will have to be made explicit. But it will be accepted that if we succeed in founding these hypotheses in both praxis and theory, and in opening up some pathways between these three psychic spaces, then it is likely that certain contents of psychoanalytic knowledge and the limits of its practice will, in turn, have to be re-evaluated.

Accordingly, the questions treated in this book should hold our attention as psychoanalysts, whether we are using the couch setting or/and other settings adapted to the analysis of linking configurations. Let us now consider how these questions have a meaning for psychoanalysts and how they find their place in psychoanalysis.

The three pillars of the psyche

The human psyche rests on three main pillars: infantile sexuality, speech, and intersubjective linking. This is the basic postulate of my research, and I suppose that many psychoanalysts will be able to share it. I must add that these three foundational pillars are closely interrelated: the long initial dependence of the newborn baby, owing to its prematurity at birth, is their geometrical locus; it influences his sexuality, his links (or ties), and his access to speech and language. Speech and language come to the *infans* (prior to the age of speaking) marked by the repression of his infantile sexuality and by the intersubjective conditions in which his first environment—the mother—brings them to him by transmitting to him her own unconscious contents and her own repression: these conditions are simultaneously both subjective (the mother's mind) and intersubjective (the encounter between the mother's mind and that of the *infans*). Correlatively, intersubjective linking is inscribed in sexuality and in speech, and it marks them with its effects. Sexuality, speech, and linking contribute in a distinct and fundamental manner to the formation of the unconscious of the subject and to the construction of his I [*Je*]. At the same time, these three pillars contribute to the formation of the unconscious psychic reality of intersubjective linking.

Freud's entire work is punctuated by propositions that do not limit knowledge of the unconscious to the sole dimension of sexuality, even though he placed the latter at the heart of his discovery and equipped himself with a paradigmatic method for exploring its consistency and for linking it up with the other pillar: namely, that of speech. The idea that others constitute, for the mind of each individual, an object, a model, a helper, and an opponent (Freud, 1921c, p. 69), that "an individual's fate depends on his relations to

other people" (1933a, p. 167), is also an insistent proposition, but
it belongs to the speculative construction of psychoanalytic theory.
It is nonetheless a strong hypothesis, for which the corresponding
theoretico–clinical concept is identification. However, with this concept alone, as with that of object-relations, we cannot construct a
psychoanalytic theory of linking for the reason that, in linking, the
other is encountered in his concreteness and cannot be reduced to
the internal world of his subjects. In order to validate the hypothesis of the three pillars of the psyche and the idea that links are
constructed within an original psychic reality that would not exist
without the intersubjective encounter, it was indispensable to test
them clinically within a setting appropriate to these objects and in
conformity with the methodological requirements of psychoanalysis.
Henceforth, psychoanalysts could feel concerned by group psychoanalytic work for at least three reasons.

The contribution of psychoanalytic work with groups
and the subject within the group to the treatment of
"otherwise inaccessible" psychic sufferings

One of the first reasons concerns the specific contributions of psychoanalytic work in plurisubjective[1] situations to the treatment of
psychic sufferings and psychopathologies that are "almost inaccessible in any other way".[2] Approaching these contributions in terms of
nosography is relatively incidental compared with the more general
factors that contribute decisively to producing them.

    The interest that psychoanalysts have shown since the middle of
the last century in the practical value of the group as a setting for
doing psychoanalytic work, and in the intelligibility of the processes
that occur there, has its place within a very precise cultural field.
To simplify: it could be said that modernity, through the ruptures it
introduces into the silent settings on which psychic life is based—
membership in communities, shared beliefs that provide certitudes,
alliances based on fundamental prohibitions—has made it necessary
to think about the *metapsychic*[3] functions of the group. By "metapsychic" I am referring to the formations and functions that surround
each subject's psychic life. They are situated *in the background* of the
individual psyche, *between* it and the larger frameworks—cultural,
social, political, religious—supporting them. The deregulation, the

failures or deficiencies of these metapsychic functions directly affect the structuring and development of each individual's psychic life. I have come to think that three major sets of failures are involved.

The first set concerns the failures or deficiencies of the inter-subjective mechanisms of the stimulus barrier [*Reizschutz*] and of repression in *the structuring of the supports of instinctual life*. Instead of the formation of stable and reliable internal objects, split and non-subjectivized formations develop, which are unfavourable to the processes of symbolization and sublimation. Intense narcissistic suf-fering is at the root of the antisocial behaviours that develop in these conditions. These failures affect the conditions of the formation of both the unconscious and the preconscious.

The second is constituted by failures in the formation processes of basic structuring *identifications* and *alliances*. These alliances go beyond the framework of intersubjective linking: they are in a *meta* position in relation to them. They consist in the pacts instituting the major taboos (prohibition against murdering a fellow human being, cannibalism, incest), in what Freud described as the shared or com-mon renunciation of the direct satisfaction of instinctual aims, and in what Piera Castoriadis-Aulagnier (1975) theorized as the narcis-sistic contract. These alliances form the frameworks or the intersub-jective bases of subjectivity; they are the metapsychic conditions and safeguards of the space in which "the I [*Je*] can come into being". They ensure the transmission of psychic life between generations. Their deficiency or their failure bespeak of the regression of con-tractual forms of linking towards power struggles that benefit groups that hold the power to define, in an arbitrary and violent manner, social norms, the place of each individual, order, and the dominant values. They lead to those who are subjected to them suffering from radical psychic and social forms of deterioration.

The third set concerns failures in the processes of *transformation* and *mediation*. The most fragile elements in any living organization are intermediary formations and connecting processes. In psychic life, they are the conditions of possibility of the work of symboliza-tion and the formation of alterity, but also the capacity to love, to work, to play, and to dream. These formations and these processes are the ones that are most threatened by crises affecting the meta-psychic safeguards. The major consequence of their failure is the collapse and disconnection of the preconscious, the crushing of the capacity to think by the collapse of verbal presentations. The work of the preconscious is always closely associated with the activity of symbolization and with the construction of meaning in intersubjective linking.

The concept of intersubjectivity and the formation of the subject in linking, unconscious alliances, and common and shared psychic spaces

A second reason for psychoanalysts to feel concerned by the psychoanalytic approach to the group and to the subject in the group resides in its contribution to the issue of intersubjectivity. This question interests the majority of contemporary psychoanalysts, but it also sets them in opposition, depending on their cultural traditions and theoretical references.

It is not my plan to make a review of the question of intersubjectivity, but I must make it clear how I have worked with this concept.[4] I use this notion in its European sense and context. By intersubjectivity I mean not a system of behavioural interactions between individuals communicating their feelings through empathy, but the experience and space of psychic reality that is specified by their relations as subjects inasmuch as they are subjects of the unconscious. Intersubjectivity is what is shared by these subjects, who are formed and bound to each other by their reciprocal subjections—structuring or alienating—to the constitutive mechanisms of the unconscious: common repressions and denials, shared phantasies and signifiers, unconscious wishes and the fundamental taboos that organize them. (For a fuller development of the question of the subject, intersubjectivity, and subjectivation, see Kaës, 1993, 1998, 2006.)

The development of non-psychoanalytic aspects of intersubjectivity stands in contrast to the weakness of the elaboration of this question in psychoanalysis, with a few notable exceptions.[5] In the field of post-Freudian psychoanalysis, several theories of intersubjectivity coexist. In the wake of post-Hegelianism, Jacques Lacan was one of the first to introduce the concept, privileging its effects of alienation on a subject essentially subjected to the desire of the other, the latter being but an inadequate representative of the big Other [*grand Autre*]. Lacan only describes the psychic reality that is produced in and through intersubjective linking, with the aim of focusing on its imaginary consistency. His critique of the group results from this.

Even if the concept of intersubjectivity does not appear as such in Piera Castoriadis-Aulagnier's work, she nonetheless pays assiduous attention to these conjunctions of subjectivities. This preoccupation can be seen in three important notions: the narcissistic contract concluded between the subject and "the ensemble in which the I can come into being" and its identificatory function; the function of speech-bearer carried out by the mother who accompanies the psychic experiences of the *infans* and the structuring of his psyche by prohibitions; states of alienation and the collective treatment of the desire for self-alienation.

In order to take into consideration the processes and formations of intersubjectivity as a whole, it is necessary to resort to another logic of psychic processes. The logic of internal processes and formations needs to be linked up with the logic of *correlations of subjectivities*, a logic of conjunction and disjunction, the formula of which might be stated in the following way: "Not one without the other, nor without the whole which constitutes them and contains them; one without the other, but within the whole uniting them." This formula maintains that we cannot *not* be in intersubjectivity. This means, as Winnicott thought in relation to the baby, that the subject manifests himself and exists only in his relation to the other, to more than one other [*plus d'un autre*].[6] This also means that the process of "becoming I", of the Freudian *Ich werden,* as well as the stumbling points and impasses of this becoming, is traced in the intersubjective relation with the other: this is true for the child, for becoming a man, becoming a woman, or becoming a father or a mother.

Intersubjectivity is not only the constitutive part of the subject held in the subjectivity of the other or more than one other. It is constructed in a psychic space specific to each configuration of linking. This amounts to saying that the question of intersubjectivity consists in the recognition and articulation of two partially heterogeneous psychic spaces, each endowed with their own logic.[7]

Understood in this way, the question of intersubjectivity gives us access to psychic sufferings and to forms of contemporary psychopathology that can only be understood, analysed, and relieved by being linked up the with the values and functions that they have acquired or continue to acquire for an other, for several others, and finally for the group of which the subject is a constituted and constituting part.

To sum up my position, I would say that the issue of intersubjectivity opens up a central question of psychoanalysis: it concerns the
intersubjective conditions of the formation of the unconscious and
of the subject of the unconscious. In these conditions, I call intersubjectivity the dynamic structure of the psychic space between two or
several subjects. This space includes specific processes, formations,
and experience, the effects of which have a bearing on the accession
of the subjects of the unconscious, and on their becoming I at the
heart of a We. This definition is very far removed from a perspective
that reduces intersubjectivity to interactional phenomena.

The epistemological transcendence of the opposition between individual and group

There is a third reason for interesting ourselves in the links between
the formations and processes of psychic reality proper to the individual subject and those of the group. Epistemological in order, it
concerns the field of objects that psychoanalysis sets out to study by
means of its specific method. It must be admitted that these objects
have never been limited to the exclusive study of the individual psyche, even if the method of access to knowledge of the unconscious
was created from the paradigmatic situation of the individual treatment. The principal basis of psychoanalytic knowledge is grounded
in this situation, but it has always been confronted, at a speculative
level or in the mode of its applications, with more wide-ranging objects and with bodies of knowledge constituted in other disciplines,
such as biology, linguistics, ethnology, and social psychology.

Among the problems that arise when one tries to think about the
articulation between the individual subject and the group in the field
proper to psychoanalysis, the opposition between the individual and
the group crops up regularly. In my opinion, it is a false problem,
and it is important to understand that the attachment to this opposition arises from several sources. One of them is historically and cul-
turally associated with the confrontation of Western thought with the
increased power of the urbanized and industrialized masses in the
second half of the nineteenth century. It led many European think-
ers to develop conceptions capable of accounting for the specific
forces and formations that organize the masses and institutions, and
which determined their madness and their deviations. The masses

are crazy and drive the individual crazy. Tarde, Le Bon, and Durkheim, Weber, and Canetti, but also Freud and Moreno on different grounds, took part in this movement. It was also necessary to account for the specific role that small groups could play as a regulating variable between the individual and the masses, and as a locus of specific processes. Although he was among the first to contribute the notion of the group mind [*Gruppenpsyche*], Freud was not interested in it at this level of psychosocial organization. It was Kurt Lewin and a few others who, later on, and with other methods and postulates, accounted for group dynamics by conceiving of groups as specific entities. It is striking that these preoccupations for the masses and for the group appeared at the same time as individualistic myths and ideologies began to establish themselves. The effects of rupture that modernity created in the continuities between the group, society as a whole, and individuals were translated essentially by an opposition of the individual to the mass, institutions, and the group.

Freud transcended this opposition, but not without difficulty, for it touched on the initial epistemological task of psychoanalysis. In order to constitute its object and to recognize the strong and disruptive identity that was forcing itself upon it, psychoanalysis treated the unconscious, and the psychic reality it generates, within the limits of intrapsychic space and of its accessibility by means of the individual treatment. The model of the individual treatment is based on the model of the dream, a paradigm of intrapsychic space and its objects. If this epistemological division called for rigorous methodological congruency, by the same token it placed outside its field any object situated outside the *first*, intrapsychic space.

Although speculative thought discovered that the theoretical field of psychoanalysis extended beyond this space—the works of "applied psychoanalysis" of the first psychoanalysts are evidence of this—the need to safeguard the practice of the classical treatment on the couch and the transmission of psychoanalysis against deviant practices, or practices feared as such, forced itself very quickly on the group of pioneers.

This fear, and the accusations of bad intentions that nourished it, were manifested notably with regard to the group: they were a constant feature in the psychoanalytic movement, both with respect to Freud when Burrow suggested that the practice of psychoanalysis be extended to groups (see Burrow, 1927; Ruitenbeek, 1966), and with respect to Klein when she warned Bion to renounce his interest in groups; and also with respect to Lacan, the great denouncer of the obscenity that the imaginary effects of the group establish and maintain.

These positions were not only measures aimed at preserving the identity of the psychoanalyst, the institutions of psychoanalysis, and the orthodoxy of the theories that it had founded concerning the exploration of the unconscious and the treatment of the internal conflicts of an individual subject. And it is true that to constitute the group as a setting suitable for psychoanalytic work, to think of it as a space where the unconscious produces specific effects that this time it was a matter not of denouncing but of studying, to conceive of their consequences in the intrapsychic space and in the formation of the subject of the unconscious, was to run the risk of introducing another paradigm into the epistemology of psychoanalysis. But taking this risk was also to open up the frontiers of psychoanalysis itself, as was the case for the psychoanalysis of children and of psychotic or borderline patients.

Taking this risk also means gearing psychoanalytic listening to group effects that have, since the foundation of psychoanalysis, been propagated in its institutions, in its groups, and in the transmission of psychoanalysis itself.

It is now clear that the opposition between individual and group is sustained by several sorts of issues. The epistemological debate is nourished by several centres of resistance—epistemophilic and institutional—to gaining knowledge of the group effects of the unconscious. It can serve as a lever of research.

Notwithstanding these resistances and their tactical expressions, the opposition between individual and group was never really upheld at a fundamental level by Freud. In the language of his epoch, he formulated the first broad outlines for overcoming this opposition with concepts constructed from the situation of the individual treatment.

Three key moments in this process may be identified here. The first appeared as early as *Totem and Taboo* (1912–13) with the hypothesis [*die Annahme*] of a collective mind [*einer Massenpsyche*]—a notion that describes both a specific psychic reality and a continuum with the psyche of individuals who compose the group. This notion was characterized more precisely as group mind (or group soul) [*Gruppenpsyche, Gruppenseele*] in *Group Psychology and the Analysis of the Ego* (1921c).

The second moment followed closely on the first: in 1914 Freud wrote, in "On Narcissism: An Introduction" (1914c), that the individual leads a twofold existence: he serves his own purposes and the other as a link in a chain, a beneficiary, a servant, and an heir. In this same text, Freud notes that a child's narcissism is grounded in his parents' unfulfilled wishful dreams. This remark may be read as a consequence of this twofold existence. It can be seen, then, that Freud is speaking not only of the individual, with his bodily and biological roots—it is a matter of the subject insofar as he is subjected to a psychic order that constitutes him: namely, the unconscious desire of those who precede him.

This first proposition implies, in fact, that the "individual's" psychic life is determined on two counts, one internal and the other external, both probably being interdependent; but the question is not posed directly in these terms. This proposition has gone more or less unheeded by virtue of the fact that the opposition between the individual and the group has persisted so strongly in psychoanalytic culture, maintaining by the same token great misgivings about introducing the "other", and more precisely the group, as one of the terms of the formation of the subject.

The third moment came in the Introduction to *Group Psychology and the Analysis of the Ego* (1921c). This Introduction is particularly precious for us: it announces that "in the individual's [*der Einzelne*] psychic life, someone else [*der Andere*] is invariably involved as a model, as an object, as a helper, as an opponent; and so, from the very first, individual psychology in this extended but entirely justifiable sense of the words, is at the same time a social psychology" (p. 69). If we admit that what Freud is speaking about is even more valid for the subject than for the individual, then we have in this text one of the founding statements of an intersubjective approach to the subject, as well as the hypothesis that the others as a whole together construct a *Gruppenpsyche*.

Though we have acquired from Freud himself the premises of a way of thinking that is searching for this passage between the individual subject and the group, these openings have nonetheless remained speculative. For the over-determined reasons that I have supposed, they were not tested clinically within a setting that was appropriate and congruent with the methodological requirements arising from the paradigmatic situation of the treatment of neurotic adults. It was only later—more than two-thirds of a century ago now—that psychoanalysts worked with group settings (then with families and couples). They then built models and concepts to account for the consistency and modalities of the psychic reality that they discovered.

An epistemological debate could have opened up at this time, not only because these concepts and models require the founding hypotheses of psychoanalysis to be revisited, but also because they call for a critical examination of the methodological conditions that surround our conceptions of the unconscious. However, nothing of the sort happened, and, to the best of my knowledge, no one has wondered why. It is thus time to engage in this debate concerning its decisive epistemological question: namely, how, with what the psychoanalytic approach to the group and the subject within the group has taught us, are we to think about the relations between the construction of the theory of psychoanalysis, its fundamental object, and the method that gives access to its knowledge and its processes of transformation. It is to be hoped that the specifically psychoanalytic issues that are at stake will appear more clearly at the end of this study.

***

I hope that I have begun to show how knowledge of the psychic reality that specifies groups within a psychoanalytic framework concerns psychoanalysts. I have distinguished three main reasons: (1) to describe the experience of the unconscious that such set-ups or arrangements make possible; (2) to conduct the treatment of the psychic sufferings that are formed in intersubjective links, alliances, and psychic spaces, and which the individual treatment can only treat through their effects in a subject considered in his singularity; and (3) to elaborate the epistemological and methodological questions that this practice engenders. The aim of this book is to develop these propositions and to throw into sharper relief the specifically psychoanalytic issues at stake in them.

The first four chapters are intended to present the general framework of the psychoanalytic approach to groups. It will first be necessary to describe the various problems that are posed by extending the field of investigation and practices of psychoanalysis. I then retrace some significant stages in the development of interest in the group within the psychoanalytic movement. Then I define the dimensions specific to a group psychoanalytic setting [*dispositif*] and situation.

Finally, the reader is given a substantial idea of the processes and formations of subjective and intersubjective psychic reality based on clinical work with a group within a psychoanalytic setting, which will form the main thread of the subsequent conceptual elaborations.

On these foundations and in the course of the six following chapters, I describe the main elements of a psychoanalytic model of the group and of the subject within the group. This model distinguishes and articulates three levels of psychic reality in which the effects of the unconscious are manifested. The first describes the group as an intrapsychic formation: the concepts of internal groups and of "psychic groupality" account for this. The second level considers the psychic reality of the group; the latter is conceived as a specific formation which at once precedes the subject and is constructed by means of the combining and adjusting of the psyches of its members and acquires autonomy in relation to them. The concepts of group psychic apparatus, unconscious alliances, common dream space, shared phantasies, joint symptoms, associative chain, and group thinking describe these formations and processes. The third level deals with processes and formations, but also with the people who form a link between the group and the members of the group, and who manifest themselves in different ways, notably in the phoric functions of speech-bearer, symptom-bearer, dream-bearer, or ideal-bearer.

When these propositions have been set out, we will be able to return to the central question that concerns us as psychoanalysts: namely, of understanding that the subject of the unconscious is inescapably part of an intersubjective set of subjects of the unconscious. The subject of the unconscious is a subject of linking. Consequently, it is not enough for the aim of psychoanalysis to be stated as "where Id was, there I [*Je*] shall be"; it is also necessary for I [*Je*] to extricate itself from the structuring and alienating formations of the group in order to come to terms with itself as heir of its history woven in intersubjectivity.

NOTES

1. I am referring essentially to the group setting conducted according to the requirements of the psychoanalytic method; concerning the criteria of this method, see chapter 3.

2. I am adopting here the terms used by Freud (1923a, p. 235) when

he defines psychoanalysis as "a procedure for the investigation of mental processes which are almost inaccessible in any other way".

3. *Meta*: when this preposition forms part of certain concepts, it indicates a change of locus, condition, or place (metaphor, metabolism, metathesis) or a succession in time or in space (*meta ta phusika*: Metaphysics comes *after* Physics in Aristotle; on the same model: metamathematics, metapsychology, etc.). It is this second sense that interests me, for it indicates that we have to think retrospectively about the background settings that surround the processes or formations that we observe, and which thus pre-exist them. It could be admitted that the level *meta* denotes a level of determination of these phenomena. It is in this sense that I speak of *meta*psychic organizations: the group space is in a *meta*position in relation to individual psychic space.

4. It is worth recalling that the concept of intersubjectivity was first constructed with the philosophical and psychological problems of consciousness and of the subject in his relations with the recognition of others. The sources of inspiration for these problems are diverse; they have arisen from phenomenology, the linguistics of enunciation, the psychology of interaction (with G. H. Mead), and ethnology. When the ethnologist and psychoanalyst G. Devereux discovered in the 1930s that he was "an other for these others" whose civilization he was trying to get to know, he opened up a new perspective on the question. These modern approaches have some antecedents: well before Hegel and Husserl, before the blossoming of the philosophies of recognition and reciprocity with Buber and Levinas, the alterity of the other was thought about in connection with internal alterity. Montaigne was ahead of us by several centuries when he wrote that "there is as much difference between us and ourselves as between us and others".

This intuition of an internal difference, of a gap between self and self at the heart of the subject, contains the premises of Rimbaud's modern maxim: "I is an Other." This is most definitely an intrasubjective formula revealing a divided subject, but one that remains to be combined with a counterpoint necessary for founding any form of intersubjective reciprocity: the experience that I is an Other is based on this prior experience that the Other is an I for another I. One may justifiably consider that this reciprocity, symmetrical or asymmetrical, is a late acquisition both in the species and for each subject. It remains the case that this conception of alterity (otherness), which involves the vicissitudes of internal alterity, defines intersubjectivity in a much less operative manner than does interactionism, which essentially refers to behavioural loops or, with Stolorow and Atwood (1992), to contextualism.

5. One may wonder why psychoanalysts have long remained in the background of this debate. Several answers may be considered. It may have been feared that posing intersubjectivity as a condition of possibility of psychic life would entail the risk of diverting the field of psychoanalysis away from the intrapsychic towards the relational or towards the interactional. This fear is partially justified, but it confuses the problem (intersubjectivity as a co-founding element, along with the body, of the psyche) with one of

its conceptual approaches (behavioural interactionism). But above all, the mere denunciation of this tendency has the result of masking a certain number of basic findings that are decisive for psychoanalysis itself: namely, that the question of intersubjectivity was put forward from the very beginnings of psychoanalysis as one of the conditions of psychic life.

6. Translator's note: this expression signifies, of course, the notion of "several others" (as in the group situation) but also stresses that there is *not just one* other, as in the individual treatment and in the usual conceptualization.

7. The prefix *inter* indicates that beyond a necessary reciprocity, symmetrical or asymmetrical, between two or several subjects, it is the gaps between these subjects that make the emergence of I's possible. Whereas in the concept of transsubjectivity the prefix *trans* designates that which occurs *through* the subjects and defines something constant and continuous, the prefix *inter* signals discontinuity, the gap and the difference *between* the subjects in relation to one another, their distinction defining their opposable relations of identity (see Kaës, 1993).

1

How the question of the group was posed in psychoanalysis

The group was first of all an "application" of psychoanalysis to subjects who were unable to benefit from analysis or individual psychotherapy in their classical forms. It appeared later that the group setting, by virtue of the processes that its specific morphological characteristics generate, was potentially of great interest in the treatment of subjects suffering from specific disorders: serious neuroses, psychoses, or borderline states. Another application of the group, employed notably by Bion, made it possible to treat, economically, psychic sufferings linked to current collective traumas—in this case, in wartime.

To these three best-known applications may be added another, where the group setting is used for the purpose of personal training in "group phenomena", especially through experience of the effects of the unconscious that occur in such a situation. Another application with training purposes concerns the learning of a particular set of training skills, or the formation of a professional identity. This is the case when part of the supervision of psychoanalysts in training takes place in a group, when the group is a temporary stage in the training of psychoanalysts (the cartel had this function in the economy of the "pass" with Lacan), or when the group is used to structure the identity and clinical experience of doctors under the leadership of medical psychoanalysts (Balint groups).

All these practices have resulted in more or less precise theoretical elaborations, but these have generally not given rise to the debates they ought to have inspired in the psychoanalytic community, or at best they have remained marginal in the debates that have taken place. On the contrary, most of these practices have aroused, and continue to arouse, reactions ranging from silent indifference to mistrustful tolerance to violent, passionate rejection. For this reason, at least, it would be reasonable to examine how the group, as a configuration of ties, an object of investments (or counterinvestments) and representations, and as a means or tool for such practices raises such important issues for the identity, transmission, and institutions of psychoanalysis.

The first task of the group psychoanalytic theories that were developed in Europe, the United States, and Argentina was to conceptualize the group as such, independently of its constituent members—that is, the group as a whole forming a specific entity. This initial approach, centred on the group, was undoubtedly necessary to gain access to psychoanalytic knowledge of the psychic reality that is constituted in it. But it also posed the question of the legitimacy of this object with regard to psychoanalysis founded on the practice of individual treatment. The question of the individual subject in his relation to the group appeared only much later on and in a relatively marginal way. From this point on, other questions were asked, though they did not become a subject of debate. The fact is that the conception of the subject changes, and with it our way of thinking about the unconscious changes, according to whether one considers it in terms of the classical treatment setting or in terms of the group setting.

It is outside the subject and scope of this chapter to review the history of these developments. Nonetheless, it is useful to describe, not the events and their sequences but, rather, the principal orientations of the research, the accentuations and tendencies that finally constituted the elements of psychoanalytic thinking about the group. I will try in particular to show how the group poses a problem for psychoanalytic theory and practice, in the hope that, by identifying its contributions and its obstacles, issues for debate will emerge concerning the fundamental objects of psychoanalysis, the extent of its domain, and the frontiers that it sets for itself in its contemporary practice.

The group as therapeutic instrument in the tradition

When psychoanalysts found that they were faced with the necessity of inventing an alternative to the individual treatment, the group setting quite quickly appeared to be adequate for certain patients. The majority of these psychoanalysts were involved in situations where they had to deal with serious psychiatric problems, within institutional settings that aggravated them, and according to a crazy logic of the apparatus of madness, with teams whose primary task was, precisely, to treat such madness: this was the case with Enrique Pichon-Rivière in Buenos Aires. Many of them, like S. H. Foulkes in London, were obliged to look for alternative techniques in the face of the failure of standard analytic treatment: at the time the necessary modifications were difficult to conceive of and, given the theoretical–clinical gaps that they produced, to square with the categories of psychoanalysis itself. Others had to take charge of urgent situations such as the traumatic neuroses engendered by war, and they had to invent economic arrangements (in the financial and psychic sense of the term) in order to be able to treat them, discovering their efficacy in so doing: this was the case for W. R. Bion at the beginning of the Second World War. There were also some psychoanalysts who were very keen to take into consideration the imperatives of public health and the management of therapeutic resources. In France, at the end of the Second World War, the development of therapeutic group practices inspired by psychoanalysis came about largely as a result of the effect of the objectives set by the emerging Social Security system and the plan for reinforcing the processes of socialization undermined by the war and urbanization. Among other attempts, many formed part of the tradition that regards the group as an instrument in the service of social or pedagogical causes.

Now, psychoanalysis has a different objective: namely, to liberate the psyche from its psychic impediments. Group psychoanalysis forms part of this task: its objective is to loosen the intersubjective links that are a source of disturbances in linking and in the subjects of linking. By opening up the way to knowledge of this part of the individual psyche involved in the "group mind" and linked to it by formations and processes that transcend each subject, these psychoanalysts were confronted with clinical, methodological, and theoretical problems that led them to the boundaries of psychoanalysis with other disciplines. The latter, based on other conceptions of psychic life, worked with hypotheses that were bound, sooner or later, to prove to be in opposition to the constitutive hypothesis of psychoanalysis: that is, of a psychosexual unconscious of infantile origin, separated from consciousness but acting on it in a specific and constant way.

The first group psychoanalytic theories were, as we shall see, not all constituted from the outset on psychoanalytic bases. The importation of extraterritorial concepts into the field of psychoanalysis was carried out at the price of sometimes hybrid theorizations and ambiguous practices, but it was also an opportunity for naturalizing problematic issues that had hitherto been excluded from the field of psychoanalytic research: the concepts of intersubjectivity, belonging, and alienation emerged from this acculturation. Depending on their cultural heritage and the specific genius of their founders, the different currents or psychoanalytic schools elaborated theoretical corpuses to account for the formations and psychic processes of which the group is the locus. However, the construction of a metapsychology of intersubjectivity and a theory of the subject of the unconscious, insofar as he is equally a subject of the group, occurred at a later stage. This is the direction that my research has progressively taken.

The pioneers of the psychoanalytic invention of the group

Enrique Pichon-Rivière and the operative group

In Argentina, the first research studies by Pichon-Rivière into the use of the group as an instrument of training and therapy preceded the initiatives of Foulkes and Bion by a few years. The initial idea had its source in his practice as a psychiatrist faced with institutional hospital dysfunctioning: he himself experienced the group as a powerful means of social action and a remarkable therapeutic instrument for the individual. This action gave rise to several practical and theoretical concepts, notably that of the operative group.

Pichon-Rivière defined the operative group as

> a group centred on the task of learning to think in terms of resolving the difficulties created and manifested in the group field, and not in each of its members, which would be an individual analysis in a group. Nor is it centred exclusively on the group as in Gestalt conceptions, except that in each *here-now-with me* of

the task, one is working in two dimensions, realising to a certain extent a synthesis of all the currents. We consider the patient who speaks about what happens in the group as the speech-bearer for himself and for the unconscious phantasies of the group. [Pichon-Rivière, 1971, p. 128]

Commenting on this definition, Bernard (see Pujet, Bernard, Chaves, & Romano, 1982) clearly shows the importance in Pichon-Rivière's work of the reference to North American social psychology: for instance, the use of group concepts centred on the task and social learning. However, with the notion of the work *here-now-with me*, Pichon-Rivière takes into consideration the dimensions of the transferential field, already recognized by Foulkes, when he distinguishes between horizontal (group) transference and vertical (individual) transference.

The guiding principles of his thought only emerged later on. Pichon-Rivière's model proposes an understanding of the group in terms that are marked more by psychoanalytic social psychology.[1] These lines, written in 1972 (in collaboration with A. de Quiroga), recapitulate rather well the principal hypotheses of his research:

The social psychology that we have in mind is part of a critique of daily life. What we are concerned with is man immersed in his daily relationships. Our awareness of these relations loses its trivial character to the extent that the theoretical instrument and its methodology enables us to investigate the genesis of social facts. . . . The social psychology that we are postulating has as its object of study the development and transformation of a dialectical relation which is established between the social structure and the unconscious phantasy of the subject, and rests on relations based on the subject's needs. In other words, it is a question of the relation between the social structure and the configuration of the subject's internal world, a relation that is approached through the notion of *linking* [*vinculo*]. . . . The subject is not only a subject in relationships, he is also a *subject produced* in a praxis: there is nothing in him which is not the result of the interaction between individual, groups and classes. As this relation is the object of social psychology, the group constitutes the privileged operational field of this discipline. This is due to the fact that the group makes it possible to look for the interplay between psychosocial (internal group) and sociodynamic (external group) dimensions by observing the forms of interaction, the mechanisms by which the roles are attributed and accepted. It is by analysing the forms of interaction that we are able to establish hypotheses concerning the determining processes. [Pichon-Rivière, 1980, pp. 205–206]

One can clearly see here Pichon-Rivière's attempt to articulate, rather than to synthesize, certain psychoanalytic hypotheses with others that are borrowed as much from psychology as from various philosophical currents: the Gestalt school, the psychology of learning, group interactionism, Marxist and Sartrian dialectics. As for psychoanalysis, several concepts are inspired by the thinking of Melanie Klein and that of Susan Isaacs, notably when he borrows certain characteristics of her conception of phantasy, though modifying it considerably. Pichon-Rivière explicitly defines the objective of the operative group as one of identifying and interpreting the underlying and emerging unconscious phantasies of the manifest task, which are condensed in the group in the form of specific fears—namely, attacks on the ego (paranoid anxieties), the loss of the object (depressive anxieties), and resistances to change. However, for Pichon-Rivière, these phantasies do not originate in the drives: they are the result of the relational experiences of the members of the group. There is an issue of debate here between this, let it be said in passing, inventive and innovative author and some of his contemporaries and successors.

S. H. Foulkes and the current of group analysis

In London at the beginning of the 1940s, S. H. Foulkes, John Rickman, and Henry Ezriel laid the foundations of what was to constitute the current of *group analysis*. This current shares the structural perspective of Gestaltism. Trained in Frankfurt, Foulkes retained the central idea of the structural approach to behaviour inaugurated by Goldstein, and he applied it to his conception of the individual and the group. At the risk of simplifying, this perspective can be characterized by three propositions: (1) the group is a totality, and the totality precedes the parts; (2) it is more elemental than they, and it is not the sum of its elements; and (3) the individual and the group form a whole of the figure–background type; the individual in the group is like the nodal point in the network of neurons.

Theoretico–clinical priority is given to the group as a specific entity. These three propositions present the group as a precession of the individual and the latter as an element of the group, not as a subject participating in the construction of the group. My conception differs from Foulkes's on this point.

From these three propositions, Foulkes derives the proposition that the group possesses specific therapeutic properties. He thus justifies the practice of group analysis, which he elaborated in London at the beginning of the 1940s:

> the idea of the group as a mental matrix, the common ground of operational relationships, comprising all the interactions of the individual group members, is central for the theory and process of the therapy. Within this frame of reference all communications take place. A fund of unconscious understanding, wherein reactions and communications of great complexity take place, is always present. [Foulkes, 1964, p. 110]

Foulkes (1964, p. 292) considers that every illness is produced within a complex network of interpersonal relations; and in this sense he considers that "group psychotherapy is an attempt to treat the total network of disturbance, either at the point of origin in the root or primary group, or through placing the disturbed individual under conditions of transference in a group of strangers." The group possesses specific therapeutic properties that are expressed by the five fundamental ideas of Foulksian group analysis: (1) the choice of listening, understanding, and interpreting *the group as a totality in the "here and now"*; (2) only taking into consideration *the transference "of the group" onto the analyst*, and not the lateral transferences; (3) the notion of *unconscious phantasy resonance* between the group members; (4) the *common tension* and the common denominator of the unconscious phantasies of the group; (5) the notion of the *group as a psychic matrix* and frame of reference for all interactions.

In the broad sense, group analysis is a method of investigating the psychic formations and processes that develop in a group; its concepts and technique are based on certain of the fundamental facts of psychoanalytic theory and method, and on original psychoanalytic elaborations required by the fact that the group is considered as a specific entity. In a more restricted sense, group analysis is a technique of group psychotherapy and a means of acquiring psychoanalytic experience of the unconscious in the group situation.

Wilfred R. Bion and group mentality

At the same time as Foulkes was inventing group analysis, and in the same hospital at Northfield, Wilfred Bion proposed another original conception of group formations and processes. Like Foulkes, who was seeking an alternative to the limits of individual treatment, Bion counted on the specific mobilization of group processes for the treatment of certain traumatic, borderline, and psychotic pathologies. Bion (1965) founded his analysis on central categories of psychoanalysis when he distinguished two modalities of the psychic functioning of small groups: (1) the work group, in which the processes and requirements of secondary logic prevail, organizing the representation of the object and of the group objective, the organization of the task, and the systems of communication that permit its realization; and (2) the basic group, in which primary processes predominate in the form of basic assumptions in tension with the work group.

The group mentality is the mental activity that is formed in a group from the unanimous and anonymous opinion, will, and unconscious wishes of its members. Their contributions to the group mentality, which constitutes the container for them, permit a certain satisfaction of their impulses and their wishes; they must, however, be in conformity with the other contributions of the common fund and be sustained by it. The group mentality thus guarantees that the life of the group is in line with the basic assumptions that organize its course.

The three basic assumptions (dependency, fight–flight, pairing), which describe the different possible contents of group mentality, represent three specific emotional states. They play a decisive role in the organization of a group, in the realization of its task, and in the satisfaction of the needs and wishes of its members. They are, and remain, unconscious, express unconscious phantasies, and are subject to primary processes. They are used by the group members as magic techniques for treating the difficulties they encounter and, notably, for avoiding the frustration inherent in learning by experience. Bion drew attention to the resemblance of their traits with the phenomena described by Melanie Klein in her theories on part-objects, psychotic anxieties, and primary defences. From this point of view, the basic assumptions are defensive group reactions against the psychotic anxieties reactivated by the regression imposed on the individual in the group situation.

José Bleger and the deposit of the agglutinated nucleus in the group

We are indebted to José Bleger for several important contributions to the psychoanalytic theory of groups, in addition to his concepts of the frame, the agglutinated nucleus, and the deposit. In the first place, we have him to thank for a fundamental distinction between two forms of sociability: syncretic sociability and interactional sociability:

> In every group there is a type of relation which, paradoxically, is a non-relation, that is to say, a non-individuation; this type of relation imposes itself as a matrix or as a basic structure of every group, and it persists to a variable degree throughout its life. I shall call this type of relation syncretic sociability, to differentiate it from interactional sociability . . . [Bleger, 1970, p. 90]

Syncretic sociability is based on an immobilization of the non-differentiated or symbiotic parts of the personality, in a group or institution; these parts are split off from the differentiated formations which, for their part, are mobilized in interactional sociability; this corresponds to an interplay of intersubjective exchanges producing individuating effects and manifest forms of interaction.

The concept of syncretic sociability includes that of the agglutinated nucleus: a few years earlier, Bleger (1967) had posited that the first contents of the infant's psyche were constituted by an agglutinated nucleus deposited first of all in the mother's psyche. This nucleus is the foundation, starting with mechanisms of projective identification, of syncretic sociability, an unconscious base that constitutes the deep infrastructure of every subsequent link or tie: this nucleus will be deposited in the couple and in the family, and then in every group and in every institution.

In these conceptual constructions, Bleger draws on studies of psychological research (Wallon's psychology of the development of social relations), but he gives them another content. The same is true of the notions of group belonging and cohesion, which he borrows from the research carried out in social psychology. For Bleger (1970), cohesion rests on the force of attraction that a group exerts on its members so that they stay together: the group thus becomes a referent for their attitudes on the basis of their sense of belonging to the group. Bleger's specific contribution is to have understood that the group identity of belonging [*identidad grupal por pertenencia*] and the dependency associated with it are constituted by the deposit of the agglutinated nucleus of its members in the structure of the group. With the concept of the deposit of the agglutinated nucleus, Bleger outlined a way forward towards taking the subject into consideration in the group. In my own language, I would say that the deposit renders the subject and the group isomorphic: I thus understand that any deviation or departure from this nuclear deposit arouses anxieties of depersonalization that may be observed in all groups but predominate in certain psychopathological organizations.

Assessment and development of the first psychoanalytic researches into the group

The first psychoanalytic theories of the group attempted to make the consistency of "group phenomena" intelligible and to establish the hypothesis that the group is a relatively independent entity from that of the individuals who constitute it, that it is an organization and a place for producing a psychic reality that is specific to it. These discoveries showed that structures and processes of different levels organize groups. Some are neurotic and are organized around the nuclear oedipal conflict and ambivalence towards the figure of the leader; others are preoedipal and pregenital and mobilize narcissistic formations, borderline and psychotic: archaic fantasies, primary identifications, primitive anxieties, mechanisms of defence other than repression, and part-object relations, especially those pertaining to the oral organization of the libido.

Nonetheless, the conception of the unconscious involved in these models still remained vague. Like Bion, Foulkes assumed that the unconscious produces specific effects in the group, but both treated it more as a quality linked to group phenomena than as a system constitutive of intersubjective formations and processes. The question was scarcely touched upon by Pichon-Rivière, but it began to acquire original consistency with Bleger.

In this first epistemological period, the primary concern was to study the group as a specific entity and to constitute it as a therapeutic setting. Clinical and theoretical attention was entirely focused on the basic concepts that were supposed to account for the "group mind". Under these conditions the question of the *subject* within the group—*a fortiori* that of the subject of the group—was not taken into consideration. However, the *individual* was not neglected, but when attention was paid to him, it was essentially as an element of the group, to the extent that he contributed "anonymously" (Bion) to the group mentality or as a transmission relay in the functioning of the group system (Foulkes). Pichon-Rivière began to reintroduce the subject, but this was essentially a psychosocial subject. From this standpoint, the first theories of the group were theories in which the subject of the unconscious disappears, along with that which singles him out—that is, his desires, his history, his place in unconscious phantasy, the idiosyncrasy of his impulses, affects, and representations and of his repression. But just as attention was not focused on the individual subject, nor was it directed at the nature of the links or ties between the subjects assembled in a group.

The methodological and clinical consequences of these conceptions are by no means negligible. If we examine them, for instance, from the point of view of interpretation, it appears that only "the group" as a whole is both the object and recipient of the interpretation. Though the interpretation is thought out and presented in group terms, its effects are discounted in each individual, owing to the ties that link him to the matrix of the group, situate him in its field of forces, and are part of a *basic assumption*. But this link, and what is involved therein for each person, is not interpreted directly. Here again, Pichon inaugurates a different position: with his notion of the work *aqui-ahora-conmigo* [here-now-with me], the two dimensions of the transferential field, horizontal and vertical, lead him to distinguish between two phases and two recipients an interpretation.

The French current of psychoanalytic research into groups

I thought it appropriate to give particular attention to the French current of psychoanalytic research into groups, inasmuch as my own work is grounded in and, to a certain extent, coloured by it. But there is yet another reason for dwelling on the way in which psychoanalysts in France have developed an interest in the group. As in Argentina and England, the local psychoanalytic culture has played an important contextual role. In France, the question of the group is inscribed within a dual cultural tradition formed by the Enlightenment and the Revolution. One of these traditions, individualism, gave greater importance to the individual subject, to the point of excluding, as pure alienation, every reference to the group in its formation and its history. The other tradition, with its roots in the socialist current, laid emphasis on the group as a means of revolution and a basic element of freedom of thought. These two currents converge in the ideologies that run through the French psychoanalytic movement, influenced more by Tarde and Le Bon than by Durkheim, and which maintain a certain mistrust of the group.

Historically, the question of—quarrel about?—the group was crystallized in the stir caused by the splits that affected psychoanalytic institutions at the beginning of the 1960s and a few years later in the mental revolutions that occurred in 1968. Broadly speaking, I would say that psychoanalytic interest in the group evolved in three stages that led progressively to ever-increasing attention being paid to the links between the subject and the group.

Interest in the group in post-war France

The first phase is situated in the context of post-war France. The effort to reconstruct the economic and social structure facilitated interest in the group in psychological and psychiatric circles. At the end of the Second World War, French psycho-sociologists discovered the ideas and methods of Lewin concerning the dynamics of groups, and those of Moreno on psychodrama. Laboratories, psychiatric hospitals, and companies—and certain educational establishments—provided the terrain for their practice and research. With regard to psychiatrists, a few of whom were psychoanalysts, some had the task of reforming the psychiatric institution and were concerned to treat as many patients as possible with new therapeutic techniques. They too were interested in the works of Lewin and Moreno and found two notable advantages in the "group techniques" inspired by them: the first was the possibility of treating a large number of patients, and the second, in accordance with the then dominant theories on the adaptive function of the ego, was the possibility of maintaining the psychic progresses of social integration. A third area of interest then began to emerge insofar as the group was seen as one of the basic means of institutional psychotherapy.

Among the first psychoanalysts, two major currents formed, and they have survived until today. The first united psychoanalysts who were keen to apply the findings of psychoanalysis to the psychotherapeutic treatment of individuals in a group situation. The techniques that were developed according to this perspective usually made use of so-called "individual" psychoanalytic psychodrama: a team of psychodramatists treat a patient using psychodrama. This first current was first inspired by Lebovici, Diatkine, Decobert, Kestemberg, and then by Lacan in the psychodrama worked out by P. and G. Lemoine in the following decade. If the therapeutic virtue of the group was observed empirically, the conceptualization of the processes underlying it seemed to be a risky adventure. One was satisfied with resorting to classical Freudian concepts to describe, justify, or denounce the mobilizing capacity of identifications, the effects of the resonance of phantasies, and the consolidation of defence mechanisms in the group context.

The psychoanalysts who formed the second current tried to identify the active unconscious processes within the group. They encountered two sorts of difficulties: The first lay in the direct application of psychoanalytic concepts with hypotheses and techniques elaborated by Lewin, Rogers, and Moreno. This "makeshift situation" bore witness to the concern to put to the test—and sometimes only to illustrate—Freud's speculative propositions concerning his "social psychology" and the group mind, but it produced a sort of epistemological syncretism that is rather dangerous. The second difficulty stemmed from the fact that the concepts used arose from the psychoanalytic theorization of the individual psyche. The work of theorization is rather weak, and during this first period, the works of Pichon-Rivière, Bion, Foulkes, and Bleger were still unfamiliar to most French psychoanalysts.

The foundational statements of the 1960s
and the first epistemological break

The rapid expansion of psychoanalytic investigations into the group was closely linked with the vicissitudes that affected the French psychoanalytic movement at the beginning of the 1960s. The conflicts and splits arising from differences of opinion concerning psychoanalytic training, the conduct of the treatment, and relations with the IPA resulted in the creation of new institutions: the *Ecole Freudienne de Paris* in 1963 and the *Association Psychanalytique de France* in 1964. These ruptures and creations were accompanied by violent group effects that were both cultivated and denounced. As their traumatic substance was not recognized, excitement that was at times activist and at times paralysing strengthened the ban—or at least the resistance—against thinking about the group and institutions with what could be learned about them from psychoanalysis. Criticism, often violent, was directed *a priori* at all those who were engaged in a group practice that claimed to be psychoanalytic.

It is certainly fitting to analyse further the reservations and resistances of psychoanalytic institutions towards the group. The persisting ignorance concerning the considerable role that the group played in the foundation of psychoanalysis, as well as the ideological power the group had over the first psychoanalysts, were issues that were not thought about and were, indeed, passed over in silence, thus maintaining and amplifying the repetition of the original traumas. The rejection of the group as an anti-psychoanalytic object and situation, unsuitable to any form of psychoanalytic elaboration, could not but maintain a dangerous split in psychoanalytic institutions, with a return of violence in the reality of institutions. (On these questions, I refer the reader to my studies on the group of first psychoanalysts: Kaës, 1994a; 2000.)

The position, more than the thought of Lacan, exerted a decisive influence in all this effervescence both within psychoanalytic groups and concerning groups. It was a paradoxical position in a man who both established the group (the "cartel") as the agency in the name of which the psychoanalyst authorizes himself (". . . from himself and from a few others") and denounced the effects of the group as the place of alienation in the imaginary of the One: "I measure the group effect," wrote Lacan (1973, p. 31) a few years later, "by what it adds in the way of obscenity to the imaginary effect of the discourse."

Paradoxically, the issue here was not one of understanding the sources of "group effects" by the means that psychoanalysis affords us, and of freeing ourselves from them by the work of analysis, notably through the group setting: they had to be denounced and—omnipotence versus anxiety—it was enough to do so. Such an absurd and categorical position is not only anathema thrown in the face of any group psychoanalytic practice, it is a ban on thinking about the unconscious issues at stake and the subjective position of psychoanalysts in groups. It always remains possible to manipulate the effects of the unconscious in groups that are set up—until the inevitable reversal occurs of the manipulator who is manipulated by his own stratagem.

Towards the middle of the 1960s, a number of French psychoanalysts, who had formerly been associated with Lacan—Anzieu, Bejarano, and Pontalis among them—proposed another psychoanalytic approach to the group. Pontalis and Anzieu criticized the direct application of psychoanalytic concepts to the group: these concepts had to be thought out again in relation to their new object. They also pointed up the contradictions and the impasses for psychoanalytic thought of the dynamics of Lewinian groups, and of Moreno's imaginary conceptions of social cure through psychodrama and sociometry.

Pontalis criticized Lewin's theory for its ideological content, based on a quest for good communication. Anzieu took up this critique in order to free himself from the group techniques used in the institution that he had founded in 1962, which consisted, at that moment, of a combination of elements borrowed from Lewin's social psychology and from psychoanalysis. Anzieu criticized Lewin's theory for not taking into account the unconscious signification of group movements. With regard to this critique it may be objected that this was not Lewin's own frame of reference but, rather, one that we borrowed from him in part. And indeed, considered from a psychoanalytic standpoint, Lewinian techniques bolster an idealization of the group leader and, correlatively, the emergence of an ideology of the "good" group. The priority accorded to performance in accomplishing the task and to the efficiency of the network of communication leads to a manipulation of the transference with these aims in mind and not to its understanding and interpretation. The psychoanalytic approach to groups thus had to return to hypotheses and objectives that conformed to the object of psychoanalysis.[2] Four main propositions underlay the studies of French psychoanalysts on the group from the middle of the 1960s; they would only be developed in the course of the following decade.

The small group as object

The work of the French school gave back to the group its value as a psychic object, as an object of instinctual investments and of unconscious representations for its subjects. Pontalis wrote that

> it is not enough to put one's finger on the unconscious processes that operate within a group, however ingenious one has been in doing so: as long as one places outside the field of analysis the image itself of the group, with the phantasies and values that it bears, one in fact eludes every question concerning the unconscious function of the group. [Pontalis, 1963, p. 1068]

This study marked a turning-point in group psychoanalytic theory.

The group, like the dream, is a means of fulfilling unconscious wishes

The group was no longer considered as the form and structure of a system of interpersonal relations wherein forces of balance, representations producing influential norms and processes, pressures to conform, networks of communication, and locations of statuses and roles were in operation.

In 1966, Anzieu proposed a model for understanding the group as an entity within which unconscious processes operate. His approach thus converged with those of Bion and Foulkes, but the path of entry was both classical and original, starting out from the dream model. Anzieu (1966) contends that the group, like the dream, is the means and locus of the imaginary fulfilment of unconscious infantile wishes. According to this model, the diverse phenomena that appear in groups are akin to manifest contents derived from a limited number of latent contents. The reference to the dream model implies that the processes that constitute the group as an object of the common wishes of its members are the same as those of the dream, and that in the group they are determining: that is, displacement, condensation, symbolic representation, and reversal into the opposite. (I have added to this list two other major processes particularly solicited in groups—namely, the diffraction and multiplication of an identical element.) According to Anzieu, whether the group accomplishes the task that is assigned to it efficiently or whether it is paralysed, it is a debate with an underlying phantasy. It is a stage upon which internal topographies are projected. Like the dream, and like the symptom, the group is the association of an unconscious wish that is looking for its path of imaginary fulfilment and defences against the anxiety that such fulfilments arouse in the ego.

Though group formations and processes obey general mechanisms that are specific to any production of the unconscious, some of them are specific to the group situation, as, for instance, the group illusion described by Anzieu (1971).

The four objects of the transference and analytic listening

Bejarano published a study in 1972 (written in 1966) in which he examines the conditions of psychoanalytic listening applied to the group context. He very quickly comes to question the system of transferences. In groups, objects and contents of the transference develop that suffer the vicissitudes of the personal multiple situation. The manifest discourse of a group and its activity must be observed psychoanalytically as simultaneously both hiding and expressing a latent discourse.

It is a question—as in psychoanalytic treatment—of deciphering this latent discourse in order to restore its meaning and, if possible, of leading the group to an awareness of this meaning. Resistance is expressed in the gap between this latent discourse and the manifest discourse. In a group context, the transferences are multiple: onto the psychoanalyst (central transference), onto the other participants (lateral transferences), onto the group as such (group transference), and onto the external object.

The group combination of psyches

During the second half of the 1960s, I collaborated with Anzieu to develop a group psychoanalytic setting in line with the methodological requirements of psychoanalysis. My first researches were closely linked to his. We tried to establish the methodological, clinical, and theoretical conditions on the basis of which the hypothesis that the group is the locus of its own specific psychic reality could be defended.

My first studies (1965–68) were centred on the study of the unconscious representations and instinctual investments of which the group is the object, in the sense that had recently been defined by Pontalis. I first uncovered the organizing nuclei of group representations and I distinguished two types: (1) the unconscious organizers at the level of phantasy; and (2) the sociocultural organizers. I described the unconscious organizers as "groups of the inside" structured according to the laws of composition that obey primary processes. Later on, I called them internal groups, while giving this concept a rather different meaning from the one that Pichon-Rivière and Diego Napolitani had attributed to it.

Then I began to study the effects of psychic groupality in the organization of group processes and to work out a model for articulating individual psychic space and the psychic space proper to the group. The conception of the model of the group psychic apparatus (1968–69) helped me to think about how the psychic reality proper to the group is produced, contained, transformed, bound, and managed by such an apparatus, its main function being to establish relations of tuning and adjustment between the intrapsychic formations and the inter- and transsubjective formations produced by the group. Among the active principles of this apparatus, the organizing role of internal groups was recognized.

The interest of the model of the group psychic apparatus is that it helps us to understand the processes of investment, production, and treatment of psychic reality in the group and in the members of the group. It contains concepts centred on diverse modalities of articulation between the subject and the group, and notably on the interweaving of group effects with the effects of the unconscious.

The development of psychoanalytic research into the group, from the early 1970s to the present day

Psychoanalytic research into the group developed at the beginning of the 1970s and went in two main directions. The first pursued the investigation of the formations and processes of which the group as a whole is the locus. I shall have to confine myself here to mentioning the main contributions of Anzieu (the group illusion, the group envelope), Rouchy (archaic processes, the notion of belonging), Avron (the notion of inter-drive processes) and Kaës (development of the model of the group psychic apparatus, ideological, utopian, and mythopoetic positions, unconscious alliances, common and shared dream spaces, associative processes, and associative chains). The majority of these researches progressively integrated the findings of Anglo-Saxon contributions, and in particular Bion's concepts

and approach: this was true of the research work of Avron (1996) and Rouchy (1998). The latter also works with concepts arising from the work of Torok and Abraham. Connected with these researches are those contributions that are involved in the analysis of group therapeutic processes, transferences, the particularities of the work of co-analysis or co-therapy, and associative processes. Other contributions are concerned with the specificity of groups of children and adolescents (Privat, Haag) and with the family group (Caillot, Decherf, Pigott, Eiguer, Granjon).

The second path of research has been much less frequented: it is interested in the position of the subject within the group and is concerned with what I have called the phoric (bearing) functions—that is to say, the locations and functions performed in the group by some of its members when they are speech-bearer, symptom-bearer, dream-bearer, ideal-bearer, or death-bearer, and so on. It also opens the way to a set of problems to which I have given particular attention because they are of vital concern to all psychoanalysts. I am referring to the role played by the group in the structuring of the psyche. I have spent several years trying to understand how the processes of anaclisis, the mechanisms constitutive of the unconscious (repression, splitting, denial), the formation of symptoms, and the return of the non-repressed unconscious, identifications, the system of narcissism, the function of thought and significance, defensive organizers, and forms of subjectivation are worked on and constructed in the matrix of the primary group, in intersubjective links. This is an exciting field of investigation and one that is still open. I have become accustomed to formulating what is at stake in it by saying that the subject of the unconscious is a subject of the group. This is not a purely speculative proposition: it is at the root of the conception of the psychoanalytic work that a subject can carry out in a group; and, above all, it is a way of revisiting our conception of the subject and of the unconscious.

I have limited my historical approach to three principal active areas in the formation of psychoanalytic thinking about the group and groupality. My aim is to show how this thinking is formed, what its content is, and how group psychoanalytic thinking and practice concerns psychoanalysts. If it were a question of accounting for all the fields of research, it would clearly be unfair to confine ourselves to these three areas. Research studies more or less inspired by these foundations, especially by the Bionian and Foulksian currents, have developed in many European countries, in the United States, in Latin America, and in Asia.

The moment has now come to examine more closely the epistemological, methodological, and clinical problems posed by the extension of the field of objects and practices of psychoanalysis.

NOTES

1. The subtitle of *El proceso grupal* is *Del psicoanálisis a la psicología social.*

2. The abandonment of psychosocial techniques was not immediate: a period of transition was necessary for the transformations to occur that would result in the establishment of a clearly psychoanalytic group setting. However, the critique of Pontalis and Anzieu acted as a sort of introductory manifesto in the break-up of the French group analytic movement with its Lewinian and Morenian roots.

2

The epistemological problem
of the group in psychoanalysis

Just like the *first* setting [*dispositif*] of the individual treatment, each
of the settings inspired by the general method of psychoanalysis is
based on theoretico–clinical principles and hypotheses. These principles and hypotheses generally remain implicit, but when extensions of psychoanalytic practice occur they come to the surface, and
sometimes in an untimely manner. It is thus important to make as
explicit as possible the elements of these principles, which serve as
a foundation for these extensions. To do this, some epistemological
and clinical considerations on the object, the method, and the frontiers of psychoanalysis are necessary.

The specificity of the object and method of psychoanalysis:
the extension of its field

Psychoanalysis was constituted by progressively constructing a field
of theoretical and clinical objects from a clearly identified methodological setting: namely, the individual treatment of neurotic adults.
In order to think about the psychoanalytic consistency of the group,
not only with the concepts of psychoanalysis but in the field of

psychoanalysis, we may start with the characteristics that Freud recognized in psychoanalysis when he defined it, in 1923, in terms of
three dimensions:

> Psychoanalysis is the name (1) of a procedure for the inves-
> tigation of mental processes which are almost inaccessible in
> any other way; (2) of a method (based upon that investigation)
> for the treatment of neurotic disorders; and (3) of a collection
> of psychological information obtained along those lines, which
> is gradually being accumulated into a new scientific discipline.
> [Freud, 1923a, p. 235]

By the same token, it may be said that in the field of psychoanalysis
so defined, the group is a method of investigating and gaining knowledge of a specific unconscious psychic reality that is otherwise inaccessible, and which is irreducible to that of its constituent subjects.
This setting is capable of mobilizing a process of psychoanalytic work
for the treatment of psychic disorders. Clinical findings are the object of a work of theorization that describes the unconscious psychic
reality and the corresponding modalities of subjectivity that develop
in the common and shared psychic space of the group.

These three propositions situate the question of the group within
a perspective that is no longer that of applied psychoanalysis. They
signify that the model of the psychic apparatus arising from the practice of the so-called individual treatment cannot be "applied" without transformation to a psychic configuration other than that of the
subject considered in his singularity. From the moment a methodological setting confers on practices "outside the typical treatment"
relevance with regard to the object of psychoanalysis, the debate
concerns fields of the knowledge of the unconscious that can today
be recognized as falling within the scope of psychoanalysis.

Including the unconscious psychic reality proper to the group
among the theoretical objects of psychoanalysis obliges us to re-
define the constitutive statements of psychoanalysis, as they were
constituted on the basis of the practice of classical analysis. It is
thus necessary to set out the propositions on which we ground our
conception of the object of psychoanalysis, its method, and its extension. Apart from the postulate concerning the three pillars of the
psyche—that is, infantile sexuality, speech, and linking—I will put
forward three main propositions.

Unconscious psychic reality

The unconscious, or that which Freud calls more descriptively "unconscious psychic reality", is the constitutive hypothesis of psychoanalysis. Freud also describes the unconscious in two ways: as a structure, topography, and economy; and as a dynamic of the psyche. This fundamental statement implies the recognition of the structural division of the psyche as an effect of the unconscious—the instinctual drives and infantile sexuality being the organizers of this division and of psychic conflicts. The unconscious must be specified by its constitutive modalities and by its specific topographies: those of the primal unconscious, the repressed unconscious, and the non-repressed unconscious resulting from splitting, denial, and disavowal. Phantasies, symptoms, and dreams are their accessible formations. Freud describes the unconscious as a quality of psychic material under the effect of the mechanisms that constitute it as such.

The foundational hypothesis of psychoanalysis, the hypothesis of the unconscious and of unconscious psychic reality, has opened up three large areas of study for research into the group.

The group as specific psychic reality

The major epistemological problem with which we are faced involves three sets of questions. The first asks whether we can conceive and describe a consistent psychic reality formed by the effects of the unconscious in a common and shared space such as the group. If this is the case, how can the hypothesis of the unconscious help us to think about the concept of the group; and, correlatively, how is the concept of the unconscious transformed by the hypothesis of the group?

I pointed out in chapter 1 how the idea was formed that there are "group phenomena" that are irreducible to the individual phenomena of the subjects who compose them. Before Lewin, Freud put forward this idea at a speculative level, and after him those psychoanalysts who were interested in the group validated it: the group psyche consists of specific psychic formations and processes and of unconscious processes operating within them. Diverse theories have accounted for this conception.

I have in turn accepted this hypothesis, while clarifying it further: if, as I think, the group comprises structures, organizations, and psychic processes that are specific to it, psychic entities are created that would not exist without the grouping. It seemed logical to describe the topography, dynamics, and economy that characterize them. This is what I have tried to do by proposing the elements for conceptualizing a "third topography".

The relation of the subject to the group and the subject's position within the group

If one accepts that unconscious psychic reality extends beyond individual psychic space, a second set of questions require consideration.

Models that were centred solely on the group as an entity (Bion, Foulkes, Pichon-Rivière, Anzieu) did not satisfy me, not because of their inadequacy in accounting for group psychic reality, but because they do not take into account, or at least not sufficiently, the question of the subject within the group. Now this articulation is decisive for explaining the part played by the subject in the group process, and reciprocally for defining the role played in the formation of the subject's unconscious by his intersubjective and group determinants. This dual point of view is indispensable for making a link with the psychoanalysis of individual processes.

Once the subject's position in the group had been taken into account, I came to think that common identifications, shared phantasies and representations, formations of the Ideal, the common dream matrix, and unconscious alliances constitute passing points and lines of rupture between intrapsychic space and intersubjective space. From this common space subjects emerge who fulfil on their own behalf and on behalf of the group the functions of symptom-bearer, dream-bearer, and speech-bearer; some are bearers of ideals and illusion, others are bearers of death (on the phoric function of the thanatophor, see Diet, 1996): all of them are go-betweens [agents de liaison]. I refer to these functions as "phoric".

The effects of the group on the subject's psyche: the subject of the group

This third field of research has particularly claimed my attention. As a psychoanalyst providing both individual and group treatment, it was important for me to understand how the subject's psychic life

is constructed through its relations with the common and shared psychic space of several subjects in the links and matrix of the primary group.

I use the notion of subject to describe a mode of existence of the individual inasmuch as he is affected by an order of reality that governs and organizes him: his impulses, his phantasies, his wishes, and his unconscious conflicts. The subject is not only divided from within, by the effect of the *Spaltung* [splitting] created by the unconscious: he is similarly divided between serving his own purposes and the place that he has to assume in the links that have constituted him. This second division is also structural, and it has a decisive effect on the formation of the subject of the unconscious.

I have put forward a proposition according to which the subject of the unconscious is constructed in the space of the primal group. Let me explain what I mean by this hypothesis: the mechanisms of co-repression or of joint denial, the contracts that are at the basis of the subject's narcissism and that of the group, and, more generally, unconscious alliances, play a determining role in the constitutive modalities of the subject's unconscious, in its contents, in the conditions of the return of the repressed, and in symptom-formation.

It is in this measure that I contend that the subject of the unconscious is indissociably subject of the group and that, correlatively, the subject of the group is a dimension of the subject of the unconscious. By adopting this point of view, I also accept that a part of the subject is "outside the subject", that the subject has several centres, that some of his unconscious formations are displaced, exported, and deposited in psychic places that are already present in the group and are used by the subject.

The epistemological problem then takes on another dimension. We have to think about the relations between the psychic reality of the group (or of any other configuration of linking), that of each subject considered in his singularity, and that which forms the psychic matter of the links between the subjects who constitute it. Here we are touching on a question that concerns all psychoanalysts: namely, what effects on the formation of the subject of the unconscious are to be attributed to the interference of these spaces?

It was with a view to conceptualizing these relations that I proposed at the end of the 1960s a model that was capable of accounting for the psychic reality proper to the group, the links of the group, and of the subject in the group. The model of the group psychic apparatus enabled me to describe the relations between the structural agencies, the economic and dynamic systems of the individual psychic apparatus, and of the group psychic apparatus.[1] With this model, psychoanalytic knowledge can be extended to the psychic consistency of each of these three spaces and to the processes and formations that unite and separate them.

An appropriate setting for the aims of psychoanalytic work

Knowledge of unconscious psychic reality is only possible through a setting that is appropriate to the twofold aim of psychoanalytic work: the transformation of unconscious psychic reality and knowledge of the unconscious. We know that the theoretico–clinical field of psychoanalysis was constituted to a significant extent from the method of the individual treatment and that it is on the basis of this practice that the theory of psychoanalysis accounts for the schemata of the construction and functioning of the psychic apparatus in its internal logic, of the accession of the subject, and of the I [Je] that assumes responsibility for it. It is worth noting that a certain time was needed to think through the correlations between the method, the clinical work that it makes possible, and the theories that it gives rise to.

However, it is accepted that the theoretico–clinical field of psychoanalysis has never been restricted to the practice of the individual treatment alone, as can be seen from all of Freud's speculations, that it is not limited by right to this practice alone,[2] and that, consequently, it regularly goes beyond it. Indeed, when clinical work confronted psychoanalysts with treating psychotic and borderline adults and children and adolescents suffering from serious disturbances, modifications were made to our knowledge of the unconscious and to the setting used for treating these disorders. We are familiar with the debates and controversies to which these transformations gave rise. They have continued to cause a crisis for the Freudian conception of the unconscious.

The problem we have formulated can obviously not be dealt with independently of its relation to the psychoanalytic method and technique in the group situation. We therefore have to establish the characteristics of a group psychoanalytic setting and to examine the conceptual transformations that are necessary for understanding how transferences and associative processes are ordered and how objects and modalities of interpretation are chosen.

We have to understand that the psychic work produced in pluris-ubjective settings is not identical with that which is made possible by the individual analytic setting. Although it is likely that transversal processes are at work in each of these settings, in the individual treatment and "outside it", what matters is understanding how work in individual analysis is affected by what we learn from work "outside it".

The controlled extension of psychoanalytic practices
is an effect of the infinitude of our knowledge of the unconscious

These problems lead us to the deepest level of the epistemological debate: insofar as we cannot fail to take into account the effects of any extension of the field of psychoanalytic practice on the theory of psychoanalysis—the treatment, at first, of children, then of psychotics, and, in this case, a psychoanalytic approach to the group—we have to think constantly about the objects, methods, and limits of psychoanalysis.

It is thus not surprising that this critical tension, which has given rhythm to the entire history of psychoanalysis and kept it alive, arose again when psychoanalytic practices were extended to the treatment of parent–child relationships, couples, families, and group relations. This extension of the practice of psychoanalysis, providing it is controlled, is an effect of the infinite nature of our knowledge of the unconscious. The epistemological import of this proposition is that the conditions of the knowledge of the unconscious are not established once and for all, and that the theoretical object of psychoanalysis, its modalities of constitution and its frontiers, have to be subjected periodically to critical thought.

In other words, each setting used by the psychoanalytic method produces, out of the clinical findings that it generates and on which it works, specific fields of theorization: this means that the knowledge of the unconscious is modified with the changes occurring in the practice of psychoanalysis. Every innovation calls for the renewal of certain previously established metapsychological conceptions, and each setting is itself founded on theoretico–clinical hypotheses the principles of which are often implicit and need to be made explicit.

I have indicated that the group psychoanalytic approach has introduced us to two other spaces: namely, those of intersubjectivity and of the subject in intersubjectivity. This space is organized by a different logic than that of the individual psyche, but between these two logics there are many points of convergence.

The complexity of the logical levels
of the psychoanalytic problem of the group

I have distinguished three logical levels in the study of group psychic reality: namely, the group, the links between the subjects who compose it, and each subject considered in his singularity. If, as I believe, the group is a common and shared psychic space, it is necessary not only to take into consideration that which pertains to the psyche of the subjects in the original formations that make up the group, but also to specify that which is singular and private, that which is common and shared, and that which remains different.

The private, the common, the shared, the different

The "private" or "singular" corresponds to the individuated psychic space that marks, by its specificity, the structure, the history, and the subjectivity of a particular subject: his drive organization, his secondary phantasies, his defence mechanisms and his repressed or split contents, his identifications, his object-relations—in short, that which singularizes his unconscious desire. However, a part of that which is "private" has its origin in what the subject has inherited, in what he has acquired and transformed, or in what has remained for him without transformation. As Freud indicates in "On Narcissism: An Introduction" (1914c, p. 78): "the individual does actually carry on a twofold existence: one to serve his own purposes, and the other as a link in a chain, which he serves against his will or at least involuntarily." It is the tension between serving one's own purposes and being a link, beneficiary, servant, and heir of an intersubjective and transgenerational chain that defines the subject as subject of the

unconscious in respect of his position as subject of the group. But the consequences of this point of view need to be taken further: the singularity of the private psychic space coexists with zones of reality that are common and shared with other subjects.

The "common" is the psychic substance uniting the members of a bond,[3] whatever its configuration may be—a family, a couple, or a group. Phantasies, dreams, desires, identifications, ideals, signifiers, illusions, and unconscious alliances are common or become so. The narcissistic contract (Castoriadis-Aulagnier, 1975) is the common matrix of the psychic life of the *infans* (i.e. prior to the stage of speech) with his mother in the primal period: the mother inscribes the *infans* there in her own narcissism; she founds him in her own psyche and in the family psychic space. There is no bond without this psychic substance common to the subjects of a bond. The "common" requires the abandonment or loss of certain individual limits of the subjects within the bond, and thus a certain lack of differentiation, but it is also the basic psychic material necessary for the subject to emerge in his singularity. The "common" knows of differences: it is equally or unequally common.

The "shared" corresponds to the *role* that each subject takes, or to the specific and complementary place that he has, in a phantasy, an alliance, a contract, or a defensive system common to the subjects of a bond. A phantasy that might take the form of "a parent is threatening/repairing a child" is both common to the members of a group and organizes the relations between the group members. Everyone is mobilized by this phantasy, and each member is in turn, or simultaneously, the passive or active actor or, alternatively, the observer of this psychic action. However, each subject can have a certain place, the place that is his own and that singularizes him in this phantasy. The sharing of the phantasy is a sign of a subjectivizing process of individuation in the common and shared space. This system of sharing ensures the terms of an intersubjective exchange.

The "different" takes into consideration the gap in the bond between the subjects at the point where their difference reveals that which can be neither common nor shared between them. In difference, the radical otherness of the other emerges, with an indication of what remains singular and private in him.

In other words, there is no bond without common material. A bond cannot rest on the exclusivity of difference. It is because there is something in common and also *différance* (Derrida) that I can share (and that I am shared).

Status of the psychic formations in the three psychic spaces

The group experience is essentially the experience of the assembling, combination, and adjustment [*appareillage*] of these three spaces—the space of the group, the space of intersubjective relations, and the intrapsychic space—and this process of combination accords a variable place to each of these four modalities. To give an example of this, I would say that phantasies or dreams do not present the same characteristics in the internal, singular, and private space, in the common and shared space, and in the transpsychic space.

   Figure 1 expresses the idea that the contents and modalities of the functioning of phantasy work in different ways in the group situation and in the individual analytic situation. In the group situation, the structural properties of phantasy are particularly mobilized, especially the locations of the subject in the phantasy scene and the locations that he allocates to the other in this scene. Another application of this proposition, which I shall come back to later, is that symptoms are produced and maintained by the group members for

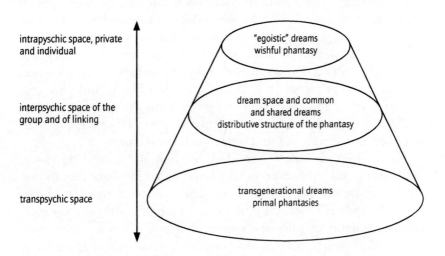

intrapsychic space, private and individual

interpsychic space of the group and of linking

transpsychic space

"egoistic" dreams
wishful phantasy

dream space and common and shared dreams
distributive structure of the phantasy

transgenerational dreams
primal phantasies

Figure 1. Status of the psychic formations in the three psychic spaces

the function that they fulfil in the psychic life of each of them and simultaneously in the group process.

For this reason, the identification of the subject's position in his own particular history is given less attention in the group situation than it is in individual analysis. On the other hand, the subject's position in intersubjectivity, in his relation to an other and to a group of others, is given closer attention in the group situation.

Epistemological principles for analysing the relations between the spaces of psychic reality included in the group

In the course of my research I have been led to define several principles of analysis for thinking about the relations between the different psychic spaces included in the group. The first four concern the organization of these psychic spaces: they have epistemological and clinical significance. I distinguish the principle of constancy and transversality of psychic material, the principle of complementarity, the principle of plurifocality, and the polyphonic principle. The three following principles are principles that organize theoretical thinking. I have selected the principle of complexity, the principle of uncertainty and the principle of multifactorial indetermination.

The principle of constancy and transversality of psychic material

This principle accounts for the relative constancy of psychic material in the three psychic spaces: the group as an entity, the group links, and the individual subject within the group. This constancy is, however, relative, for the system formed by these different spaces is not totally closed. Here we can turn again to the example of phantasies or dreams: their material is constant; they traverse the psychic spaces, but their organization and the modalities of their functioning are different in the group psyche and in the individual psyche. Another example of this proposition is that the unconscious is inscribed several times in each of these spaces, with distinct forms and effects. It may be considered that psychic material traverses these different spaces while simultaneously transforming itself, and that it remains relatively constant independently of the specific forms that psychic reality takes in each of these spaces.

The principle of complementarity

This principle gives further clarity to the principle of transversality: the group forms a psychological entity and is itself in a complementary relationship with other organizations of psychic life. This principle is very useful to us in psychoanalytic investigation when we are seeking to gain knowledge of the unconscious in the diverse spaces in which it manifests itself.[4] One application of this principle is that psychic formations and processes are disposed in different ways and they fulfil different functions when they are mobilized in each of the spaces. This is how certain properties of phantasy are used in linking situations with specific effects, notably as their organizer.

The principle of plurifocality

Notwithstanding the common idea that the group is a circle that possesses a single attracting centre, it has to be acknowledged that in fact it possesses several, and that some are active while others are latent. Only the phantasy of the One and of the Centre make us believe in this unifocal conception. Bion, on the contrary, worked on the ternary principle of basic assumptions. I subscribe to this idea and adopt the principle of plurifocality to contend that psychic space in the group possesses a plurality of organizing centres (or systems). We are dealing here with a mutation that corresponds to the equivalent of the transition from Copernican cosmology (the centre of the world is not the Earth but the Sun) to Kepler's cosmology, which allows for several organizing centres of the universe. It marks the end of heliocentrism.

The polyphonic principle

This principle is a consequence of the three principles of constancy-transversality, complementarity, and plurifocality. By *polyphony*, following the theories of Mikhail Bakhtine, I mean that in the psychic space of the group, as in any linking configuration, several voices and several statements addressed to several recipients are heard. The central notion here is one of resonance, independently of any quest for harmony or unison. This principle comprises a hypothesis concerning the topography of the unconscious and clinical implications for the psychoanalytic conception of transferences and associative processes in groups. It organizes our listening from the diverse places where the unconscious expresses itself in linking. (I should add that polyphony means not harmony but the combination of several voices of different frequency: cf. Kaës, 2002b.)

The principle of complexity

This principle helps us think about the processes of organization and reorganization of the spaces of the psychic reality of the members of the group (or of any other linking configuration), between the members, and within the group. With the group—as with any linking configuration—we are dealing with a complex object, but one that is conceivable as such on the basis of the three fundamental propositions of complex thinking: the dialogical principle, which considers a unit of n opposing and complementary elements in almost permanent tension; the recursive retroactive loop of effects on causes; and the hologrammic principle, which states that each element contains to a reduced degree the totality of which it is a part.

It is easy to see that the intra/inter/transpsychic triad creates disturbances (disorganizations) in each of its components owing to the modalities of adjustment between these diverse psychic systems. The regulations (organizations) and original creations (reorganizations) that are necessary make use of and transform each of these systems.

The theories of complexity and chaos have contributed valuable schemata for thinking about the organization, dispersion, and reorganization of psychic energy and representations in the group. Thinking of the group as a dynamic system comprising episodic processes of organization that are more or less stable, fluctuating, and random, as proposed by chaos theory, allows us to envisage complexity from the processual angle. According to the theoreticians of chaos theory (e.g. Fogelman Soulié, 1991; Morin, 1990; Nicolis & Prigogine, 1989), such systems possess two fundamental characteristics: sensibility to the initial conditions and the existence of attractors. The first signifies that small variations can result in unpredictable behaviours of the system (the classic example is that of the fluttering of a butterfly's wings, which is the distant and non-linear cause of storms). Attractors are temporary organizers, whether repetitive or not, of the system: they attract the system towards a given organization.

From this perspective, complexity is the result of the degradation (entropy) of the group as an initial system, to the benefit of its constituent elements (the subject-members), returning eventually to the more complex reorganization of the group itself. In other words, the process of subjectivation, the starting point of which is the group, finds its matter and energy in the episodic decline of the group's attraction for its subjects; the liberated energy and representations are transformed into complexity in a way that is specific to each subject, and are susceptible to being reinvested in the group whose organization thereby acquires greater complexity.

To this extent, complexity is to be understood as a problem posed for our knowledge of the articulations between psychic structures, those of each subject linked to other subjects in an organization of linking, and those of this link itself. The principle of complexity is confronted with the processes of reducing complexity, both in the process of knowledge and in the process of regulating complexity.

The principle of uncertainty

The principle of uncertainty, as I am using it here, is inspired not by the concept of relations of uncertainty formulated by Werner Heisenberg, but by the meaning that it has acquired in probabilistic theories under the name of subjective probability: that is, a normative theory of probability in which all the judgements made by a hypothetical subject necessarily stem from the assumptions that he freely makes in conditions of uncertainty. In the situation that concerns us, the conditions of uncertainty reside in the fact that each subject-member of the group is faced with the complexity of diverse and plural psychic organizations, and with the fact that they are ordered in a way that is not systematically foreseeable—that is, in a partially aleatory manner. The impossibility we find ourselves in of predicting with certainty the conduct of the other—and *a fortiori* of more than one other—does not mean that we cannot understand the logic of it retrospectively. In the group situation, the conditions of uncertainty require the employment of reductive processes of uncertainty so as to diminish the perplexity (Pujet, 2002) associated with it.

The principle of multifactorial indetermination

It follows from the two preceding principles that the processes and formations that govern the relations between the subjects in the group (or in any other configuration of linking) and the group itself are determined in an interdependent and multifactorial way. The psychic space of the subject considered as such is itself affected by this type of causality.

Particularities of clinical practice on the boundaries of intra- and interpsychic spaces

The diversity and heterogeneity of psychic forms and processes define the complexity of the clinical work we are faced with in groups. These spaces are heterogeneous; their consistency and logic are distinct, but they are inter-communicating. We get a measure of this when we try to understand how the common and shared transferences in the group and the specific transferences of each subject are articulated. Our psychoanalytic listening encounters this complexity when it situates itself on the boundaries and zones of interference of the three psychic spaces that I have distinguished.

We generally reduce this complexity by focusing our attention on just one of the levels of the psychic reality involved in the group: that is, we focus either on the subject in the group, or on the links or ties between the subjects, or on the group as an entity or as a "totality". Bion, Foulkes, and Anzieu focused their attention and their theorization on this last level (historically the first). Pichon-Rivière began to articulate two terms: the subject as the "emergent" or *portavoz* [speech-bearer] of the group and the group as a whole.

Conclusion

Having arrived at the end of this chapter, we have been able to pinpoint one of the issues at stake in the question that we want to establish. The psychoanalytic approach to groups concerns psychoanalysts to the extent that the knowledge of the unconscious to which the group psychoanalytic situation gives us access offers a new understanding of the relations between the several psychic spaces. It is

ultimately a matter of finding in psychoanalysis the matter and reason for a general theory that can have meaning for the understanding of both the individual psyche and the psyche of configurations of
linking, of which the group is one of the paradigmatic figures.

It remains for me to describe the methodological setting by
means of which group psychoanalytic practice manifests itself. I will
then need to explain how the clinical findings on which my conceptual developments are based are themselves polarized by hypotheses
and by theoretical models that form the background to our evenly
suspended listening.

NOTES

1. I describe further on (in chapter 6) their processes, functioning, and
principal formations, but I want to emphasize at this point that the group
psychic apparatus is not to be confused with the individual psychic apparatus: it is not an extrapolation of it.

2. "The use of analysis for the treatment of the neuroses is only one of
its applications", wrote Freud (1926e, p. 248.)

3. In *Totem and Taboo* (1912–13, p. 135) Freud defines kinship as the
"participation in a common substance" uniting the members of a clan.

4. The adoption by Devereux (1972) of Niels Bohr's notion of complementarity forms part of the field of method and epistemology: Devereux's
constant point is that psychological discourses and sociological discourses
are mutually irreducible and that a relation of complementarity exists between them.

3

The group as a psychoanalytic situation

In chapter 2 we saw that the extension of the field of the theoretico–clinical objects of psychoanalysis has always entailed an epistemological crisis: the fundamental requirements of the psychoanalytic method have had to be adjusted in order to make the knowledge of new objects accessible, and this knowledge has resulted in modifications of the theory.

The group as an artefact did not escape this rule: the extension was carried out on the basis of the methodological principles that structured the inaugural model of the individual treatment, but with the transformations imposed by the morphological characteristics of the group—that is, plurality of subjects, prevalence of the face-to-face situation, and interdiscursivity. These three morphological characteristics determine the specificity of the psychic reality of the group, and of the psychic reality mobilized in the members of the group; they confer particular inflections on the transferences, the associative processes, listening and interpretation; they influence the manner in which the fundamental rule is received and how it functions, and, finally, the psychoanalyst's way of working in the group psychoanalytic situation.

In this chapter, we examine the methodological principles on which the group psychoanalytic setting was built. We will thus be able to establish how it is similar to, and differs from, the model of the individual treatment.

The method of psychoanalysis: general considerations

Generally speaking, the method opens the path to knowledge of a reality that is otherwise almost inaccessible. By psychoanalytic method, I mean a set of procedures for acquiring knowledge of psychic reality and for treating psychic disorders. One must be careful not to accentuate the impersonal character of the method. On the contrary, the psychoanalytic method includes, in a decisive way, that which is specific to the analyst's personality.

Three propositions concerning the method of psychoanalysis

To my mind, the following three statements form the root of the psychoanalytic method:

1. The *aim* of analysis is the treatment of "otherwise almost inaccessible" psychic disorders. It is important to recall that this aim is "therapeutic in kind", but it is not limited to the realization of this aim alone. Indeed, this treatment requires a psychoanalytic process to develop during which an authentic experience of the unconscious is possible in the transference that is created, received, and unravelled in the psychoanalytic situation. The treatment of neurotic adults was the *first* form of psychoanalytic treatment; it is the first paradigm of the method of gaining access to the unconscious.

2. Psychoanalysis is produced in a *situation* suited to mobilizing, knowing, and working on the processes and formations of the unconscious of a subject considered in the singularity of his structure and his history. This situation develops from a setting, a frame, and a limited number of structuring rules accepted as the "fundamental rule". The activation by the analyst, who acts as their guardian, of the setting, the frame, and the fundamental rule generates processes that identify this situation as psychoanalytic.

3.   The efficacy of the *psychoanalytic process* lies in the statement of the fundamental rule, in the movements of the transference and countertransference, and in the function of interpretation in the psychoanalytic situation. Everything that happens in the psychoanalytic situation—symptoms, dreams, and associations—are related to the transference, its modalities, its objects, and its contents, and to its relations with resistance to the psychoanalytic process. The analyst exercises the function of interpretation, and he is attentive to how the analysand receives it. In point of fact, interpretation is produced in the transference–countertransference field and returns to it, while transforming it.

The relations between method and theorization

Psychoanalysis built its theory by virtue of this paradigm and situation. It elaborated models of intelligibility concerning psychic phenomena that became knowable thanks to the properties of the *first* situation. The latter functioned as a situation of reference when it became necessary to modify the basic protocol in order to make other forms of psychoanalytic work possible.

As a general rule, two principles govern a method: the principle of possibility and the principle of limitation. These two principles define the field of its theoretically knowable objects.

According to the principle of possibility, the method has the function of tracing a path that leads us towards the object to be known, framing it within the setting in which it occurs. By so proceeding, psychoanalysis framed its theoretical object methodologically, and this framing made it possible to acquire knowledge of the organization, formations, and processes of the unconscious. Freud sought to render the most typical manifestations of the unconscious—dreams, symptoms, repetition, and transference—congruent by means of the method capable of opening up the "royal" road to its knowledge, and to the treatment of its pathogenic effects. This framing of the object is a requirement of the method: without it, the order of the formations and processes of the unconscious could not become manifest, and its effects could not be recognized for what they are, for an individual subject, in this psychoanalytic situation.

According to the principle of limitation, the method allows for the subsistence—beyond the framing that it institutes for tracing the

path towards its object—of a "remainder to be known" and, by definition, of the unknown. This remainder to be known of the unconscious, which can find a path of access if an adequate methodological
adjustment is made, belongs hypothetically to the field of objects
theoretically knowable by psychoanalysis. This is what happened with
the invention of a method of psychoanalytic treatment for children,
and for psychotic or borderline patients. The same question is posed
when psychoanalytic treatment by means of the group calls for modifications of the method.

The stakes of the methodological problem

In fact, when the psychoanalytic aim gives itself a new object—no
longer the individual subject but the group and the individual subjects who make up the group—it is imperative that it constructs
a setting capable of responding both to the characteristics of this
object and to the criteria of every psychoanalytic situation. It is thus
appropriate to examine how the morphological characteristics of
the group and the fundamental rule mobilize certain effects of the
unconscious and define a specific space of psychic reality.

Thus posed, the methodological problem we are faced with does
not concern "applied" psychoanalysis, nor the urgency of verifying
whether Freud's speculations on the group and the "group mind"
can be maintained. The problem is one of constructing a new psychoanalytic object using an adequate methodology. The issue, then,
is to define this situation to the maximum of its heuristic power.

Psychoanalytic setting, situation, and frame

Before specifying the conditions under which the group setting meets
the requirements of the psychoanalytic method, I must explain how
I am using the concepts of setting, situation, and frame.

The *setting* [*dispositif*] is a working apparatus constructed with a
certain aim. It is an artifice, a construction. It is the arrangement of
spatio–temporal elements and materials appropriate to an objective
of knowledge and transformation. It is thus inscribed not in the absolute, but in the relative suitability of an object or an instrument to
a task or to a certain state of things. The setting is both *that which the*

analyst has at his disposal and *that which he puts in place* for practising psychoanalysis: the artifice that he sets up reveals a certain order of the psychic reality that is otherwise indiscernible, and no operation aimed at transforming this psychic reality would be possible without this setting. To produce this effect, one has to introduce a break or rupture into the course of things, operate a reduction of that which is diffuse, and neutralize the orders of reality that interfere "naturally" with the order of psychic reality, whose manifestation is supposed to be favoured by the setting.

For the fundamental reason that lies in the object of psychoanalysis, the setting only produces effects of analysis by virtue of being proposed and sustained by the psychoanalyst, who, in his threefold function of transference object, guardian of the setting, and interpreter, is himself subject to it. The relevance of the setting may thus be evaluated according to several criteria: the aim, method, ethics, theory, and practice of psychoanalysis. The latter cannot be dissociated from the personal equation of the psychoanalyst.

The psychoanalytic *situation* is developed on the basis of a setting governed by the necessities of the method. It may be defined in two ways: (1) in terms of the aim pursued: that is to say, the experience and knowledge of the unconscious of an individual subject; and (2) in terms of the psychoanalytic processes that the setting has set in motion. These processes develop from the announcement of a limited number of structuring rules (known as the "fundamental rule") of which psychoanalysis is the guardian. They consist essentially of the set of movements of repetition and creation that specify the transference–countertransferential field and of a discourse called free association. It is therefore important for the capacity to feel, to put into words, and to interpret that which manifests itself in the psychoanalytic situation to be established and preserved. The formations of the unconscious are only knowable under these conditions, without which the very possibility of analytic practice disappears.

The concept of the frame [*cadre*] must not be confused with the invariants of the setting [*dispositif*][1] of investigation, treatment, or research. The psychoanalytic concept of the frame was progressively constructed from the writings of Bleger, who, in his article "Psychoanalysis of the Psychoanalytic Frame" (1966), put forward the idea that the frame gathers up and stabilizes the psychic contents

emanating from the "psychotic part of the personality". This psychotic part is essentially a topographical place split within the ego:
it does not have much to do with clinical psychosis, nor with the
destructuring of the ego and its delusional restoration. The frame is
essentially the place where these archaic elements are deposited and
settle. It is first constituted by the psychoanalyst's psyche and then
by an extension of the latter in the psychoanalytic space. The essential function of the frame is to attain stability so that there is *process*,
movement, and creativity. However, no frame is perfectly stable: owing to the analysand and the psychoanalyst, the frame is subject to
transformations that reveal its function and contents. Thus the frame
is dialectically related to the process.

The frame is the receptacle not only of the archaic, but also of the
primal: there are thus grounds for reflecting on the relation of the
frame with the primal violence that "lies in it". Nevertheless, certain
elements of the frame are associated with oedipal difficulties, insofar
as the frame defines limits and prohibitions.

I have distinguished six functions of the frame. The first is the
containing function described by Bleger when he says that the frame,
a "receiver of symbiosis", contains "the psychotic part of the personality". Within this first function, we may distinguish the *capacity* as
a receptacle or as a constraint; the *deposit*, a consignment pure and
simple, or the *depository*—that is, the place where one disposes of
certain objects to preserve them or keep them safe; and the *crypt*,
which receives what is hidden and archaic.

The second function, that of *limitation*, protects the distinction
between the "ego" and the "non-ego". The frame is the guardian of
the subject's limits, of his bodily and psychic space.

The third function of the frame is *transitional*: constituting a
boundary between the ego and the non-ego, the frame articulates
the inside and the outside; the frame participates in this space conceptualized by Winnicott where paradox and indecidability prevail.
Found–created, the frame is neither subjectively conceived nor ob-
jectively perceived. One of the resulting problems is that of maintaining the contractual dimension of the frame confronted with that
of its adequacy and its adjustment. This problem partly defines the
content of what I have called transitional analysis (Kaës, 1979).

The frame fulfils a fourth function of *support* and *anaclisis* on the
model of leaning against the object in the background: the contribu-

tions of James Grotstein, Joseph Sandler and Geneviève Haag have demonstrated the role of this object in the formation of the sense of security and identity.

The fifth function is that of the "*container*": it corresponds to the function of representing and transforming object- and affect-presentations into word-presentations, which are made possible by the frame.

If these five conditions are fulfilled, the frame can have a sixth, *symbolizing* function, a major condition of the formation of thought.

I use the concept of *metaframe* (on the concept of "meta", see Introduction), or frame of the frame, to account for the fact that every frame is itself framed by a frame that contains it, maintains it, encroaches on it, or impedes it. This notion is very useful for understanding the relations between the psychoanalytic frame of the individual treatment, the psychoanalytic frame of supervision, and the psychoanalytic frame of the psychoanalytic institution.[2]

The group as a psychoanalytic setting, situation, and frame

In order to clarify the conditions under which the group can constitute a methodological paradigm that is able to render manifest the psychic reality of the subjects in the group and the psychic reality of the group, I must first describe the morphological properties of the group situation.

The morphological characteristics of group situations

I distinguish four morphological characteristics of the group psychoanalytic situation: the precession of a desiring and organizing principle; the plurality and simultaneous presence of persons; a face-to-face position; and the plurality of discourses and interdiscursivity. These characteristics are common to all group situations, whatever their aim and their technique—therapeutic groups, training groups, psychoanalytic psychodrama groups, group analysis—the duration and rhythm of the sessions, or the modalities of openness or closure of the group (a slow-open group or a closed group).

The precession of a desiring and organizing principle

I share Missenard's idea that the psychoanalyst who brings a group together for psychoanalytic work is placed by the group members in an imaginary position as the group founder. Nonetheless, it is worth recalling that it is the psychoanalyst who announces the rules that give rise to the process of symbolization. This precession, as we shall see, has remarkable effects on the question of the origin, content, and functioning of the transference and countertransference.

The plurality and simultaneous presence of persons
who are strangers to each other

Plurality is a remarkable characteristic of group morphology. It generates a combinatory system of relationships whose effects are inscribed in the objects of the transferences, in the associative processes, in the diversity of the forms of linking (couples, trios, sub-groups), and in the resources available for the figuration of psychic scenes.

In the settings that we use, the group is composed of several subjects who are total strangers to each other. Each subject who is about to become a group member finds himself immediately facing a multiple and intense encounter with several others: for him, these objects of drive investments, emotions, affects, and representations all enter into complementarity or antagonism, into resonance or dissonance with each other. One may suppose that in such a situation a significant amount of excitement will be produced, and probably maintained by the excitement of others, in a very complex interplay of reciprocal projections and identifications.

Plurality thus provokes effects of internal co-excitation and mutual co-excitation; it develops transitory experiences of being swamped and a failure of the capacity to link up the exciting stimulations with representations. These experiences are potentially traumatogenic if the stimulus barriers are insufficient. If it is accepted that there is a constant relation between the intrapsychic components and the intersubjective components of the stimulus barriers, then it may be assumed that, in groups, certain conditions that govern the formation of the primal unconscious obtain. Freud's hypothesis that primal repression probably comes into operation when the stimulus barrier is overwhelmed finds an interesting field of observation here.

One of the defence mechanisms used by group members for dealing with a precarious situation of swamping and no-linking to which their egos may be exposed is to reduce the multiple situation to a known situation, or to a more restricted regressive situation that can be controlled better—for instance, a dual relationship. Another mechanism, identified by Missenard (1972), is that of *urgent identification*, the notion of urgency connoting the precarious situation of swamping. The group members identify with one common object capable of maintaining an intrapsychic link and of reducing the sense of panic; they thereby re-establish the containing capacity of psychic reality that has momentarily broken down. The object of the urgent identification is not just any object: it is an object that is chosen for its defensive function, which will be able to mobilize in each person diverse modes of identification, adhesive or projective.

I have identified a third mechanism for dealing with the initial dangerous situation. From the very first moments of the group encounter, the group members, without realizing it, set up shared and common defence mechanisms by tacit agreement. The repression, denial, or splitting of dangerous representations, and the repression of disturbing affects, contribute to the early production of unconscious contents linked to the group situation. This is where the origin, principle, and functions of *defensive unconscious alliances* are to be found: that is to say, negative pacts, common denials, and shared rejections.

These formations are of great importance, since the unconscious contents of these initial defensive alliances will make their return in the group, along paths that are specific to each person, but also via the group modalities of the transferences, the formations of symptoms, and the associative process. These defence mechanisms should thus be considered a constitutive part both of *group links* and of the ties of *each individual to* the group, but also of the psychic reality of the group and of the subjects in the group.

The outcome of these different ways of dealing with plurality is that an unconscious arrangement of psychic zones where linking is possible is produced. Via these processes, plurality is transformed into grouping, furnishing itself with a unifying object and a common space on the basis of which the first delimitations of inside and outside occur.

The face-to-face situation

This third characteristic also distinguishes the group situation from the psychoanalytic situation of the classical individual treatment. With the analysis of Dora, Freud set up a spatial setting such that the analyst was out of the analysand's view. The necessity of resorting to speech rather than the specular scene thus opened the way to word-presentations and to the scene of phantasy. In these conditions, it has sometimes been objected that positioning subjects face-to-face in the group situation is placing them in a space and time that is pre-psychoanalytic.

For my part, I fear that these are purely speculative objections. Clinical experience shows us constantly that if the face-to-face situation mobilizes modes of nonverbal communication, and if the visual investments find within the group space a privileged stage for the specular aspects of identifications, the necessity of speaking about what is happening here and now on the group stage opens the way to word-presentations and to speech that is proffered and heard.

The plurality of discourses and interdiscursivity

In the group situation, the utterances of speech and the signifiers associated with facial expressions, postures, and gestures constitute a plurality of new discourses. These are organized around a dual axis, synchronic and diachronic, individual and intersubjective. In point of fact, when the members of a group speak, their statements are always situated at the nodal point of two associative chains: one, specific to each member, is governed by individual purposive ideas; the other is formed by the statements as a whole and is governed by the organizing unconscious representations of the group links.

I call *interdiscursivity* the status of the discourse that is constructed at these two intercurrent levels—that is, the discourse of each subject and that which is formed by their discourses as a whole (Kaës, 1994b). The enunciations and utterances are determined by this dual axis. The associative discourse in the group is organized in such a way that each subject uses it to bind or unbind his own representations with those of the others. The outcome is a mode of functioning of the associative process that is different and more complex than that which obtains in the individual treatment, even though each of these situations may be considered as the locus of processes of co-thought described by Daniel Widlöcher (1986).

I have often described the group associative process as a means for stimulating and transforming the preconscious activity of the members of the group. Certain unconscious representations that had previously not been able to find paths of access towards the preconscious can become available and useable. The analysis of phoric functions (speech-bearer, symptom-bearer, and dream-bearer) has also opened up new paths for understanding preconscious activity and the intersubjective conditions of thinking.

A particular aspect of this interdiscursive property of the associative process is to inform us about the conditions that facilitate the construction or reconstruction of individual memory in the presence of the group[3]: events that "affect" the group lead to the return of the repressed in the group members and stimulate thought activity, insofar as the stimulus barriers function. This property may be used when working with patients who suffer from disturbances of memory or psychic traumas of diverse origins.

The structuring rules:
transference and countertransference in the group situation

These four morphological characteristics of the group setting are interdependent. They have an effect on the rules of the psychoanalytic method—free association, abstinence, or spatio-temporal *setting* of the sessions—and on the psychoanalytic process. Let us now examine some of the consequences of plurality.

Transference in the group situation

Transference is the result of the property of the situation and of the specific transferred content that is activated in it. This proposition, which is valid for the individual treatment, is also valid for the group. Nevertheless, in the group situation, the complexity of the levels— intra-, inter-, group levels—at which the psychic processes occur sometimes makes it difficult to identify clinically the movements of transference and the contents transferred from one level to another. We are dealing with a very particular economy and topography of transferences, which require a precise reading of the interaction of these different levels. One of the points of interaction consists in the phoric functions, for they are emerging transferences.

The first consequence of plurality is that the group is a locus for the emergence of *particular configurations of the transference*. It is not only objects that are transferred, but object-connections with their relations. What Freud noted in the treatment with regard to the analysis of Dora is relevant for the group. The group space allows for a synchronic actualization of *Schaltstücke* ["connecting pieces"] (Freud, 1895d, p. 293) and the relations that the subject maintains with and between his unconscious objects. This model of connection was subsequently to be applied to dream-thoughts, symptoms, and transferences and is borne out in relation to the group. For one and the same subject, these transferences are interconnected: an example are the complementary "harmonics" of the Oedipus complex and the fraternal complex. Their dynamic organization and their economy are the object of the work of interpretation.

Another characteristic of the transference in the group situation is that the contents transferred in synchrony are *heterogeneous* psychic organizations: archaic, primal, neurotic, psychotic, symbiotic. They develop there in a mode that is both synchronic and diachronic, whereas, allowing for exceptions, they manifest themselves successively in the individual treatment.

The exception that I have just referred to has led me to take a different view of the theory and interpretation of lateral transferences and of the splitting of transference in the individual treatment: they are generally analysed as resistances *to* the transference, whereas in some cases they are resistances *within* the transference. One could say that lateral transferences are the normal mode of functioning in group situations: they occur in synchrony, according to the primary process predominant in the *diffraction* of the transference. These diffracted diachronic transferences thereby furnish a figuration of the *transferred object-connections*—that is to say, of what I call an internal group.

The distribution or diffraction of the transferences onto the group members as a whole, onto the group, and onto the analyst is thus not a dilution of the transference. It would be truer to say that in the group situation the plural, multilateral, and interconnected transferences are diffracted onto objects predisposed to receiving them on the synchronic group stage.

This characteristic of the transference in the group situation describes the group as a location of psychoanalytic work for subjects who would not be able to tolerate a single transference object: such is the case of psychotic, borderline, or antisocial patients. The diffraction of the transference is also an economic distribution of the instinctual charges linked with the transference object.

I should add that the concept of diffraction–distribution of the transference is one of the specific contributions of the group approach to the understanding of the psychic transmission between generations: we can observe how, for a given subject, the synchronic deployment in the transference of objects transmitted and received in the subject's intersubjective history occurs.[4] The clinical example presented in chapter 4 provides an illustration of this.

In groups, as in individual treatment, the transference is only analysable in the gap between the analyst's position and that of the other members of the group in the transference–countertransference field. The analyst preserves his analytic function when he maintains this gap for analysing the transferences, whereas the participants treat themselves as others and respond in reality to the transferences of which they are the object. Maintaining this gap is the condition for recognizing and analysing the unconscious alliances that the subject members of the group conclude.

The group develops other modalities of transference as well. The members of a group are in a transferential relationship towards each other, which is different from that which each of them would establish with his analyst in the individual treatment situation. Owing to group morphological necessity, the psychoanalyst in the group is the object of simultaneous or successive transferences of several subjects, and he is not the *only* object of transference. Moreover, as I have pointed out, the psychoanalyst's precession in the group situation, in addition to the fact that the group members have been brought together by the psychoanalyst, confers this precession from the outset with an imaginary foundational value; it mobilizes *ipso facto* phantasies about origins and the question of the primal. These two characteristics have a bearing on particular aspects of the psychoanalyst's countertransference in the group situation. In particular, they play a considerable role in the particular modalities of the transference and countertransference when two or several analysts choose one another to take on the psychoanalytic function of the group. In this case, the psychoanalysts have to elaborate what I have called the intertransference (Kaës, 1982).

Intertransference

The intertransference describes the state of the psychic reality transferred between the psychoanalysts insofar as it is induced by the group situation, by the transferences they receive, by their own countertransferential dispositions, and by their choice of working together. The intertransference can thus not be treated independently of the transference and countertransference. It is made up of the same constituents, the same issues with regard to the process of increasing awareness: it is simultaneously both repetition and creation, resistance and path of access to the knowledge of the movements of unconscious desire.

Intertransferential analysis is the elaboration characteristic of the psychoanalytic function of the analysts in the group setting. It concerns the transferential locations allocated by each psychoanalyst to the other psychoanalyst in the group situation and the countertransference effects that each person has on each other person: such an analysis is in certain cases a necessary condition for elaborating the interpretation.

Although with regard to this particular aspect of technique, conducting a group psychoanalytically is different from conducting an individual treatment, the issue of the intertransference can throw light on certain aspects of the intersecting points of the transferences involved in the psychoanalytic situation and process of the individual treatment, and in the processes of control and supervision. All these situations bring into play conjunctions of subjectivity, unconscious alliances, pacts, and contracts that affect the countertransference and its effect on the elaboration of the transferences.

Three propositions by way of conclusion

The group psychoanalytic setting is a method that enables the subject to experience the effect produced by him and within him in the encounter of his unconscious with that of the other, or of more than one other, in a configuration of linking such as the group. This setting gives access to an organization of psychic reality that is otherwise inaccessible: namely, that of the group as such.

In order to show how the group psychoanalytic setting has traced new contours and new contents for the notion of psychic reality, it has been necessary to describe the means employed for gaining access to it. I have thus characterized the specific mode of functioning of the transferences and associative processes on the basis of the traits of group morphology.

As a result of these reflections on the method, the following hypothesis takes on sharper focus: in the group, as in every intersubjective relationship, the unconscious is inscribed and manifested several times, in several registers, and in several languages: those of each subject, those of the intersubjective relationship, and those of the group.

NOTES

1. I define the psychoanalytic situation, on the basis used by Bleger himself, as a process that includes the totality of the phenomena included in the psychoanalytic relationship. In the broader sense in which Bleger defines the frame [*cadre*], what I call the *dispositif* [setting]—that is, the technical constants, the stable elements—forms part of the frame but does not coincide with it entirely. I maintain the notion of a difference between *dispositif* [setting] and *cadre* [frame], drawing on the psychic specificity of the frame highlighted by Bleger: the frame receives the psychotic parts of the personality. For me the frame has other properties—for example, that of constituting a limit between the inside and the outside.

2. It is also useful for analysing, in a psychiatric hospital structure, for instance, the relations between the therapeutic setting, individual or group, and the institutional setting. In many cases of institutional suffering what is necessary, when the relations between the different settings have become antagonistic and destructive, is to recognize and re-establish their reciprocity.

3. This is different from the question of collective or group memory: the problem is to understand what constitutes a trace for a group (on this question, see Kaës, 1989b).

4. Studies based on these situations derived from the individual treatment have advanced research into the contents and modalities of the transmission of psychic life between generations; this has a number of consequences for the theoretical conceptions that psychoanalysis has formed of the structuring of the psyche and of the subject of the unconscious (Kaës, Faimberg, Enriquez, & Baranes, 1993).

4

Clinical psychoanalytic work
in the group situation

A clinical example will help us to understand how group psychic reality is formed, how the combination and adjustment [*appareillage*] of psyches occurs, and which processes are at work in the psychic work of the subject in the group situation. This example will provide us with the tangible material for the conceptual and theoretical developments that I present thereafter.

It concerns a group of short duration whose aim is to make it possible for the participants to experience, and be in a position to think about, certain effects of the unconscious in themselves, between themselves, and in the group. In this type of group, the psychoanalysts do not set out to transmit to the participants a form of knowledge about the group, or to train them in conducting groups, or to improve their communications, or to offer them an experience of ego-adaptation to the norms of the group. It is clear that such learning effects can occur. Nor are these groups proposed as groups with a therapeutic purpose, however much the demand of the participants may have its origin in a form of psychic suffering. One observes, however, that therapeutic effects do occur during this experience. Lastly, such groups are not proposed as psychoanalytic groups, in the sense of Foulkesian group-analysis—that is to say, as a group psychoanalytic treatment. However, for some subjects it can be seen that real psychoanalytic work does take place in this type of setting and that it has a deep and lasting analytic effect on their psychic organization. I have noticed this sometimes before some of them get into individual treatment or, and in certain conditions, during their treatment, or alternatively after the treatment.

I have chosen to present a clinical experience of this type of group because it intensifies the processes of the group's psychic organization and mobilizes the individual processes that are the most sensitive to group effects.

I have also chosen it for another reason. Its richness and complexity have given me the opportunity of proposing an analysis of it at several levels, and it illustrates rather well the hypothesis that, in groups, we are concerned with three psychic spaces: that of the group as a specific entity, that of the links between the group members, and that of the individual subject in his intrapsychic groupality. I think that these three spaces are mutually heterogeneous, that their consistency and their logic are distinct, but that they are intercommunicating.

The main theme of my exposition is therefore the articulation between the psychic process of this group and that of several participants. I begin by giving a detailed account of the first four sessions, and then I summarize certain significant moments in the subsequent sessions. I have chosen to proceed in this way because an exhaustive account would be practically impossible; and if I were to venture to provide one in spite of everything, it would be tedious and would very quickly become confused, owing to the complex levels of organization of the psychic reality involved. I am going proceed, then, like Akira Kurosawa in his film *Rashomôn*, by proposing in this chapter, and in the course of the following chapters, several points of view concerning this group. I study it from the standpoint of phantasy considered as an unconscious psychic organizer of the psychic reality of the group. I then analyse it from the angle of group associative processes, dream activity and its effects in the group, affects, and transmissions of affect, and, finally, I examine how the process of subjectivation of certain participants in the work of the group is set in place.

Group presentation

Groups of this type are generally made up of about a dozen people. They do not have familiar, familial, or hierarchic relations between them; they are not selected by interview beforehand. The sessions are spread out over 3, 4, or 6 days, with four 75-minute sessions per day, two in the morning and two in the afternoon. A half-hour break separates the two sessions of each half-day. The participants meet in the same room, at the times agreed in advance; they are seated face-to-face, generally in a circle, either because the seats are so arranged or because they themselves arrange them in this way.[1]

The first five sessions

Ten participants had enrolled in this group for 16 sessions spread out over four days. Two psychoanalysts conducted it, Sophie and myself.

First session:
misunderstanding, disorientation, losing one's points of reference— feeling "beside oneself"[2]

When they arrived at the first session, these ten participants were ten strangers to us and to each other. Some of them were already waiting in front of the door of the room when we arrived to open it; others arrived when we were already seated, in silence, waiting a few moments for the latecomers. Nine of them were present when Sophie and I opened the session: we welcomed them, reminded them that they had asked to be enrolled in this group, and described the unvarying elements of the setting—that is, place, times, duration of sessions. Then we explained the rules underlying our work: they are invited to say—and only to say—whatever crosses their minds, as it occurs to them, without criticism or restriction. Correspondingly, the analysts will only relate to them verbally, and only during the sessions. These two statements constitute the fundamental rule and the rule of abstinence. They are the two indispensable rules.

To these, two further recommendations are added: one of discretion, the other of "restitution"—the first recommends that each participant should remain discreet outside the group with regard to the persons encountered in this group; the second proposes that whatever is said between the participants outside the sessions, during the breaks, should be brought back into the following session.

A long silence followed the announcement of the rules and recommendations. It was interrupted by Jacques, who asked if we could "do a round of first names so that we know whom we are addressing, who is speaking to whom". He needed these "bearings" to be able to move on.[3] Marc introduced himself by saying: "I'm called Marc"; then he remained silent until the middle of the session.[4]

Jacques' request was left hanging for a while. Sylvie talked about the strange experience she had had at the beginning of the session, before Sophie introduced herself as the group's co-analyst. Sylvie talked about her "misunderstanding": she had wondered who Sophie was, and hesitated between two women; pointing to them, she asked them to give their first names. Michèle gave hers readily, Solange with reticence.

Seizing the opportunity, Jacques suggested that they continue "the round of first names", but no one took him up on this. Several participants were more mobilized by Sylvie's "misunderstanding", saying that they had asked themselves the same question at the beginning of the session. Now they knew and were , like Sylvie, reassured. I wondered why Sylvie's question mattered to the others, why it was so urgent to identify the woman in the pair of analysts, and what it was that she wanted to reassure herself about. I supposed that it was an urgent identification, but against what danger? And was it the same for the women as for the men? I also wondered what Sylvie was signalling by speaking about her misunderstanding, and what effect this had had on Sophie. It was remarkable that the group had begun with such a strong movement of transference ("taking one person for another"). But for the time being I really had nothing to go on, and the silence that set in was probably entirely bound up with the repression of this fleeting and dangerous recognition in Sylvie of a movement of transference towards Sophie. It became clear later on that from the very first moments of this group the participants were caught up in a transferential and resistant unconscious alliance, the meaning of which was to unfold subsequently.

The silence was broken by Marc: he said he was feeling vaguely uneasy; he could no longer think, put two ideas together: his head was empty. Boris expressed the same feeing: he no longer knew clearly where he was, or who he was. Both of them were in agreement with something Jacques had said, which had been taken up and completed by Marc; namely, that they had lost their "bearings" [*repères*] and felt "beside themselves" [*hors de soi*]. This sense of unease was shared by Sylvie and Anne-Marie, then by Solange and Michèle. A rather long associative sequence emphasized the feelings of confusion, the loss of bearings, and diverse experiences of misunderstanding.

I noted, without expressing it, the polysemy of the French expression "*hors de soi*": it refers to a disorientation of the ego, but it also expresses the anger felt in this chaotic disorganization. This rather untimely irruption of a sense of malaise lasted until the end of the session. The idea I had at that moment was that the participants had indeed lost their "identificatory bearings" and were trying to recover them; I was attentive to the violence of Marc's and Boris's expression of malaise and the intensity of Sylvie's transference onto Sophie.

During the break Sophie also spoke to me about her uneasiness about the participants' anxiety and the massive transferences that she was the object of, from the women in particular. She told me that she was afraid she was not "up to it" and counted on me to help her deal with the situation. We went back over the session together, hoping to find a leading thread to this narrative activity.

Second session:
the double and the mobilization of a violent the primal scene phantasy

At the beginning of the session Solange repeated her first name: "this time voluntarily", she added for Sylvie's benefit. She went on to say that she had been intrigued, bothered, and even rather anxious about the fact that Sylvie had taken her for Sophie. She wondered what part she herself might have played in this misunderstanding. Sylvie replied somewhat enigmatically that there was perhaps something more between Sophie and Solange than the first syllable of their first names.

Solange took up the idea of misunderstanding to speak about her expectations of this group. She said she had enrolled to learn to "speak properly"—that is, to speak with ease; she needed to be able to do this in her profession. But she had just realized that the reason why she was here at the moment was perhaps not because she wanted to learn to "speak properly". She was here to find the words she needed to express what she felt, words to name what was making her suffer, a "packet to undo", of which she could say nothing, not even *to herself*. This discovery had occurred to her when Marc had said that he was feeling "*hors de soi*"; she had then translated this as *à côté de lui-même* [*next to, beside himself*], as if he had a double. And she had been struck retroactively by the fact that she had been the object of a misunderstanding when Sylvie had imagined that she might be Sophie—her double, as it were. This had made her anxious. Someone said to her that she had not heard what Sylvie had suggested to her about the initial syllable of their first names, but several others could not remember this either, and the group was once again in a state of confusion.

Solange said that this misunderstanding had led her to experience a certain sense of disappointment about the group. Sylvie suggested: "Disappointment about not really being Sophie?" In a weak voice and a defensively disaffected tone, Solange replied that she would indeed like to be Sophie. She very swiftly put on a more dynamic voice and said that she had decided to stay in this group in spite of this disappointment: something was happening in it that was different from what she had expected, and she was surprised by this. She was very interested by what had happened between Marc and Boris, by their way of coming back at each other and telling each other what they were feeling, that they had lost their bearings: like them, she no longer knew where she was.

Owing to this trait she had in common with them, Solange very quickly identified the relationship between Marc and Boris as one of doubles: she was herself caught up in a relationship of this kind with Michèle and Sophie. This was no doubt what Sylvie had wanted to make her understand. Solange was suddenly confronted by Sylvie with her identification with Sophie. I supposed that she was anxious about being confronted directly with what this relationship between doubles represented for her: she was being faced with both her homosexual identifications with the similar other—the sister—and with the maternal imago of her idealized oedipal wish, "*hors de soi*" ["outside" herself, out of her reach], at a distance that caused her anxiety, probably because she had to share it with rivals who deprived her of it. Obviously I did not transform this thinking into an interpretation: it would only have been an individual interpretation, which I did not yet know how to link up with the group process. Moreover, it would have had the effect of stopping the process that was underway.

The way Solange had found a solution for getting out of her brief descent into depression confirmed that it was useful to wait. In a new and sudden change of tone and language, Solange began to criticize sharply what she referred to as our "welcome": she had expected us to introduce everyone, and we had not responded to Jacques' request. She would have liked some real leadership, and we were particularly passive. She knew very well that what she had not got had allowed her to discover something else; but she was still expecting us to be "real leaders". Some participants asked her to clarify what her expectations were, but she could not—or would not—say anything more.

Solange's criticism was especially significant in that she voiced aloud the complaints that the others were not formulating at that moment but would acknowledge later on as their own. Solange and the entire group fell silent, probably out of anxiety that Solange's criticism would cause us to abandon the group. The affect of anger and the fear of being abandoned were transformed into aggression towards Solange: she was talking too much, invading the group, criticizing everything, and so on.

I commented on this displacement: Solange was being attacked because she was revealing hostile feelings towards us. My interpretation hit the mark: it triggered new reproaches towards us: "you don't say anything and you are deserting the group"—an expression of abandonment anxiety. Fresh reproaches came our way in which, strangely enough, Marc, Sylvie, and Solange took no part. The criticisms concerned the arrangement of the room (a long, narrow room!), the colour of the carpet (it was red, aggressive, and dirty!); the disordered way in which the tables and chairs were piled up "making the bedroom [*chambre*] look like a battlefield [*champ de bataille*]" (*chambre* and *champ* sound similar in French). Michèle voiced her impression that not only was there "a big mess", but that there were "people everywhere, too many of us in the room", and that we "should have restricted the number of participants". Sophie drew attention to the power over life and death that was being attributed to us.

The portrayal of the room (*salle* [*sale* = dirty]) as a "*chambre de bataille*" ("battle–bedroom") needed linking up with the phantasy that we had deserted the group: we had abandoned it to have children, too many children. I did not point out or interpret this slip of the tongue. Had I done so, I would have added to the sense of persecution and would probably have stimulated the defences against an over-direct evocation of the underlying phantasy that was still too repressed; and furthermore, I would have overloaded the interpretative path opened up by Sophie.

The work continued in a highly interesting way, for the slide in meaning from room to bedroom was picked up by the participants themselves. It had two opposing effects: for some of them (Marc, Boris, Anne-Marie) the slip of the tongue added to the experiences of confusion, and anxieties about violence and death. For others, on the other hand, it paved the way to playing with words, to investments in pleasure and life. Jacques—who was trying to link up ideas and to establish links with the others—transformed the expression *perte de repères* [loss of bearings] into "we have also lost our *repaires* [hideouts]". This reference to a protective space brought back into the associative chain the image of feeling "beside oneself". I wondered whether these affects of violence, disorientation, and anger had not been there since the very beginnings of the group. My sense was that they were beginning to form links with each other. It therefore seemed possible to me to point out to them that certain words used in the first session were now being used again with new meanings: *perte de repère* and abandonment anxiety [*repaire*]; feeling "beside oneself", which condenses the confusion and anger towards us; *chambre* [bedroom] transformed into *champ de bataille* [battlefield].

My intervention was possible thanks to the effects of Sophie's interpretation concerning the power over life and death that was being attributed to us. But I did not go so far as to say that their anger was that of children excluded from the battle–bedroom where the "parental couple" had taken refuge, and that their confusion was to do with being confronted with the chaos of their prolific mating. I think that they were still caught up in the affect of feeling "beside themselves".

Sophie's interpretation and my intervention were to have other effects: coming back to what Solange had said about her expectations of the group, several participants explained why they had enrolled in this group. Sylvie confined herself to giving one bit of information: one of her friends had taken part in a group with Sophie—hence, she added, her urgent need to know who Sophie was.[5] After pointing out that there remained fifteen minutes until the end of the session, Mark said that he had come to do this group with me, that he had enrolled "because of my name", giving rise to laughter and questions. The phrase was surprising, as was the way he had introduced himself. But Marc did not comment on this.

The end of the session was entirely taken up with a play on the signifier *repère* [bearings], *repaire* [hideout], *re-père* [re-father], *re-paire* [re-pair] (Sophie and I?) The session stopped at the point when Marc observed that the series of "re-"s indicated a repetition, as in *re-père*. He wondered whether the same was true of my first name (Re-né).

During this session, a primal scene phantasy was mobilized, whose function as an unconscious organizer of the group psychic reality and group links is worth noting. In the intrapsychic space, this phantasy was the scene of an action, with internal protagonists and corresponding subjective locations. In the group space, this phantasy brought a representation and locus for the origin of the participants in the group—namely, a battle–bedroom, a figurative image of the founding primal violence in which "Sophie" and "I" were supposed to have conceived them, in which they still felt immersed, disoriented, and confused, feeling that they had lost their bearings and that they were "beside themselves" with anger.

At the break, during the meal, Sophie and I did not talk much about the group: we reflected on our interventions, those that we had outlined during the session, and on the various thoughts that had come to us. We spoke about certain participants, about Marc ("who had enrolled because of my name, but was lost between his *re-pères* [re-fathers]"); about Sylvie (her misunderstanding and the sway she held over Solange); about Solange (divided between speaking about herself, for herself, and speaking for others). We also spoke about our holidays, accidents that had happened to close relations, about the difficulty of writing up the clinical material of psychoanalytic treatments, about a film that we were planning to go to see that same evening. After the meal, I withdrew to make notes and also to be able to let myself associate freely.

Third session:
Marc's enigmatic confession

Right at the beginning of the session, Marc said that he felt bound to confess to the group as a whole an "event that had marked him a lot", about which he had spoken to some of the participants during the break. He was thus obeying, he added, the "rule" of restitution that I had formulated. This "marking" event was the traumatic shock that he had suffered in a similar group to this one. He then evoked, in a confused, vague, and elliptical manner, a wild "interpretation" that had been given to him by the psychoanalyst who was conducting this group, *fifteen minutes before the end* of the last session. He said that this interpretation had made him feel as if he had received a blow on the head, leaving him stunned and disoriented, and he had still barely got over it.

This "confession" surprised us and astonished the participants. They—like us—wanted to know more: why, how, what had been said, and so on. But Marc kept quiet; he did not respond to any of the questions that were put to him, and obviously we did not question him about it. He repeated his "confession", emphasizing the "mark" received, the "marking" event that had "marked" him, the "fifteen minutes before the end". I noted the insistence of the signifiers "mark" and "fifteen minutes before the end", the violence of affect conveyed by his voice, the impossibility (or the refusal?) of communicating an idea or image of the content of the incriminated interpretation. The term "confession" supposes a feeling or an act that has long been held back, very likely a guilty feeling or act that has to be kept hidden.

Marc added that that he had chosen the two analysts of this group "because he hoped that with their help he would be able to get over this". We all understood that his presence in this group was sustained by a clear demand for reparation, and that this demand was addressed to me in particular. It will be recalled that at the end of the previous session, when pointing out that there remained fifteen minutes until the end of the session, Marc had declared that he had come to this group "because of my name", without giving any further details in spite of the questions that were put to him at the time. We knew that he had noted a repetition in my first name, one of a "renaissance", and thus of a death traversed or denied. I made the hypothesis that his first name, mine, and my family name were for him major signifiers of a drama that he was reliving in the transference. My associations led me to the formula he had used when introducing himself: "I'm called Marc". I supposed that an unconscious phantasy had become frozen in this traumatic scene, which had been reactivated in the last quarter of an hour of this last session.

Only the violent affect from this scene had remained active. If we are attentive to what Marc was not only saying but *doing* with what he was saying, we can understand that he was trying to *make* the others—particularly Sophie and me—*experience* what he was experiencing repetitively himself. He was seeking to transmit his affect by arousing an affective identification in the others.

While listening to Marc in the silence of the perplexity and astonishment that followed his "confession", I wondered what he might be feeling guilty about: His violent phantasy? The pleasure he had experienced from being subjected to this "marking event"? We had to wait and see what would follow. For the moment, I made the assumption that Marc had never had at his disposal, either in the past—but when?—or in the present, the word-presentations needed to express his emotions and to symbolize whatever had been brought into play for him by this "marking event". This event only acquired its full weight from the phantasy that he was actualizing and realizing unwittingly, fulfilling its destiny "outside himself"; and it was in order to link up the threads of this destiny again that he had come to the group because of my name. But I had to wait until what was being conveyed through affect, in order to be experienced, had first found its way into the participants' associations before Sophie and I could say something about it in an attempt to unravel the enigma by analysing the transference.

After the silence that had followed Marc's confession, Boris expressed once again the sense of malaise to do with being disoriented, of having lost his bearings, of no longer being able to think. The experience of finding it difficult to think was probably one of the effects Marc was unconsciously trying to achieve: it was expressed by Boris, and it was felt by most of the participants. The entire group was in the process of forming links with each other through the repetition of affects of anger and through anxieties to do with disorientation.

It seemed to me that it would be useful to draw attention to the connection between this difficulty, the breakdown of the associative process, and its roots in the transference by making an interpretation. I realized that I was counting on Sophie to make this interpretation: I was feeling too burdened by Marc's transference towards me. I think that, at that moment, I was afraid of repeating the "blow on the head"—unless, that is, I was restraining myself from dealing him a blow because of my own aggressive countertransference feelings towards him. But Sophie did not intervene: she did not feel any urgency to do so. I did, and I resented the fact that she was leaving me to deal with the situation alone, unable to find the best way of extricating myself from it. At the same time, I could not leave the traumatic effect of Marc's violent confession without words, without representing it in the form of words.

So I intervened to underscore the fact that what was being repeated now, after Marc's confession, was the sense, already expressed, of losing one's bearings. Marc had referred to a shock, something that had happened elsewhere—in a group like this one—and he had spoken about it in a powerful and allusive manner, which was perhaps arousing the fear that the same thing might occur again here in this group. Each participant was reacting to this something with emotions that were their own, and which were perhaps putting them in touch with something that was "outside them". But it also seemed that these emotions, these anxieties, and the sense of losing one's bearings were common to, and shared by, the group as a whole. What this sense of unease and disorientation were about was for each one to say: perhaps the fear of receiving "wild" interpretations, as Marc said he had received *in extremis* his blow on the head, was preventing them from speaking about it?

The immediate effect of my intervention was a period of silence—continued until the end of the session: not for fifteen minutes, but for a few minutes.

During the break Sophie and I talked about the emotion—in fact, the astonishment that Marc's confession had caused in us. It was as if we had to defend ourselves against the allegation that he was making, which was confronting us, each in our own way, with our violent impulses towards the participants, and the phantasy that we might be savages in this group of savages. We spoke about my expectation that Sophie would intervene, about her silence infused with Marc's enigma, about the analysis that I had made of my countertransference feelings and of the interpretation that followed from it, about the sense of relief that my intervention had produced in her, and perhaps in the group, notwithstanding the silence.

I continued to question myself about what was being repeated insistently and about the sway that Marc's "confession" was having over the whole group, as well as over us. The effect of this confession, the affective trace that it rekindled in the participants, clearly gave the telling of this "event" a group dimension.

Fourth session:
Solange, speech-bearer

This very quiet session seemed to me to be heavy and chaotic. I felt discouraged and was unable to let associations develop or to maintain an "evenly" and sufficiently suspended attention. What was said was repressed or erased without my realizing it, and Sophie also noticed that she could no longer remember exactly what had been said during this session.

Then, once again, something was repeating itself: Solange also declared, about fifteen minutes before the end of the session, that she felt obliged to speak now, that she could not put off much longer becoming the "speech-bearer" for what Anne-Marie had confided to her during the break: namely, that Anne-Marie's daughter had been hospitalized for a few days to have a test that was supposed to confirm whether or not she had cancer. This event had overwhelmed both the mother and the daughter to the point that Anne-Marie's participation in this group had been uncertain. After speaking to the doctors and assuring themselves that the young patient would be in good hands, they had decided together that Anne-Marie would come to the group: she had enrolled a long time ago and was expecting a lot from it.

The account Solange gave of this situation on Anne-Marie's behalf was not linear. Solange was invaded by powerful emotions. While she was speaking for someone else, the memory suddenly came back to her of a threat that her own mother had once made to her: the young Solange would get cancer if she continued to smoke so immoderately. At the time, Solange was approximately the same age as Anne-Marie's daughter. She had forgotten this threat until this day.

Anne-Marie, who was very moved too, thanked Solange for having spoken on her behalf, as she had asked her to do. Anne-Marie and Solange cried, while tears came to Jacques' eyes, too. Solange said that she could understand the burden that Anne-Marie needed to get off her chest: she herself was feeling relieved. Anne-Marie said how guilty she had felt for wanting to come here, and how much her daughter, by accepting her absence, had helped her to feel less guilty. But who would believe in this exculpation? Anne-Marie stated that she might have to leave the group if her daughter's condition were to deteriorate.

During this sequence Solange and Anne-Marie maintained eye contact with Sophie, though they did not speak to her. The associations that preceded the end of the session concerned the decisive weight of certain remarks made by parents to their children: in particular, the devastating though sometimes saving effects of the things mothers say to their daughters.

The end of this session threw light retrospectively on the sense of unease at the beginning of the session, and most probably in the very first session, and perhaps also the frequent breaks in the associative process. A new "confession" outside the session, and the realization, *in extremis,* of the mission of the speech-bearer, was necessary for it to become clear to what extent death-anxieties were being mobilized in this group: the significant repetition of the confession of the "last fifteen minutes" was evidence of this. But we have not finished with this signifier.

The fifth session:
Michèle's dream

The following day's session was punctuated by Michèle's telling of a dream she had had during the night: *"I was making love in a very untidy room with Marc's father, or perhaps with my own father; they both had greying hair."* Disturbed by her own account, Michèle added that she didn't know what she was saying (laughter, except Marc).

Each element of the dream was the starting-point for several series of associations. The first series was organized around the uncertainty about the father's identity (was it Marc's or Michèle's?) and the common feature of greying hair. The associations stopped when recognition of what was at stake in the transference towards me became imminent (the same greying hair as that of the fathers in the dream), and the depiction of the incestuous wish towards the father became too embarrassing. It was still too early to interpret resistances. Marc was silent and ill at ease when the role of his father in Michèle's dream was mentioned.

The second associative series began with the "very untidy bedroom". This scene was the depiction in Michèle's dream of a day residue: the dissolute love-scene referred to the day before, the proliferation of babies, and the hallucinated blood stain on the carpet in the battle–bedroom [*chambre de bataille*]. Marc participated actively in the associations by "marrying" couples whose relations he was observing. He gave a wife to the men with whom he had a defensive conflict. He "saw" Sophie and me as a harmonious couple, attentive to each other. He "married" Sylvie and Jacques, who, according to him, also complemented each other perfectly. He saw Jacques as a sort of son who, he imagined, was in conflict with a distant, learned, threatening, and attractive father whose strength and understanding of the "things of life" he admired. Several participants spoke about a film (*Les Choses de la vie*, by Sautet) whose central theme involved a car accident and amnesia.

The third associative series was formed around the idea of catastrophe and accident. Several traumatic events were mentioned: a father's sudden and premature death; the loss of a very close friend in a mountaineering accident; a mother's paralysis following a car accident.

A fourth associative thread took its source in the libidinal re-investment brought about by this reference to death. It was bound up with the central theme of the dream: "Can the participants make love without transgressing the prohibition against incest, or does the rule of abstinence only apply to the relations between the psychoanalysts and the participants?"

Michèle's dream faced Marc with an incestuous scene in which his father played a part. We have seen how he defended himself against this by "marrying" several couples. By making Jacques his son, he threw light on the position that he occupied in the phantasy of the son's seduction by his father and the defence he had erected against this phantasy. This threatening phantasy concealed a violent scene, which broke out when Jacques protested against this imposed filiation. Marc behaved aggressively towards Jacques by threatening to make an interpretation of his resistance to hearing what he was saying to him—namely, that he loved him like a son!

I immediately pointed out the repetition of the threat of a "wild" interpretation and the repetition in the transference of a configuration of father–son ties in which Jacques, Marc, Boris, the "wild psychoanalyst", and I were involved. I added that these issues of desire, seduction, and threat also had to be seen in relation to the incestuous resonances (daughter–father) contained in the narrative of Michèle's dream. Is to love a man as one's son to love him as a father loves his son or as a son loves his father?

How are we to understand that Michèle had integrated Marc into her dream by depicting his father as the object of the displacement of her own incestuous wish? Michèle dreamt for herself and for an unknown part of herself; in the dream she represented pictorially her own wish. Her dream was made up of what she had absorbed from the psychic contents formed the day before in the group. Michèle's dream was also an interpretation of what she had unconsciously perceived about the phantasies involved in the traumatic "event" reported by Marc and about Marc's unconscious psychosocial conflicts. These phantasies concerned her because they were linked to her phantasy of being seduced incestuously by the father.

I will have the opportunity of coming back to the analysis of Michèle's dream, but I would like to emphasize right away that Michèle's dream was produced in the dream matrix of the group and for a set of recipients: it was addressed to Marc for what he represented for her and for me, present/hidden in the dream. It was addressed to me for what I represented for her and for Marc. It was also addressed to Sophie for what she represented for her and for me.

As a result of Michèle's dream, a transformation occurred in the core of the group's organizing phantasy. The phantasy of reprisals against the "wild" interpretation that Marc allegedly received was associated with phantasies of seduction, beating, and the primal scene. We were getting closer to the meaning that the "marking" event had acquired for Marc, but this meaning could only be revealed gradually in the transference and the group associative process once the common and shared symptoms had been sufficiently repeated.

Work on the signifier "last quarter of an hour"

During the following sessions, the signifier "last quarter of an hour" was to establish itself as a "symptom supported on several sides" in each member and in the group. Some sessions started or ended with a silence lasting a quarter of an hour; a forthcoming absence was announced a quarter of an hour before the end of the last session of the third day.

I interpreted the association of absence–silence–death and "last quarter of an hour", pointing out once again the repetition and the connection it had, it seemed to me, with Marc's "marking" event. My intervention got the associative process moving again. There was mention of the end of the world. Boris got involved in a complicated obsessional calculation to do with the *extra* quarter of an hour of the

group session (an hour and a quarter) compared with the one-hour
time unit, and the quarter of an hour *less* corresponding to the individual analytic session (45 minutes). Michèle took up her dream
again, evoking the "good fifteen minutes" of the orgasm and asking,
with false naivety, what this *extra* and *less* was all about and who made
one come the most: men or women? Jacques associated to the signifier "last quarter of an hour" and to death, which introduced the
themes both of separation and of confusion.

The rest of the sessions were centred on the analysis of sexual
relations and relations between the generations as they had taken
shape in the group through the transferences. Marc then came
to understand what had been traumatic for him in the preceding
group: confronted with his phantasy of being seduced by his father,
he had feared its realization in the transference onto the analyst,
and, at the same time, he had accomplished it *in extremis* by accusing
him of a wild interpretation.

Analytic perspectives

As announced, I continue the analysis of this group in the course
of the chapters to come. I would like, however, to open up a few
perspectives concerning my conception of the psychic reality of this
group.

The unconscious psychic organizing phantasy of the group

The psychic reality of the group and the group process are *organized by an unconscious organizing schema*, the formula of which here is
the fantasy: "*A parent is threatening/repairing a child.*" This organizer
maintains the identifications and the link between all the subjects of
the group: it is the actual representation of a "marking" traumatic
event, no doubt primal, outside time, outside thought and speech,
inaccessible to each member directly.

This phantasy organizer (Figure 2) corresponds to what I call an
internal group: its structure defines the correlative, complementary,
and reversible positions of the subject, the object, and the action.
Its generic formula is that of a grammatical sentence: *subject–verb–
complement.* The subject (parent) and the complement (child) can

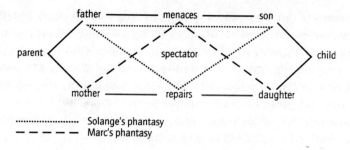

Figure 2. Generic structure of the organizing phantasy of the group

permutate, and the verb can be active or passive (threaten/be threatened). This internal group functions as an organizing schema of the way in which the psyches in the group are combined or assembled, as a structure of attraction and psychic locations. The formula of the principal organizer of this group can be developed into twenty theoretically possible statements. Some statements are not actualized in the group; others are actualized for several subjects at the same time or at different times; several statements can be actualized in succession for one and the same subject.

The organizing phantasy is an attractor of phantasy scenarios and subjective locations

The phantasy functions as an organizing schema of the combination of the psyches (or the way the psyches adjust to each other) in the group. Each member of the group participates in this organizer according to the particular version of his personal phantasy. The phantasy *"A parent is threatening/repairing a child"* is an attractor of phantasy scenarios and subjective locations. It has the effect of constructing the psychic consistency of the group, but its formation is preceded by mobilizations of phantasy that converge and organize themselves progressively.

It will be recalled that during the first session, Sylvie's "misunderstanding" led to confusion; the affect associated with this massive transference was expressed, identifications through affect occurred, activating phantasy scenarios whose offshoots were manifested in the shared and common symptoms of a sense of "losing one's bearings" and feeling "beside oneself", but the source of these affects remained unconscious. I noted that for Sylvie, as for Marc and Anne-Marie, a fomenting of phantasy had already occurred before the first session: imaginary places had been attributed in advance to several group members, in particular the analysts.

These chaotic psychic movements might be gathered together under the formula: "We're seeking an origin." This formula came in various versions (Who is Sophie? Whom are we addressing in this group?) without an organizing phantasy establishing itself. What we were dealing with, rather, was unstable affective states and identificatory movements. Sylvie's question to herself about Sophie and the confusion of thought experienced by Marc, Boris, Sylvie, Solange, Michèle, and Anne-Marie were certainly not unrelated to these states, marked by uncertainty and perplexity. The expression of anger (being "beside oneself") was linked to this uncertainty; it was what provoked Solange's attack against the analysts and against the frame. Solange herself was treated aggressively for having treated us aggressively.

In pointing out the displacement of the transference, I uncovered another phantasy whose formulation expressed the anger of being excluded from the parental bedroom: *Parents are making love in a battle–bedroom. They are having too many children.* The (paranoid–schizoid) sadistic primal scene phantasy was accompanied by a (depressive) phantasy of abandonment and exclusion.

When the confession of the "marking" event occurred at the beginning of the third session, all the participants were mobilized by the question of origins (the primal scene) and death (the blow on the head, the last quarter of an hour). This confession came after Marc's announcement that he had enrolled "because of my name", after his question about re-naissance, and his demand for reparation. The injection of affect triggered identification through affect, which, failing representation, contributed to the sense of confusion and threat.

In my countertransference and in the intertransference with Sophie, I was concerned by this phantasy at several levels: by the position of threatening and repairing parent in which I was being placed by Marc; and by my expectation of a salutary and protective interpretation from Sophie against my phantasy of repeating the "blow on the head". I managed, however, to shake this phantasy off by virtue

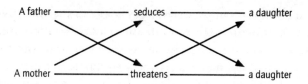

Figure 3. The second organizing schema

of having recognized in time its relation with Marc's phantasy and that of some of the others.

The fourth session offered quite a convincing indication that a common and shared phantasy was being formed: Anne-Marie's story and the return of the repressed in Solange when, taking on the role of speech-bearer, she became a co-actor in the scenario "*A parent is threatening a child: we are looking for someone to repair, restore him.*"

Michèle's incestuous dream account the following day was based on this intersubjective phantasy navel. Let us recall the words she used: "*I was making love in a very untidy room with Marc's father, or maybe my own father; they both had greying hair.*"

The dream brought both an imaginary answer to the reparation—namely, incest—and it clarified the nature of the threat: the risk of death. Indeed, though the manifest content is explicit, "*A daughter (a son) is making love with a father (a parent?)*", the associations bring more complex connotations: questions about the father's identity; defensive measures against the incestuous scene (Marc marries couples, gives himself a son, threatens him); remembering traumatic events and the death of close relations; a request for reassurance concerning the taboo on incest (between brothers and sisters).

A second organizing schema took shape, transforming the first. Seduction comes to the fore, with its correlate, the threat. (See Figure 3.)

Access to the individual phantasy and the process of subjectivation

The following sessions were organized around the signifier, "last quarter of an hour", linked to death anxieties associated with the phantasy of castration. The interpretation we gave of this sparked thoughts about the difference between the sexes, bisexuality, and symbolic castration. From this moment on, psychic work was accomplished which decondensed the principal core of the organizing phantasy, allowing each participant to identify his own particular phantasy. Even though it has often been objected that the identification of the subject's phantasized position in his own particular history is given less attention in the group situation than in individual analysis, the example of this group, as far as Marc is concerned, partially contradicts this idea. Traversing an organization of common and shared psychic reality, such as this group phantasy, is necessary if the group is to function. But through the group process the variations of this phantasy produce an important transformation: each subject is singularized in his secondary phantasy. The phantasy ceases to function in an impersonal and anonymous mode and gives way to an individual version that marks accession to the process of subjectivation.

This transformation occurred in Marc, but not without resistance. In the generic structure of the phantasy he was able to oscillate between the various positions of victim (passiveness), silent observer, seducer, and active persecutor of his "son" Jacques. In each of his scenarios he assigned the others to positions complementary to his own, but without being able to recognize himself in the unconscious desire that was moving him. The formula of the secondary phantasy specific to Marc's subjective position was disclosed at the same time as it was recognized in the vicissitudes of the transferences and in their analysis: *"My father, in the past and elsewhere, but who is still present for me here, is seducing/threatening/repairing his son, who finds his 'mark' in this phantasy."*

How the group process gives Marc access to his history: the work of intersubjectivity

Let us dwell for a moment on Marc's story in this group. Above I proposed the idea of the psychic work of intersubjectivity to describe this elaboration. I would like to show through this example how this notion functions with the model of analysis I am proposing, which comprises two basic concepts.

The combination of intrapsychic organizations

The group is an apparatus for transforming trauma through the work of the unconscious combining or assembling of psyches, which constructs the psychic space of the group and organizes the links

between the group members. Original psychic processes and formations are set in place and, among these, from the very first moments
of the life of the group, the repression, denial, rejection, or splitting
of dangerous representations. These defence mechanisms constitute
the material and reason for unconscious alliances.

We can see how Marc polarized the unconscious psychic movements that would organize the group. After Sophie, he became a
second object of urgent identification insofar as he offered the initial
situation of confusion and chaos psychic material with traumatic
content. His "confession" cleared the way for word-presentations and
linked them up with earlier representations that were hitherto inaccessible to several participants: anxiety about losing one's bearings,
affects of anger and dejection, misunderstandings and confusion
over identity, nomination without subject. At the same time as he
increased the traumatic charge, Marc contributed to the breakdown
of the stimulus barrier and maintained the identifications through
affect. What had assumed for him the value of an unthought event
became an experience that was shared by several members of the
group and organized the psychic reality of the group through the
unconscious alliances.

The effects of these defence mechanisms can be identified in the
content and modalities of the transferences and associative work:
unconscious contents return in ways that are specific to each group
member, but also through the psychic productions of the group as
a whole.

The adhesion to the traumatic object has as its correlate the
hopeful expectation in a repairing object capable both of reducing
the fear of being overwhelmed and of mobilizing positive transference movements. Marc's demand for reparation triggered a demand
in the others that also concerned an event that had taken on traumatic dimensions because it had not been possible to give meaning
to it at that moment.

The work of associations and the functions of speech-bearer open the way to the return of the repressed

The psychic work of intersubjectivity rests on a second idea: namely,
that the group associative process, dreams in the group, and phoric
functions are "nodal points" that bind the psyches together; and they
are also passing points from one subjectivity to another.

Solange designated herself and was designated as speech-bearer, not only for Anne-Marie but also for several group members, Marc in particular. The "confession" of a secret through speech of which another person is the bearer for an other, memories of violent behaviour in the relations between parents and children, issues of life and death are carried by the group associative process. Later, the narrative of Michèle's dream, which dramatizes an incestuous act with Marc's father, would reveal other components of Marc's drama.

In order to understand more clearly the function of speech-bearer and group discourse, we can observe that the group is the bearer of speech that is only available to certain of its members, but it is also speech that is important for others, and whose terms are used by the speech-bearers unwittingly. When the missing sense or meaning has become the concern of several group members, the missing speech may appear in the intersubjective arrangement of the group discourse. Under these conditions, the group associative process clears the way for the return of the repressed.

Marc discovered three things through the psychic work of the group: (1) that what he presented as his traumatic experience, his "marking" event, was the effect of his phantasy of being seduced by the father, of the threat of primary homosexual beating (being beaten and seduced by him) and the intense castration anxiety associated with it; (2) that his first name bore the trace—*the mark*—of the inscription that his position in a phantasy, probably shared by his father, had acquired for him; and (3) that he repeated the scenario in groups, both for the sake of pleasure and to obtain reparation for it.

Some remarks on the aim and processes of psychoanalytic work in the group psychoanalytic situation

The clinical case I have presented makes it possible to characterize *the aim of psychoanalytic work* in the group psychoanalytic situation. The objective is to render the experience of the unconscious possible in the forms and processes that manifest themselves in the group for the subjects who are a constituent part of this group. The movements of transferences, the organization, and functioning of the associative process give access to this experience.

The analytic work concerns the links that have been formed in relation to the object of their primal group, which are repeated, tuned, reorganized, and transformed in the group space of the transference and countertransference. But the group psychoanalytic situation comprises another essential characteristic in that it is an encounter with unknown persons, with the unknown and the unforeseeable. It is in this dual register of repetition and random encounter that the relations the subject maintains with his own unconscious objects, with the unconscious objects of others, and with common and shared objects may be worked on.

NOTES

1. I have used other spatial arrangements, in which the participants and the analyst are placed in a circle, but out of sight of each other: that is, back to back. With visual support being provisionally suspended, other perceptual processes—auditory, olfactory, thermic sensibility, etc.—are intensely mobilized (cf. Kaës, 1994b).

2. Translator's note: the polysemy of the French expression "*hors de soi*" is explained a little further on. I have translated it sometimes as "beside oneself" and at other times as "outside oneself", depending on the context.

3. Such a proposal is frequently made during the first session: around the table introductions are solicited: it is a classic measure for creating a protective shield to reassure oneself about the worrying aspects of what is unknown. Jacques used an unusual expression by insisting on first names, and my attention was momentarily focused on it; it was mobilized by the fact that his proposal "to know who is speaking to whom" entered into associative resonance with a concern that I had at that time, and one I had felt when coming to this group, about how the associative process functions. Surprised by Jacques' formula, I recognized that he knew nothing of my interest in this question: but I did not exclude the possibility that when I had announced the fundamental rule, certain intonations might have given away a sign that was barely perceptible, except to him, of my investment: though the hypothesis was plausible, the question remained, why him?

4. In the account given of this group, all the first names have been disguised, except Marc's, for reasons that will appear quite clearly later on.

5. This does not explain why this identification was urgent for other participants.

5

The group as an intrapsychic formation: psychic groupality and internal groups

The clinical analysis presented in chapter 4 illustrates how the founding hypothesis of psychoanalysis—that is, the hypothesis of the unconscious and of unconscious psychic reality—has opened up three areas of research into groups. I will recall them briefly.

The first is based on the notion that there exists a group mind or psyche, that the group comprises structures, organizations, and unconscious psychic processes that are specific to it and are not produced without the grouping. Clinical analysis has given an intuitive idea of the way in which group psychic reality is constructed and transformed.

The second focuses on the relations between the subject and the group. We have been able to confirm the hypothesis that, for its subjects, the group is an object of instinctual investments and unconscious representations, and we have noticed the functions that they carry out in the subject and in the group process. The group is the stage on which the psychic formations and processes that belong to the members of this group are externalized. Clinical analysis has shown how the relations between each subject's internal space and the common and shared space of several subjects in the group are organized.

The third area of research concerns the effects of the group on the subject's psyche. It investigates the way in which his unconscious formations and processes are organized and transformed, if it is accepted that his psyche is structured in the matrix and intersubjective links of the primary group. The group is also the *meta*psychic, active frame of the formation and transformation of the subject.

Internal groups and psychic groupality

In this chapter I begin to set out more systematically the main concepts that make up my psychoanalytic conception of the group, intersubjective relations, and the subject of the unconscious.

Groups are not only specific entities relatively independent of the subjects who constitute them. Groups are within ourselves: each of us is a group. I have called those intrapsychic formations and processes whose properties are active both in the internal space and in the group space "internal groups".

On the couch, analysands teach us many things about these internal groups: the effects can be identified in the structure of phantasies, in the network of identifications, in the organization of object-relations, in the oedipal and fraternal complexes, in the body image, and even in the organization of dreams.

The work of literary creation—that of the novel in particular, but also other forms of creativity, children's drawings, for example—teaches us that these internal groups fulfil important functions in the organization of an *œuvre*. Finally, psychoanalytic work in the group setting has led me to the concept of the internal group to account for psychic formations mobilized electively in the organizational processes of group links and of common and shared psychic space.

I would like now to retrace in broad outline the path that led me to take this route, and to set out the principal results.

Internal groups

My first researches were concerned with studying the group-object inasmuch as it is an object of instinctual investments and unconscious representations. I attempted to identify the organizing schemas that govern these investments and representations: initially I called them "groups of the inside" [*groupes du dedans*], then "internal groups", and I described the role of unconscious psychic organizer played by seven principal internal groups in forming the group-object. These are: the body image, primal phantasies, the systems of object-relations, the network of identifications, the oedipal and fraternal complexes, imagos, and the agencies of the psychic apparatus, especially the ego.

By so identifying these internal groups, and by looking at things from the subject's point of view, I acquired the notion that the group is first and foremost the form, function, and process that it occupies in the space of internal psychic reality. I wondered if it was pertinent to speak of internal groups or only, as Freud proposes with respect to identification, of a "multiplicity of psychic personalities" [*Mehrheit der psychischen Personen*] (Draft L, 2 May 1897, in Masson, 1985). It seemed to me that the internal groups that I was describing could not be reduced to the plurality or multiplicity of psychic objects united in a mere assemblage. Indeed, what confers on a group its specificity and its own character, whether internal or intersubjective, is the link between the elements of which it is composed and, above all, the structural, dynamic, and functional unity that these links establish between these elements and with the whole. Freud's first definition describes not a mere assemblage, but an internal group formed by the network of identifications of the subject's ego.

The thorough analysis of two groups conducted with Anzieu in 1965 and 1966 led me to think that internal groups do not only play an organizing role in the representations of the group-object. Their group organization confers on them a decisive role as unconscious organizing schemas of the group process, the unconscious psychic reality of the group, and the group links.

Psychic groupality

In 1980 I brought together under the concept of psychic groupality all the specific characteristics of internal groups, broadening their scope and clarifying their content. I wanted to question the idea, too restrictive in my view, that internal groups are merely the analogical reproduction of intersubjective groups, or the pure introjection of the intersubjective objects and relationships constituted in the family group. By integrating the notion of internal group within the concept of psychic groupality, I was proposing a more precise model of functioning.

I eventually came up with the idea that psychic groupality designates intrapsychic formations endowed with a structure and functions of binding between the drives, objects, representations, and agencies of the psychic apparatus, insofar as they form a system of relations that links up their respective constituent elements.

However, this definition did not account for a characteristic that seemed to me to be yet more important. The work that I have carried out into associative processes and dreams, both in individual analysis as well as in groups, has led me to consider psychic groupality as a general property of psychic material. Its property is to associate, unbind, and level psychic objects, forming ensembles out of them according to the laws of composition and transformation, under the effect of the instinctual movements of life and death, under the effect of repression, or defence mechanisms other than repression, such as splitting, denial, or rejection. This extension of the concept backed up my initial idea that psychic groupality is the form, function, and process occupied by the group in the space of internal psychic reality.

Debate on the conception of internal groups

When, in 1966, I began working on the "groups of the inside", I did not know that my investigations would converge with those elaborated in different theoretico–clinical contexts by Pichon-Rivière and, later, by Napolitani. Although we were not aware of our respective work, all three of us had formed the idea that "internal" groups are reactivated in the group process. It is interesting to consider this convergence from the standpoint of the genesis of the explicatory hypotheses: each of us had tried to articulate intrapsychic formations with the psychic organization of the group.

The treatment of psychotic patients led Pichon-Rivière (1971) to adopt the idea of "the existence of internal objects, of multiple 'imagos' which are linked together in a world constructed on the basis of a progressive process of interiorisation". The Kleinian orientation that he espoused at the time led him to describe "the intersubjective relations or structures of relationships internalized and articulated in an internal world". However, what Pichon-Rivière calls internal world or internal group is the intrasystemic reconstitution of the relational network, through the process of interiorizing the system of intersubjective and social relations from which the subject emerges. For Pichon-Rivière, this subject is a social as much as a psychic subject.

Napolitani's (1987) conception of the internal group is quite similar to Pichon-Rivière's: the internal group is "a relational structure" (p. 165), that is to say, the network of relational modalities of which the individual has been part, the representation of the relations of each subject to the other and to the environment, and the significations and codes linked to these relations. The internal group is formed by the interiorization, via identificatory processes, of all the relationships in which the individual has participated since his birth, notably through the introjection of the objects and imagos constituted in the family group and of the prevailing values within the family. Napolitani adds that internal groupality "is a structure which codifies the world and relations to the world" (p. 48).

The Kleinian orientation in Pichon's and Napolitani's work, and the Freudian reference in my own, has led us to utilize quite a similar notion. Each of us thinks that internal groups are organizations of interiorized internal objects that orient action towards others in intersubjective relations. But beyond this similarity, our conceptions can only be partly superposed. Our sources are different, and the concept has not given rise to the same developments in each case. For Pichon-Rivière and Napolitani, internal groups result from the interiorization of psycho–social relationships, but they do not take into account their specifically endopsychic genesis; nor do they describe their structure or functioning.

The group organization of psychic material

My conception of internal groups differs from theirs on two important points. The first is that internal groups are not only reactivated in the group process; more fundamentally, they are the principal unconscious organizers. The second is that internal groups are an organization of psychic material.

This is where our main difference lies: internal groups are not exclusively the result of the internalization of relational experiences,

an interiorization of object-relations, and an organization of identifications. They arise from an organization inherent in this property of
psychic material that I have just mentioned—namely, of combining
and organizing itself into groups.

I arrived at this idea along three paths. The first is anecdotal, but
only in part: at the beginning of the 1970s, when Jacques Lacan's
theses were expanding rapidly, I proposed the formula that "the
unconscious is structured like a group". What was meant as a sort of
joke at the time was transformed by a fresh reading of the "Project
for a Scientific Psychology" (1950 [1895]): Freud's speculations on
split psychic groups and the organization of the primal unconscious
lent support to my hypotheses concerning internal groupality. The
third path, which I have just mentioned, was opened up by the attention that I was beginning to pay simultaneously to the group organization of dreams and associative processes in individual treatments
and in groups. These investigations transformed my light-hearted
"Lacanian" proposition into a working hypothesis of more general
import, to the effect that psychic material strives to organize itself
structurally and dynamically according to a group model.

Forms and processes of internal groups

The unconscious as a primal internal group

As early as the "Project for a Scientific Psychology" (1950 [1895]) and
the *Studies on Hysteria* (1895d), the group appears first and foremost
as a model of intrapsychic organization and functioning: it is a form
and a process of the individual psyche. A century before Edelman's
neuronal groups, Freud employed the term "psychic group" [*die
psychische Gruppe*] to denote a set of elements (neurons, representations, affects, instincts . . .) bound together by mutual investments,
forming a certain mass, and functioning as attractors of binding.
The psychic group is endowed with specific forces and principles of
organization, a system of protection, and a system of representation–
delegation of itself by a part of itself. The psychic group establishes
relations of tension with isolated or unbound elements that are,
for this reason, capable of modifying certain intrapsychic balances.
Freud's first outline of the representation of the unconscious is one
of a split psychic group [*eine abgespaltene psychische Gruppe*].

It is likely that all living matter is a group—that is, a movement of grouping and ungrouping, under the effect of Narcissus, Eros, and Thanatos. To restrict myself to the domain of psychic life, I retain the notion of *primal psychic group* to account for the primal binding of objects in a structure and in forms that constitute the unconscious. The unconscious, structured as a group, is constantly recombining itself in its figures, its energy, its formations and its effects.

Phantasy as the structural paradigm of the primal internal group

The clinical example in chapter 4 showed us how the structural approach to phantasy illustrates the concept of the primal internal group. This approach brings to the fore its major property, which is intimately linked to its distributive, permutative and dramatic structure: namely, that phantasy is a scenario for fulfilling unconscious desire. This scenario governs the organization of correlative psychic loci and action. Considered from this point of view, phantasy clearly manifests its property of dramatizing different versions of the subject's relation to his objects, to his desire, to an other, and to more than one other.

The structural analysis of the Rat Man's phantasies (1909d) explains how Freud's patient depicts himself as having three split and disintegrated personalities: the Rat Man places fragmented parts of the "cruel captain" in other characters, also fragmented, or in his dreams, the ultimate psychic containers of what his body cannot tolerate.

This structural approach to the organization of phantasy has been familiar to us since the analysis of Schreber's phantasy. Freud (1911c [1910]) brought to the fore its linguistic organization by developing the idea of a transformation of the "fundamental language" of one and the same phantasy statement into different psychopathological organizations arising from paranoia.

The analysis of the phantasy "A Child Is Being Beaten" (1919e) led Freud to explore the variations of the subject–action–object correlation in terms of the same model of transformation. The usual French translation of the formulation of the phantasy as "*On bat un enfant*" instead of "*Un enfant est battu*" ["*Ein Kind wird geschlagen*"] clearly indicates the imprecise identity of the one doing the beating in the formal structure of the phantasy. The phantasy is a *script* in which the subject depicts himself as taking part in the scene, "without it being possible to assign a place to him" (Laplanche & Pontalis, 1964, pp. 1861ff). While always being present in the phantasy, the subject can be there in a desubjectivized form—that is, in the very syntax of the phantasy sequence.

The structure of the phantasy is a structure with multiple points of entry whose fundamental statement is the representative of a series of statements obtained by derivation, through substitution, through reversal (masochistic or sadistic), from each syntactic unit. This structure is worked on by various primary processes: condensation, displacement, permutation, negation, inversion, and diffraction.

This structural and dynamic conception of phantasy is attentive to the principles that govern its transformation. Moreover, it contributes a more precise content to the notions of interfantasying and phantasy resonance.

Primary internal groups

Primary internal groups are acquired through interiorization, internalization, or introjection: they are the network of identifications, the group of object-relations, the group structure of the ego, the oedipal and fraternal complexes, and the body image. They can be analysed according to the dynamic structural approach that I have proposed for the primal internal groups. In all the internal groups, the subject represents himself in his relations with other parts of himself or/and with his internal objects. I have commented (Kaës, 1993, pp. 26–30) on three varieties of these—the network of identifications, the system of object-relations, and the complexes—and summarize them here.

The network of identifications

Individual treatments confront us with the hysterical identifications of some of our patients. In the course of the same session, one of my patients made me hear successively several voices: the voice of a man, that of an affected and plaintive little girl, that of a tantalizing lover, that of a refined woman, or that of a vulgar woman. Various accents (of a Parisian, or of a Southerner) reproduced the traces of past encounters. At other moments, as in the classical epoch, it was her body that was the scene of possession by several personalities. Thinking of Bion, I said to myself that she was by herself a woman-group [*une femme-groupe*] and that she would offer me a depiction of it, just as she did in the groups she frequented: she used to give me a complacent account of the effects of her aptitudes for transforming herself on other people in such groups. I also thought about Woody Allen's film, *Zeelig*. This character taught me something essential about the human "*seelig*": precisely this capacity to be a "plurality of psychic personalities", personalities whose relations remain unconscious for the subject. They can sometimes be split off from each other and sometimes united within the same internal group, whether conflictual or consensual. It also taught me that the space of individual treatment, like that of the group, could be a scene where several characters are called upon to represent (in the transference) for her (and no doubt for each of them), a shared drama, maintained, and regulated by her bisexual phantasies. As an analyst, I had to welcome and to recognize these characters and their internal links, to name them down to their source, and not to get stuck to just one of them.

I have often pointed out that Freud's first formulation on identification defines it as a "plurality of psychic personalities". This first outline of a conception of the internal group formed through internalization takes on more clarity in *The Interpretation of Dreams* (1900a) when Freud analyses the hysterical identifications operating in dream-formation (in the dream known as the "dream about caviar" or "the butcher's wife"). This same dream was the inspirational source of Freud's concept of shared phantasies, while Dora's analysis brought him the notion of identifications through the symptom: these are two decisive hypotheses for thinking about the concept of psychic groupality.

In the context of the second topography, the second theory of identifications is still more related to a group model (multifaceted identifications, multiple or dissociated personalities). It is linked up more precisely with a group theory of the ego and the superego (Freud, *Group Psychology and the Analysis of the Ego*, 1921c; *The Ego and the Id*, 1923b).

The system of object-relations

The system of object-relations is one of the forms of psychic groupality. With the term "system" I want to emphasize the network of object-relations and their interdependence.

In this chapter it is not possible to offer an outline, however brief, of this concept.[1] What is important here is to understand how the notion of object-relation describes an internal group. In the notion of object-relation, the word *relation* assumes a meaning that includes not only the way the subject constitutes his objects, but also the way these shape his activity. This interrelation implies the co-constitution of the subject and the object: speaking of a relation *to* the object signifies the pre-existence of one or the other.

On this basis, I consider that the system of object-relations functions as an internal group inasmuch as it results from the introjection or incorporation of objects and the relations between the objects: the Other of these objects (André Green) in their relations to the subject; others in the object (Kaës) on which the drive is supported; and the identifications of the ego and its mechanisms of defence.

This group of object-relations is reabsorbed through fusional defensive regression in the symbiotic state of linking: Herbert Rosenfeld noted that this type of omnipotent narcissistic object-relation is always particularly mobilized in groups.

The Oedipus complex and the fraternal complex

The complex is an internal group. It is an organized set of representations and unconscious investments constituted from phantasies and intersubjective relations in which the person takes his place as a desiring subject in relation to other desiring subjects. This is true of both the Oedipus complex and the fraternal complex. The structural conception of the complex inscribes it within a *triangular* intrapsychic organization, in which each element is defined by the special relationship that it has with each of the other elements and by the relationship from which it is excluded. This last point emphasizes the fact that it is necessary to take into account the negative or non-relationship as a dimension of the complex, as well as the way in which it is represented in the complex.

In my research I have worked particularly on the fraternal complex, in individual analysis as well as in groups and institutions (Kaës, 1992). The fraternal complex designates a fundamental organization of loving, narcissistic, and object-related wishes, of hate and aggressiveness towards this "other" whom a subject recognizes as his brother or sister. This broad definition shows that the fraternal complex does not necessarily correspond to the *real* existence of fraternal ties, as is shown by the analyses of subjects who have been single children, and notably in the studies of Bion (1950) on the imaginary twin, and Benson and Pryor (1973) on the imaginary companion. Though the complex is partly based on the interpersonal and intergenerational links constituted in infantile history, it must not be confused with these links.

Secondary internal groups

Some internal groups appear in the intrapsychic space with all the attributes of external groups: in dreams, for instance, in the form of a heroic group, a group of friends, or a sports team. Others have a less precise form: that is, that of a crowd, an aggregate, or a mere gathering. These groups are representations of the objects of the dreamer and of his ego: they borrow traits that belong to groups in external reality, but they are put to the service of figurability (for example, of the drives: thus the internal horde) and unconscious realizations (of narcissism: cf. the "narcissistic gang" described by Meltzer) or ideals (for example, internal heroic groups).

The processes of psychic groupality

Internal groups are governed by the same general processes that operate in the psychic apparatus. We can mention the primal processes, which function according to the model of the pictogram "union–rejection" described by Castoriadis-Aulagnier (1975). The main primary processes (condensation, displacement, permutation, or inversion) participate in the figurability of the instinctual representatives, object-representations, and ego-representatives. Some primary processes are, however, electively mobilized in the internal groups: I have underscored the very specific role played in these by the diffraction and multiplication of an identical element.

Condensation and the internal group "Irma" in Freud

Condensation is one of the major processes of dreams; it is also one of the principal processes of internal groups. The analysis of the dream of Irma's injection offered Freud the opportunity of discovering and illustrating this process in certain condensed figures that appear in this dream: he calls them collective or composite figures [*die Sammel- und Mischpersonen*]. We can understand that such figures form one of Freud's internal groups; thanks to condensation, the representation of his patient Emma Eckstein is simultaneously both dissimulated in Irma of the dream and connected with other female figures (Anna, his daughter; another Anna; his wife Martha, another patient). All these figures of the feminine are thus identified with each other, and by means of this procedure Freud is able to remain unaware of his own wish in the disastrous operation, carried out with Fliess, on his patient's turbinate bones.

Diffraction and the "group–Dora"

The primary process of diffraction is in a certain way antagonistic to that of condensation, but both of them organize in a specific way the multiple figuration of aspects of the ego represented by its characters and its objects, which, together, form an internal group.

Freud points allusively to the process of diffraction in his text, *On Dreams.*[2] He writes:

> Analysis reveals yet another side of the complicated relation between the content of the dream and the dream-thoughts. Just as connections lead from each element of the dream to several dream-thoughts, so as a rule a single dream-thought is represented by more than one dream element; the threads of association do not simply converge from the dream-thoughts to the dream-content, they cross and interweave with each other many times over in the course of their journey. [Freud, 1901a, pp. 652–653)]

The diffraction of the dreamer's ego, his objects and his thoughts, produces a "multifaceted" group figuration, an effect of the multiple or many-sided identifications [*mehrfache oder vielseitige Identifizierungen*] of the ego.

The process consists, then, in a de-condensation of the ego that is represented in the multiplicity of its impulses, objects, images, and part-ego(s), each element representing an aspect of the whole and entertaining with the other elements relations of equivalence, analogy, opposition, or complementarity.

Considered from the point of view of the internal economy, diffraction is a process of distributing instinctual charges onto several objects. From this perspective, it must be differentiated from a defence mechanism employing fragmentation against the dangerous character of the object.

Diffraction is operative in dreams, in transferences, and in group relations. The analysis of Dora's transferences suggests that they are organized through the diffraction onto Freud of her internal group, composed of her sick father, her mother contaminated by her father, Frau K, Herr K, the cousin, and the governess. All these internal characters are interrelated in diverse ways, and the ensemble forms what I have proposed to call the "group–Dora". It was this group that arrived in Freud's consulting room.

The different members of a group can represent for a given subject the different aspects of his internal group. For each subject the group is the stage for representing his internal groups, the elements of which are divided up into diverse psychic places, for diverse reasons: topographical and dynamic representation, but also economic, owing to the unburdening or fragmentation of instinctual charges.[3] The diversity of the psychic places in which the internal groups are diffracted raises the problem of an "ectopic" topography.

An analysis of the processes at work in internal groups teaches us that alongside the diffraction and condensation, the repetition or multiplication of the identical element, there are also processes that are in the service of dramatization, of intrapsychic staging, and the demands of censorship.

Internal groups and the transference

The concept of psychic groupality sheds light on certain modalities of transference in groups, and particularly on the relationship between the configuration of transferences and the structural properties of the group setting. In this sense, I have emphasized that the notion of a dilution of the transference has prevented us from understanding that in the group we are dealing more with a diffraction of the transferences and with the connections between the objects of unconscious desire. Among the traits that characterize the group as the locus for the emergence of particular configurations of the transference, we should be equally attentive to the fact that the psychoanalyst, owing to group morphology, is not the *only* object of the transference.

Connection and diffraction of transferences

In the treatment relationship with Dora, Freud approached the question of transference by thinking of it as the successive or simultaneous reproduction onto the psychoanalyst of the objects and persons of unconscious infantile wishes. However, it is not just a question of the patient replacing one person with the person of the psychoanalyst: the patient also replaces successively or simultaneously the *relationship between several persons* with the relationship with the doctor. Freud does not only think of the transference in terms of its plural dimension: *die Übertragungen*, transferences. There are reasonable grounds for thinking that the model of the group is also present in his conception of the *connections* between the transferred objects.

This group conception of the transference in the analytic situation defines a constant trait of the transference in the group situation: the morphological properties of the group predispose it to the manifestation of this type of transferential configuration, in a dynamic process that is served by the processes of displacement, condensation, and diffraction of internal groups.

In the group situation, we are dealing with a twofold process of the *diffraction* and *connection* of transferences. I have emphasized the first process. Rouchy (1980, pp. 55–56) has underscored the importance of the second by writing: "It is thus not only part-objects or characters, but the recomposed elements of the networks of family interactions which can be transferred in the group. This substitution can even bear principally on these relations themselves: that is, it is the connections that are transferred."

Psychic objects transferred in the group situation

The concepts of internal group and psychic groupality open up an avenue for thinking about the objects and processes that are transferred electively in the group situation. What is mobilized in groups, then, are the archaic and oedipal forms of psychic groupality, constellations determined by infantile objects and the links between these objects, and the repetition of infantile experiences during which the objects and processes of internal groups are constituted. The objects and the object-constellations transferred are also transindividual, transgenerational, and transsubjective forms and processes that do not belong specifically to each subject in his singularity, but to his membership of the primary group and the social ensemble out of which he constructs the subjectivizing version of his psychic history.

In conclusion

I have introduced the concept of psychic groupality to describe remarkable unconscious formations and processes, which I have called internal groups. I have described their structure, dynamics, and economy in internal space with reference to the clinical work of analysis. I then took up one of Freud's intuitions and developed the idea that internal groups designate a property of the unconscious—namely, of forming itself as a split psychic group, an attractor of repressed and non-repressed contents.

Analysis of transferential configurations in the group situation has shown that certain primary processes of psychic groupality (diffraction, condensation, access to figurability through dramatization) are electively solicited. The group is a setting that makes it possible to experience and identify the correlations between the objects of the transference. Internal groups contain repressed, denied, or rejected material that was constituted in the group matrix and in the subject's primary relationships; they bear the trace of unconscious alliances.

I hope I have begun to give consistency to what at first was an intuitive formula: namely, that "we are groups", and that, owing to this groupality, we become "singular–plural" subjects, that "the unconscious is structured like a group", and that the subject of the unconscious is subject of the group.

We have made further acquisitions. The concept of internal groupality brings us a partial answer to the question: How do subjects form groups? We have assumed that internal groups function as psychic organizers of the group. We now have to show how.

NOTES

1. I will draw on the synthetic definition proposed by Laplanche and Pontalis (1973, p. 277) whereby it is conceived as "the subject's mode of relation to his world; this relation is the entire complex outcome of a particular organization of the personality, of an apprehension of objects that is to some extent or other phantasied and of certain special types of defence." This post-Freudian notion has taken on increasing importance since 1930, and it forms part of a broader movement of ideas: the organism is considered no longer in an isolated state, but in interaction with its surroundings. It is worth noting that this point of view had already been put forward by Freud in the *Three Essays* (1905d), and clarified in the notes added in 1915. The object is indeed the aim of the drive, but it is held in a relationship that I call co-anaclisis [*co-étayage*] with the objects of the mother.

2. Though the notion was established in 1901, the analysis of it was furnished in several dreams in *The Interpretation of Dreams* (1900a): for example, in "The dream of the young unmarried man" (p. 494) and in "The dream of the orthopaedic institute" (pp. 199–200).

3. Springman (1976) has described this mechanism in groups in terms of fragmentation aimed at avoiding contact with the object: fragments of object and ego are scattered in the external world without necessarily finding a container for receiving and transforming them.

6

Forms and processes of group psychic reality: the group psychic apparatus

The idea that there exists a group psyche, and a psychic reality corresponding to it, may come as a surprise to psychoanalysts who are generally only familiar with individual psychic reality. It may be of interest to them if we try to articulate these two organizations of psychic reality.

There are several arguments for making this hypothesis and for discussing it: we can take up the propositions on which, after Freud, Pichon-Rivière, Bion, Foulkes, Anzieu, and a few others based their research into the group. They built pertinent theoretical models to account for the idea that the group is an original entity in which its own specific psychic reality is produced, endowed with specific processes and formations: basic assumptions and group mentality (Bion), group matrix (Foulkes), contextual, reflexive, and organizational schema (Pichon-Rivière), dream model of the group (Anzieu), and group field (Neri). (An overview of these models may be found in Kaës, 1999b.)

They nonetheless left to one side two questions that are, in my view, decisive: the first concerns the formations and processes of the psychic reality of the individual subject in the group, and the second concerns the common and shared psychic formations and processes that perform an intermediate function between the group and each subject in the group.[1]

My research was oriented in both these directions. I wanted to elaborate a conception that would integrate these two questions and would, consequently, introduce greater complexity into our conception of the unconscious.

The model of the group psychic apparatus

Towards the end of the 1960s I elaborated a general conceptual framework for integrating and distinguishing within an overall conception the relation of the subject to the group, the ordering of their psyches in the group links, and the consistency of group psychic reality.[2] The model of the group psychic apparatus was built in order to achieve this objective, but its ultimate aim was to understand the reciprocal relations between the formations of the unconscious in groups and in intrapsychic space.

The model of the group psychic apparatus does not correspond to something concretely observable any more than that of the "individual" psychic apparatus: it was built for heuristic purposes and for the sake of intelligibility; it is a "fiction", as Freud says (1900a, p. 598), about his own metapsychological construction.[3]

I have chosen the Freudian notion of *psychic apparatus* because it seemed to me the most suitable for accounting for the psychic work that is operative in the group. The idea that the psyche can be thought about as an instrument and a process of binding and transformation was of great importance in my exposition on account of its clinical implications.

The basic statements of the model
of the group psychic apparatus

The basic statements of this model are the following: (1) There is not only a collection of individuals but a group, with specific phenomena, when a common and shared psychic construction has occurred between the individuals constituting this group. The group psychic apparatus is the means of this construction and the result of a certain combinatory arrangement [*appareillage*] of the psyches. (2) The group psychic apparatus carries out a specific task: it binds, assembles, tunes, and conflictualizes parts of the individual psyche mobilized for constructing the group. (3) The group psychic apparatus is not an extrapolation from the individual psychic apparatus: it is a structure that is independent of the psyches that it assembles according to its own laws; it possesses its own organization and its own functioning. The processes governing the common and shared psychic reality depend on a logic that is different from that which governs the individual. (4) It is such a combinatory arrangement that constitutes the psychic reality *of* and *in* the group. This psychic reality is organized according to modalities whereby that which is "common" and "shared" prevails over that which is "private" and "different". (5) The individual psychic apparatus is formed, partly, within this combinatory arrangement; it proceeds from it and is transformed in it; it differentiates itself from it and, under certain conditions, acquires its own autonomy.

The determinations of group psychic reality

The psychic reality specific to the group is defined by the common and shared psychic spaces that are constructed in it and by the processes and formations that develop in it under the influence of three orders of determination. The first pertains to the structure of the group itself: this structure pre-exists the subjects and, at the same time, it only exists through them and for them. The second has its source in the contributions of the subjects to the group when they become members of the group: among the intrapsychic formations and the processes electively mobilized, internal psychic groupality plays a determining role. The third order of determination proceeds from the links or ties between the members of the group.

The psychic reality of the group cannot be reduced to that of each subject, nor to that of the intersubjective relations formed in the group. But in the group, the psychic reality of each member is traversed by that of the group. It is always important to bear these distinctions in mind, for they account for the diversity, heterogeneity, and complexity of the psychic formations and processes that we have to deal with when working clinically with groups.

This model integrates the heterogeneity of psychic spaces and recognizes it as the principal motive force of the psychic movements in the group. But at the same time it admits that certain processes and certain psychic formations are common to and shared between them, while others are specific to each of them. Finally, it asserts that certain formations and certain intrapsychic processes only appear, and are only transformed, in the group situation. This model thus furnishes a complex response to complex findings.

The concept of psychic apparatus, whether individual or group, is a fruitful concept of metapsychology. But it has the disadvantage of leaving aside the question of the unconscious in its relation to subjectivity. I reintroduced this question at the end of the 1980s, when I began to criticize the limits of this first model insofar as it did not allow one to think about the question of the subject of the unconscious and of intersubjectivity in the group.

The subject's relation to the group
according to the model of the group psychic apparatus

The model of the group psychic apparatus comprises propositions for thinking about the relation between the subject and the group. I shall summarize them in five statements.

The group is an object of instinctual investments
and unconscious representations

Here I am taking up Pontalis's hypothesis that the group is an object of instinctual investments and unconscious representations for its members. The group is invested by diverse impulses and the corresponding unconscious representations and affects that may or may not be bound to these representations: impulses of *attachment* (ocnophilic and philobatic), *oral* impulses (the group is a mouth, a breast, a toilet–breast), *anal* impulses (it is a cloaca, a belly), *genital* impulses (it is a penis, a vagina, a uterus, a "matrix"). The group is invested by the self-preservative instincts of the ego, by the narcissistic impulses (it is a mirror), and by the diverse manifestations of the death instinct. I conclude from this that the nature and force of the impulses mobilized in the group members determines the quality and the power of the bindings and unbindings in the assemblage of the psyches.[4]

In a group, these instinctual investments (and the unconscious representations corresponding to them) vary according to the moments of the group process, and they are different for each subject. The question is to understand how the functioning of the group permits the impulses of each member to find their support and their object in it; how they enter into tension and conflict in each subject and with those of the others; and how they are tamed or remain wild. The impulses cannot diverge or become dispersed too much without altering the adequate consistency of the group psychic space. The question, then, is one of understanding how they are reconciled and combined, and how the subjects accept the "renunciation" [*der Verzicht* (Freud, 1930a)] of their direct satisfaction, so that the community that provides security and love for everyone (1930a, pp. 101–103) may come into being.

Internal groups are the unconscious psychic organizers of the links to the group and of the group psychic apparatus.

As I said above, while I was researching into the group-object, I discovered that the instinctual investments and the unconscious representations of the group are sustained by psychic organizations presenting structural and functional characteristics that have led me to describe them as internal groups. I then discovered that these same internal groups function as unconscious organizing schema of the group links and of the group as a whole. The scenic, dramatic, and syntagmatic properties of internal groups define locations that are predisposed to being occupied by the subjects of a group, according to the issues at stake in, and the necessities of, the psychic dynamics and economy of each subject and of those of the group as a whole. By virtue of these properties, internal groups guarantee the basic structure of the combinatory arrangement of the psyches in the group.

The group as scene, scenario, locus of a psychic action,
a dramatized figuration

An important aspect of the subject's relationship to the group lies in the fact that, for each of its members, the group is the locus and the scene of an externalization of certain objects and certain processes of their internal world. Anzieu proposed in 1966 the idea that the group is the "projected topography" of its members. This fruitful idea needed, in my view, to be clarified and completed. The group is not only a plurality of "projected topographies": it is the ensemble of the combined topographies; the links between the group members rest on a specific tuning of their "topographies", but also of their psychic economies and dynamics.

The combinatory arrangement of this plurality is organized into a psychic scene and action, according to a scenario whose paradigm is phantasy and whose formula is: one (or several) subject (s), a verb (active/passive), one (or several) complement(s). The group I described earlier illustrates this proposition in the formula "a parent is threatening/repairing a child". One or several internal groups can be made use of as organizing schema of the group scene. The group is the scene of a psychic action whose scenario exerts an attracting function for the psychic locations of the group members.

It is on this stage, and in function of a predominant attractor, that the topographies of the subjects who compose the group are organized according to diverse modalities (projection, deposit, rejection, exportation). The psychic formations of the subjects are given figurative shape there in a double external–internal register, and this figurability makes special use of the combinatory arrangement and economy of plurality. Pride of place is thus given to the mechanisms of *dramatization, condensation* ("one represents all"), the *displacement* of one element towards another, and the *diffraction* (one represented in several elements) or *multiplication* of *identical elements*. The same primary processes that are mobilized in dreams, symptoms, and their transferences are effective in the group scene. It is on this basis that the hypothesis may be made that the group is this other stage of the unconscious on which the subject represents himself or has himself represented.

The same questions arise here that arose in relation to the instinctual investment and representations of the group. In a group, the internal groups and the attracting scenarios are diverse, and they differ from one subject to another. Under these conditions, it is important to know how they are combined, reconciled, or excluded; and if they are combined, how the figurative depictions of singular psychic formations are organized into common psychic formations. In order to answer these questions, a further question must be raised: what are the unconscious aims of the subjects who are attracted by these scenarios?

For its subjects the group is a locus and means of psychic realizations

To this question, Anzieu had supplied the following answer: the group is like a dream; it is a means of realizing in a hallucinatory mode the unconscious wishes of its members. However powerful and pertinent this answer may be, it does not exhaust the question: the group is also a locus and a means of experiencing dependency, of defences against bad objects, of messianic expectations, as Bion suggested with his *basic assumptions*. Furthermore, the group is a means of protection against solitude and fear (Géza Róheim), an object of believing expectations, of the sharing of common ideals and illusions, a locus for structuring identifications, a space "where the I can come into being" (Castoriadis-Aulagnier), a metapsychic container, the space where the structuring, defensive, offensive, or alienating unconscious alliances are formed.

Once again we are faced with the same question as before: in a group, a locus and means of psychic realizations, how are the diverse, common, and different investments of each subject fulfilled? How are their singularities maintained? On what conditions, and at what price? And how can they combine, organize, and be reconciled or, alternatively, enter into conflict and show themselves to be incompatible?

The subject in the group and the subject of the group

The subject's relation to the group must be treated at another level—the most important from my point of view—that is to say, at a level at which the question of the subject of the unconscious is posed, properly speaking (Chapter 11 herein is devoted to this subject). It is

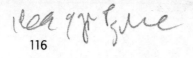

posed, in fact, from the moment one takes into account the effects that the formations and processes of the unconscious in groups have on the unconscious of the subjects of the group. The existence of such effects is quite easy to demonstrate when one observes the vicissitudes of repression and the most archaic mechanisms of defence that the group imposes on its members in order to form a group. Moreover, each subject imposes such defensive measures on himself for internal reasons linked to his group membership and links, and also to fulfil unconscious realizations that are inaccessible except in the group situation.

Among these group formations, unconscious alliances occupy a dominating position. According to the bifocal analysis that I am trying to carry out, the group is simultaneously both the locus of the formation of the subject of the unconscious and the locus that mobilizes, receives, and transforms the unconscious formations and processes of each subject.

The organization of the psyches by the group psychic apparatus

Let me recapitulate briefly on the principles of the model: the group psychic apparatus mobilizes, binds, and tunes formations and processes of the psyche of each group member in the psychic work that is demanded of them in order to construct the group. From this point of view, the formation of group psychic reality draws on the psyche of its members; it is constructed with its material, its organizers, and according to its processes. But the group receives them, captures them, uses them, manages them, and transforms them according to its logic and its own processes. It functions as an autonomous entity endowed with a specific psychic reality. The psychic reality so produced can be common to the group members and to the ensemble that they form; it can be shared, split or separated, impinged upon or invaded.

The two series of organizers: psychic and sociocultural

Two series of organizers are mobilized in the process of psychic combination. The concept of group psychic organizer was introduced into my research to denote relatively complex formations that make possible, maintain, and organize the integrated development of group ties: they are the principal paradigmatic internal groups I have identified.

The second series is constituted by sociocultural organizers. These are the schema of figurability and signification constructed socially by the work of culture, of which myths are the most accomplished representatives. Emblematic examples may be found in the mythic group of the Knights of the Round Table or of Ulysses' companions. By providing models, religious groups (the group of the Twelve Apostles, the group of the Prophet's companions), the group of disciples of a Master (the group of the first psychoanalysts), heroic groups (the Bounty Mutineers, the shipwrecked of the Medusa's Raft, the group of the Acali Expedition, survivors of an air disaster), groups of innovators (groups of painters, musicians, the surrealist group, such-and-such group of mathematicians), sports groups (such-and-such football or rugby team), military commandos, and so on. These sociocultural organizers have a dual function: they contribute normative and secondary process models to the unconscious psychic organizers. They form a prop for the narrative and legitimizing function that every group employs to represent itself, to identify itself, to construct an origin for itself and to differentiate itself from other groups.

Each group is characterized by a predominant pair of psychic and sociocultural organizers on the basis of which its identity and the identifications of its members are stabilized.

The unconscious psychic organizer of the group: clinical pointers

Let us look now at how these organizers functioned in the group with Marc.

The group process was governed by an unconscious phantasy organizer, the formula of which varied around this central statement: "A parent is threatening/repairing a child." We have been able to establish that this organizing phantasy is an attractor of phantasy scenarios, and that its effect was to give consistency to the common and shared psychic reality of the group. It supported the identifications of all its members. The bond that was established between them was organized around the actual representation of a "marking" traumatic "event", a primal trace (a primal trace of the eruption of desire), outside time, outside thought and speech, of which each one had his/her own version, but which remained inaccessible to each member directly. This trace found in the group a locus, a scene, and the psychic material brought by several participants necessary for its figuration.

I have tried to show that the basic phantasy structure of this group was transformed, and that variations were introduced in the succession of organizers. These variations are necessary if an important process is to occur—namely, that of singularizing the secondary phantasy of each of the subjects in the group. This change indicates that the subject has been able to extricate himself from the organizing group phantasy and that he or she has been able to accede to the subjective version of his/her own phantasy. We have seen that this process of subjectivization did not occur without arousing resistances in Marc and in the group. But it was to culminate for Marc in the discovery of the formula of the phantasy that was specific to him: *"My father, in the past and elsewhere, but who is still present for me here in this group, is seducing/threatening/repairing his son who thereby finds his 'mark'."* Marc and the others owed this discovery to the work of the group process.

In this group, the sociocultural organizer did not manifest itself with as much legibility as the unconscious psychic organizer. But it was not absent: the idealization, of which Sophie and I were the object, the correlate of the persecutory anxieties that they felt towards us, gave rise to the representation that their group was a heroic group, on the model of that founded by Anzieu, of which Sophie and I were members. All these movements were heard and interpreted in the transference.

The work of combination in the initial phases of the group

The work of psychic combination does not begin at the moment when the subjects encounter each other for the first time. Before meeting each other, the participants of a therapeutic group, a training group, or an analytic group have already formed certain ideas about and made certain investments in the group, as an object that concerns them personally and as an object that they will have in common. This work of expectations is also one in which pre-transferences are set in motion. This work was to manifest itself when Marc, Sylvie, Solange, and Anne-Marie spoke about the thoughts that they had had before the group began, and about what had led them to take part in it.

However, the actual encounter with a plurality of others, with strangers who are not yet sufficiently familiar, arouses turbulent feelings and uncertainties in each participant, which they will have to manage and diminish in several ways.

The necessity of protecting oneself against instinctual co-excitations by setting up an efficient and tempered stimulus barrier is always a measure of priority. Indeed, at this initial point in the group's formation, the internal stimulus barriers are insufficient or excessive. They will be so, moreover, each time the group structure becomes disorganized prior to transforming itself. There is a constant conjunction between the moments of disorganization or change in the organizers–attractors and the disintegration or reinforcement of the stimulus barriers.

The analyst's announcement of the constitutive rules of psychoanalytic work, along with the initial elements of the transference, contributes to establishing a shared and common protection. But experience shows that this is not enough and that other measures are necessary. Among these, urgent identification is particularly (and transitorily) effective because it gives everyone a sense of certainty about the presence of an object within themselves and within each of the other participants. Not only is an object once again available in each one but, above all, this object is identical, common, and sharable, and it forms a bond between them. Urgent identification is thus not simply a protective measure against stimuli: it triggers the process of combination and assemblage in a remarkable way: for the first time, internal space and the group space coincide momentarily, and the subjects become members of the group through this first solicitation of their internal groups.

Was this really how things happened in the group with Marc? From the very first moments of the first session, Sylvie and several others had an urgent need to identify Sophie, because they were trying to identify a reassuring object in her. The misunderstanding merely reinforced the urgency, and the disturbance that it aroused led to the suggestion of making a "round of first names" and to each participant introducing themselves. This procedure is standard practice and has the manifest aim of identifying who is speaking to whom, of providing reference points; but its deeper aim is to reassure and protect the ego, as well as the group that is beginning to take shape, against anxiety in the face of the unknown, both external and internal. But in this group this measure was not enough: the internal flooding, the experience of temporary depersonalization, of losing one's limits, made the identification with a double (Marc–Boris, -Sylvie–Solange–Michèle) imperative. But this new measure produced the contrary effects of reassuring familiarity and uncanniness.

It is clear that this group was struggling with the difficulty of forming a sufficiently reassuring common object. During the whole of the first session and a good part of the second, what dominated was the confrontation with an uncontrollable traumatic object: an empty head cannot fill itself with good objects and good thoughts. Furthermore, urgent identification occurred in a paradoxical mode: the more it is necessary to find the object, the more danger there is of mistaking the object. And if the object cannot be known, then they cannot know whether it is good or bad. The formula brought to the group by Jacques gave meaning to this uncertainty and provided a first point of agreement: they felt "*hors de soi*" [outside/beside themselves], the inside was on the outside; they were without references and felt mistreated.

Other measures would thus be necessary for the group to be able to form itself on a viable basis. One of them is remarkable because it participated in the formation of the unconscious psychic reality in the group, in the links between the participants and for the members of the group. I am referring to the unconscious alliance that was formed between the participants, already in this initial period, with regard to the repression of the movement of transference from Sylvie towards Sophie. It was strengthened when Marc confirmed the danger of the threat by his "confession", the object of which remained ambiguous. In order to repress the dangerous representation, Marc proposed an object to counter the menace: the very one who threatens can repair and provide "points of reference" [*repères*].

Let us sum up what we have established: the psychic work of combining and assembling the psyches of the subjects begins well before the participants meet: once the group has assembled, the first measures of this combinatory arrangement are those that fulfil the function of stimulus barrier and establish the first unconscious alliances. According to the model of the group psychic apparatus, the group is an attractor of investments and representations: it functions as a structure of attraction towards the psychic locations necessary for its functioning and for its maintenance. It is in these locations that the objects, imagos, agencies, and signifiers that the group members bring to the group are represented, and from thereon they are governed and transformed by the organization of the group. The group is thus formed and constructed according to two principal dynamics, one of which mobilizes the resources of the subjects composing the group, while the other is the dynamic of the group that organizes itself by making use, through attraction and coercion, of the psychic resources available to its participants. The principle of the combinatory arrangement rests on the synergy between these dynamics.

The formation of the group psychic apparatus and the demands for psychic work required for the combination to occur

However, I have only described part of the process: I must complete my analysis by taking into account the demands for psychic work required if the combinatory arrangement is to occur. In point of fact, the group imposes on its subjects, and the latter impose on themselves, a certain number of psychic constraints.

More broadly, a certain psychic work[5] is required by the encounter with the other, so that the psyches, or parts of them, can associate and combine, so that they can become aware of their differences and enter into a state of tension, so that they can regulate themselves.

Today I distinguish four principal demands for psychic work imposed by the combinatory group arrangement. The first is the obligation for the subject to invest the group with his narcissistic- and object-libido so as to receive in return the necessary investments for being recognized by the ensemble and by the others as a member of the group. This demand for work is based on the model of the narcissistic contract described by Piera Castoriadis-Aulagnier (1975). (See my exposition on the narcissistic contract in chapter 10.)

The second demand is the putting into latency, or the renunciation or abandonment of certain psychic formations proper to the subject. Freud had indicated (1921c) that to become a member of a group, the ego has to abandon a part of its identifications and personal ideals in favour of common ideals and in exchange for the benefits expected from the group and/or leader. More generally,

122 Linking, alliances, and shared space

the group imposes obligations of belief, representation, perceptual norms, adherence to ideals and common feelings. The combinatory arrangement does not only imply that certain psychic functions are inhibited or reduced and that others are electively mobilized and amplified. Enlarging the scope of this second demand, it has to be admitted that it is also a demand for psychic non-work. Some groups expressly require abandonment of thought, the effacement of ego-limits or of a part of the psychic reality that specifies and differentiates each subject. This is the case with sectarian groups and ideological groups. But we must admit that the question is more complex, for it also has to be considered from the standpoint of the processes of self-alienation put in the service of these group demands.

The third demand concerns the necessity of carrying out operations of repression, denial, or rejection so that that the ensemble is formed and the links are maintained. These operations do not only concern the metadefensive props that the members of a group can find in it, as Elliott Jaques once showed (1955). They concern the group or any other configuration of linking that ensures and maintains the metadefensive measures necessary for its self-preservation and the realization of its aims. They are thus required both by the group and by the personal interests that the subjects find in contracting them. Such are the status and the function of *defensive* unconscious alliances. They are processes that produce the actual unconscious in the group; they form the neurotic and psychotic knots of linking and, for all these reasons, play a major role in the formation of group psychic reality.

The fourth demand is related to the fundamental prohibitions in connection with the work of civilization [*Kulturarbeit*] and the processes of symbolization. Freud (1927c, 1930a) insisted on the necessity for mutual renunciation of the direct satisfaction of prohibited instinctual aims in order to establish a "lawful community" guaranteeing stable and reliable relationships. The result of this demand is *structuring* unconscious alliances, in which category may be counted the narcissistic contract, the pact between the Brothers and with the Father, and the contract of mutual renunciation. The result of this demand for work is the formation of meaning, the activity of symbolization and interpretation, but also the capacity to love, play, think, and work.

If one adopts the standpoint of the group, these four demands contribute to the creation of a common and shared psychic space.

Considered from the point of view of the subject on whom they are imposed, these demands are structuring and conflictual. The central conflictuality is situated between the necessity of serving one's own purposes and that of being a subject in the group and for the group. By doing this psychic work, the members of a group claim or receive benefits and obligations in exchange. An economic balance is established, positively and negatively, concerning what is gained and lost in satisfying these demands.

In a certain way we do not have the choice of eluding these demands. They are demands to which we must submit in order to form links with others and to exist as a subject. But we also have to free ourselves, to unbind ourselves, each time these demands, and the unconscious alliances that seal them, contribute to our self-alienation and the alienation that we impose on others, frequently without anyone realizing it. I think that it is from this perspective that it is possible to define the practical field of psychoanalytic work in the group situation.

The processes of combination

Several processes organize the combinatory arrangement of the psyches in a group. Some are specialized in the work of binding and unbinding; others in assemblage and separation, others in similitude and differentiation, and others, finally, in tuning or division. All these primal, primary, secondary, and tertiary processes are mobilized in this construction.

The primal, primary, secondary, and tertiary processes

According to Piera Aulagnier's theorization, the pictogram of union–rejection characterizes the primal process; it is the very first activation of the search for complementary objects and the common substance that binds the mother and child together in a shared somato-psychic locus, the breast–mouth space. This process is at work in all groups, at different moments of the group, and not just in the initial phase. In the group I have presented, it can be identified when Sylvie searches for a zone-complementary object in Sophie: an object of union, anaclisis, and identification. If the object is not there or if one is mistaken about it (about its capacity for being there), it is rejected. This is what happens when Marc injects the affect linked to the mention of the trauma.

The pictogram is taken up and transformed in the primary process: in the group, the phantasy of threat/reparation, and then the phantasy of abandonment and exclusion are its avatars. The primary process governs the course of unconscious representations, dreams, phantasies, and symptoms: it manifests itself in the diverse modalities of displacement, condensation and diffraction, dramatization, and reversal into the opposite. The primary process governs the logic of internal groups.

The secondary process regulates the course of rational, discursive, logical thought according to the principle of non-contradiction, which is itself subject to the reality principle. It implies a separation of its objects from those that are governed by primal and primary processes.

The tertiary process may be described in two ways: according to André Green (1972), it guarantees binding between the primary and the secondary, whereas for Eric Dodds (1959) it describes how myth obeys both social and cultural logic and the logic of dreams. This conception is valuable for understanding the double psychic and sociocultural consistency of mythopoetic organizers.

All these processes are at work in the development of associative chains, in the formation of the dream space and the narrative structure, and in the formation of symptoms and phoric functions.

The processes of identification

Identifications form a second set of processes. We know, since Freud, that they are the libidinal binder of group ties and that they must be distinguished from incorporation. I have already specified the diverse modalities of identification mobilized in the work of combination: adhesive, projective, and introjective identifications. These processes are at the basis of the phenomena of phantasy resonance or interphantasizing. In the group, the most significant example is that of the resonance of the phantasy "A child is being threatened/repaired": the identifications with Marc become more clearly identifiable as identifications and counteridentifications with the protagonists of the common and shared phantasy—that is to say, of the attracting internal group.

Here is another example: numerous observations show that a group—whether its aim is therapeutic or training-oriented—organizes itself or tunes itself in relation to a subject who is considered by the group members to be sick or fragile, but is invested positively by them. Most of the group members can identify with this person. In a psychodrama group that had experienced quite intense anxieties of fragmentation, Laura, who had until then been very attentive to the others, a bit withdrawn and often anxious, announced that she did not feel well in the group and was thinking of not coming to the sessions any longer. No one asked her why, but a doctor who had just come back from a conference on ethnopsychiatry spoke about a session of traditional therapy referred to in a lecture. A role play was then proposed: a shaman has the task of healing a little girl; he gets the parents and the girl together, but he needs a translator because he cannot speak their language. Two of the participants offer to play the role of the parents and ask Laura to be the little sick girl. She accepts and plays the part of a little autistic girl, who cannot speak and is completely absorbed by her swaying movements and rhythms. After a while, the whole family is swaying with her rhythm, and the translator "translates" clearly (interprets) the incomprehensible words of the shaman and the parents. Hearing the little girl beginning to speak about her solitude is an intensely emotional experience.

This psychodrama gave the group real psychic consistency again by organizing its members around the need to care for its suffering parts: the participants were able to invent a rich transference situation, to pose the problems of the sick part of each member, to "treat" Laura and, through her, other participants, to find the right words, and to get beyond confrontation and regressive movements.

Projection, deposit, exportation, rejection: unconscious alliances

A third set of processes is constituted by the mechanisms of projection, deposit, exportation and rejection. These individual defence mechanisms are active in the first moments of the process of the combining and assembling of psyches. They give rise to combined defence mechanisms that constitute a part of the metadefensive and alienating unconscious alliances.

Phoric functions

Certain members of the group fulfil intermediate functions between the intrapsychic space, the intersubjective space, and the group space and thereby contribute to the process of combination. These subjects embody significant figures, such as those of the Ancestor, the Child King, Death, the Hero, the leader, and the scapegoat. They also fulfil the functions of speech-bearer, symptom-bearer, and dream-bearer in groups: they are bearers of ideals and illusions, of death or life. They are agents of binding. These figures, these functions and locations, which may be subsumed under the concept of phoric functions (Kaës, 1993), are to be understood simultaneously and correlatively from the point of view of the subjectivity of the subjects who embody them, from the point of view of the intersubjective relations that they serve, and from the point of view of their functions in the structure of the group.

The modalities of combination

The group psychic apparatus develops in a state of tension between two principal poles that structure the relations between each subject and the whole. Between these two poles oscillates an unstable, chaotic field that corresponds to the periodic disorganization of the attractors.

The isomorphic pole

The isomorphic pole corresponds to the situation where the group organizer is identical in all the members of the group. The exact correspondence, term for term, leads to the formation of a common and undifferentiated psychic space, the result of the imaginary fusion of the individual psychic spaces and the group psychic space. In this measure, the isomorphic pole describes an experience of complete coincidence between the object (the group) and its complementary zone in the internal space. The formation of this pole implies the loss of the individual boundaries of its members. There then exists for the members of the group only one single homogeneous psychic space, and not distinct psychic spaces.

This imaginary, narcissistic, undifferentiated pole of the combinatory process already functions in the initial stage by employing the primal processes of union–rejection, urgent identifications, and the multiplication of the identical element. It reappears at other moments of the group's life. Each time the group is faced with a situation of crisis or serious danger, it attempts to adjust itself by binding its members together in the flawless unity of an "esprit de corps". It functions in the metonymic mode of "one for all, all for one". Alternatively, when a moment of collective creativity occurs, there is a sort of dilatation of the ego in the group and of the group in the ego. The psychodrama group that invented the session of healing with the shaman is an illustration of this.

A typical example of this mode of combination is what Anzieu has described as "group illusion"—that is to say, the shared belief by all the group members that the group they form and their idealized internal group coincide. Shared illusion is necessary for the formation of the group. It articulates two processes: the idealized coincidence is the individual and group answer to the urgency of identification. In a setting structured by the psychoanalytic method, the group is the experience of this transitory illusion and of necessary disillusionment.

The isomorphic pole is periodic, but it can also be a lasting or permanent modality of the group's organization. When this type of fixed and frozen adjustment prevails, the gap between the group psychic space and the subjective psychic space is constantly and structurally denied or abolished: everything that happens in one space is experienced as happening in an identical way in the other space; everything that happens inside also happens outside, and vice versa. Should one element of the group change, this change will threaten each subject and his links with the whole. This coincidence obliges each person to fulfil the place and function assigned to him in the group or to which he has assigned himself of his own accord, but each person must also see to it that no one changes places or function. Metonymic thinking predominates: it confuses the part with the whole and makes all the spaces coincide in imagination, rendering them homogeneous and undifferentiated.

This system of co-inherence[6] between internal groups and the intersubjective group characterizes the psychotic functioning of intersubjective relations in all the other configurations of linking: in the family, the couple, and the institution.

The homeomorphic pole

The homeomorphic pole, on the contrary, is characterized by the differentiation between the individual spaces and the group space, between the internal group and the external group, but also between the members of the group themselves. However, a certain similitude is necessary for minimal correspondence. The combinatory arrangement of the psyches is thus established on the basis of a relationship of tension between the similitude and difference between the psychic spaces. The gap between the spaces makes it possible to think about the heterogeneity and similitude of their contents and the logics that govern them.

The integration of the differences is the consequence of gaining access to the symbolic and the prevalence of relations of metaphorical thinking. In order for this pole to be set up, structuring prohibitions must have been announced and integrated; the group law must be able to engender and contain conflicts, to accommodate feelings of ambivalence, and to allow for separations. Individual speech can emerge as long as it is regulated by reference to the law rather than by the omnipotence of a cruel and deadly Ideal embodied by a tyrant or by the group itself.

The "whirlpool" and the chaotic moment

Between these two major polarities is interposed an unstable field that oscillates between them like a whirlpool, resulting from the chaotic instability of the tuning of the psyches. This moment corresponds to a change of attractor or to a conflict between the organizers.

I introduced this intermediate modality to account for difficulties I had encountered in clinical work. During the initial phase of one group, the participants were unable to combine and assemble themselves around any organizer, nor could they establish any stable and satisfying link between their internal space and that of the group: this failure was infused with intense excitation. The chaotic movements that predominated at this moment in the group's life were the result of a conflict between the impulses of self-preservation and the impulses turned towards the group. In another group, chaos appeared to be the effect of a paradoxical treatment of the combinatory process: the participants were tuned to each other in the mode of non-tuning, establishing a link/no-link that—whirlpool-like—was constantly attacked and displaced.

I had already been confronted with this disorganizing moment in the group with Marc. During one of the last sessions, the participants constantly exchanged places in the initial phantasy ("a child is being threatened/repaired"), which was suddenly remobilized. They did not change places in order to explore these places, which had already been the case earlier. Clinically, this whirlpool corresponded to a manic organization of the group psychic apparatus and implied a mode of functioning corresponding to internal groups in the group members. This chaotic moment set in just as a process of subjectivation was getting underway in the group, characterized by the subject's encounter with his place as a subject in the phantasy that was his own. In this appropriative encounter, which could be described in Bion's terms as the catastrophic moment of the encounter in "O", the phantasy sometimes becomes rigidified, or it whirls. This encounter is not an immediate discovery; it does not happen all at once. Through the whirlpool experience and its erratic effect, through this peregrination, the subject discovers that he cannot occupy all the places, successively or simultaneously, but only his own.

All these modalities of the whirlpool and chaos manifest themselves in moments of transformation corresponding to the group psychic space and the intrapsychic space. The whirlpool can appear when the combination or assemblage does not take place, either for lack of an organizer or because there are too many gaps between the group space and the internal space, or because these spaces are split, or when the combinatory arrangement is too invasive and it is necessary to free oneself from it. The whirlpool and chaos also occur when there is a change of attractor. In all these cases, paranoid or depressive anxieties predominate and bring into operation manic defence mechanisms that alternate with defences through apathy.

The two poles I have described have antagonistic relations, and the tension that is established between them may be considered a good indicator of the psychic work carried out in the group. The oscillation between these two poles is necessary: the psychic work of transformation takes place through the movements of binding and dissociation, unification and conflictualization of the group psychic apparatus.

Three positions of group mentality:
the ideological position, the mythopoetic position,
and the utopian position

Groups organize themselves around three principal mental positions, which correspond to world views [*Weltanschauungen*]: the ideological position, the utopian position, and the mythopoetic position. These positions do not correspond to a progressive order but are formed and stabilized at certain moments of the group's mental organization. All these positions convey representations about causality and form a more or less open explanatory system of the world, of the origin, the end, and the aims of the group.

The ideological position is under the sway of the omnipotence of the Idea, the supremacy of the Ideal, and the tyranny of the Idol (of the fetish). Conveying absolute certainties, it is governed by a rigorous narcissistic pact that does not tolerate any transformation. It is imperative, suspicious; it admits of no difference, no otherness, and pronounces prohibitions of thought. It is based on the isomorphic pole of the combinatory process. Underlying it are anxieties of imminent annihilation and grandiose phantasies of a paranoiac type. It is also a defensive measure against chaotic moments. (On the ideological position, I refer the reader to my research into this theme: Kaës, 1980, 2003b.)

The mythopoetic position upholds a mentality based on the activity of representing the origin of the group and on the encounter, in this activity, with the uncertainty that goes with it. It is also a position whose advent depends on a crisis, deterioration, or loss of meaning. The mythopoetic position creates new meaning, which includes the representation of catastrophe. It is a sort of factory of meaning open to its uncertainties, to its complexity, and to its own process of production: that is to say, its genealogy. Consequently, it is tolerant of different versions of the myth.

The utopian position is also based on an experience of crisis and a representation of catastrophe. But the modalities of elaboration are different from those of the ideological position. It oscillates between "play and reasoning madness", between the potential space and the screws of delusional reason. It imagines the locus of a catastrophe that has not occurred, which is, at the same time, the locus of a possible catastrophe. It can thus transform itself either into an ideological position, when the possible becomes the imperative—it then becomes systematic and seeks to become incarnated in history—or into a mythopoetic position when it maintains a dream space, when it remains punctual and maintains a task of becoming: in other words, when it recognizes the thinker's power of thought.

These three positions of group mentality are collective creations. They form the backdrop to our psychic life, but they also form one of its horizons.

The theoretical and clinical interest of the model of the group psychic apparatus

The moment has come to discuss the interest of the model of the group psychic apparatus. This model has been conceived and conceptualized with the terms of psychoanalysis, with the structures, places, economies, and dynamics of the psyche at the point where the subject's psychic reality and group psychic reality conjoin. Its function is to furnish a descriptive, heuristic, and, eventually, an explicatory model. It thus has a certain usefulness in the theory of psychoanalysis when the latter extends its field, and it is in this respect that it can be of concern to psychoanalytic practitioners.

A first point of theoretical interest of the model of the group psychic apparatus is that it allows us to think about the consistency of group psychic reality in a way that does not simply consider it as pure speculation. This reality is specific: it is constituted by formations and processes that are inaccessible outside the group setting.

A second point of theoretical interest is that it enables us to understand that the group psychic apparatus is common to the subject and to the group. This model informs us about the relations of co-anaclisis and reciprocal structuring of the individual psychic apparatus and the group psychic apparatus. The assemblages, conflicts, and transformations that result from this combinatory arrangement affect, correlatively, the group and the psychic apparatus of the group members. They affect in particular—and this point concerns the specific object of psychoanalysis—the unconscious of the subject insofar as it is informed by group processes and group ties.

The clinical interest of the model resides in the attention it gives to the psychic processes and formations mobilized and worked on in the individual subject in the group, in intersubjective links, and in the group as such. By limiting my remarks to the point of view of

the subject, I would say that the main clinical interest of this model
is one of conceiving the group as an apparatus for transforming the
psychic reality of its members. What is transformed is the particular
configuration of internal objects, specific to each subject, which
the group mobilizes and which becomes allied with other internal
groups. The model attracts the clinician's attention to the contributions of each subject to the construction and functioning of the
group psychic reality. The formation and function of the unconscious alliances inform us about the combination of the interests of
each member and of the group. The model also draws attention to
the specificity of the associative processes that develop in the group.
All these processes, which concern the subject, are to be thought
about in terms of the dynamics and economy of the transferences
that unfold in the group space.

On the basis of these considerations, the principal objective of
psychoanalytic work in the group situation may be formulated as
follows: to make possible the experience of the unconscious, in the
forms and processes that manifest themselves in the group, for the
subjects who are a constituent part of the group.

NOTES

1. Claudio Neri's work (1997) is an exception to this judgement: his
book is organized around a model of intelligibility centred essentially on the
"naturalization" of field theory in the psychoanalytic understanding of the
group. The writings of Madeleine and Willy Baranger introduced the basic
idea that the unconscious phantasy of the analyst–analysand "couple" is an
organizing form and force in the psychoanalytic process. By extending the
notion of bipersonal field to the group psychoanalytic situation, Neri's research is in keeping with Bion's investigation into the psychic characteristics
proper to the group space. This "naturalization" transforms considerably
the issues of intelligibility of interpersonal processes and the methodological setting that makes it possible to think about them and work with them.
Another innovation is the concept of commuting, which Neri uses to describe the transition and relations between the dimension of the individual
and the dimension of the group. I share with him this task of accounting for
this exchange between the intrapsychic spaces and the group space. With
the concepts of field, commuting, and semiosphere, we are working with
the logic of the reciprocal implications between subject and object—"you
can't have one without the other"—a logic that renews our understanding
of the psychic apparatus.

2. This overall model was published in a book entitled *L'appareil psychique groupal: Constructions du groupe* (Kaës, 1976). Subsequently, other investigators have extended the relevance of this model to the analysis of psychic reality in the family, in the couple, and in institutions.

3. "Understanding what is going on around us boils down in reality to constructing models and confronting them with our observations", write Nicolis and Prigogine (1989, p. 279). This statement is applicable beyond physics and chemistry; it concerns any work of theorization. Charcot's idea that psychoanalytic praxis is not intelligible without a background theoretical model is sound, but too simple.

4. The instinctual point of view is not taken into account in other theories of the group; it is rejected by Pichon-Rivière.

5. The notion of demand for psychic work is proposed by Freud in the *Three Essays* (1905d), and then in "Instincts and Their Vicissitudes" (1915c). Considering the question of instinct from the angle of psychic life, Freud writes: "an 'instinct' appears to us as a concept on the frontier between the mental and the somatic, as the psychic representative of the stimuli originating from within the organism and reaching the mind, as a measure of the demand made upon the mind for work in consequence of its connection with the body" (Freud, 1915c, pp. 122–123).

6. "Co-inherence" is the term used by R. D. Laing (1969) to describe the perfect coincidence between the internal "family" and the family group in psychotic patients.

7

Associative processes in groups

For psychoanalysis as it is applied in the individual treatment, free association is a-social in the sense that the social effects of enunciation and listening are suspended, leaving room solely for utterances determined by the effects of the unconscious. The "a" in a-social is not privative but suspensive: it signifies the methodological aim of the fundamental rule—that is to say, knowledge of the unconscious, inasmuch as the latter manifests itself through its effects in repetition, in the discourse of free association, and in the transference. Though the psychoanalytic setting is organized in such a way that the social effects of the discourse are suspended, their determinations are not abolished; they persist, and sometimes become insistent, in a way such that they must be recognized for what they are: they are distinct from the determinations of the unconscious but sometimes influence them.

When the fundamental rule is announced in the group situation, the conditions, processes, and contents of the associative chain are modified. Nonetheless, the methodological aim is always the same: namely, to make it possible, by virtue of the fundamental rule, by analysing the transferences, and by interpretation, to gain knowledge of the effects of the unconscious. But we are in a group situation rather than individual treatment, so we must expect the mode of associative functioning to have some specific features.

Specificity of the associative process
in plurisubjective ensembles

In the group psychoanalytic situation we are dealing with a plurality of interwoven discourses, a plurality of transferences, and the imbrication of psychic spaces with different structures. Speech utterances coexist with bodily signifiers: mimicry, postures, and gestures. The associative process is affected by several orders of determinants: intrapsychic, intersubjective, and group determinants. It is formed according to a twofold temporal axis, synchronic and diachronic, and is characterized by its interdiscursivity.

Our problem is the following: how are we to hear and understand these discourses, their principal organizers, and their effects, and to what knowledge of the unconscious do they give access?

The plurality of discourses, interdiscursivity,
and the nodal points of associative processes

The associative discourse in the group situation produces two associative chains: that of each subject in the group and that of the group. Each of them is marked by the effects of the unconscious.

The double determination of the associative process
and its nodal points

When the members of a group speak, and all the more so when they are bound by the rule of free association, their utterances are always "situated" at the nodal point of a double associative chain. One is formed out of the succession of the singular utterances of each subject and is determined by the purposive ideas and connecting paths that are proper to it. This chain is traversed by the associations that precede it, but when we understand its diachronic development, it constitutes an original discursive ensemble, which, at this level, bears the inscription of the effects of the subject's unconscious. Although the successive utterances in the group emanate from distinct subjects, they form a second associative chain, which is also a vehicle of the effects of the unconscious. It is governed by the unconscious organizers of the psychic reality of the group, and it interferes with the associative chains of each subject.

All the utterances and signifiers are available for everyone: they can be used by another subject, who then finds in these associations the facilitation [*die Bahnung*] of the passage of his unconscious representations towards the preconscious. The associative process in the group functions, then, as a medium of transformation and metabolization, which, by virtue of the activity of the preconscious, allows for the symbolization of the representations barred by repression.

This associative process can be illustrated with reference to the group with Marc and the others: a member of the group brings out in the associative process something that is enigmatic for him. He adopts a position of waiting for the associations of the other group members to what he has said, and as they are being developed, he hears in them a path of access to his enigma: his resistances are thus strengthened. The members of the group have associated by developing their own utterances, while remaining in touch with this person's enigma. As he listens to what they are saying, and when his resistances have given way, he finds in their words the signifier he is lacking. One can see from this example how interdiscursivity organizes the acts of enunciation and contextualizes the utterances along a dual axis. An association only exists by virtue of other associations, in the double network of associations that are specific to each subject, or which come from the other or more than one other. Particular attention must be paid to the nodal points produced by this interdiscursivity. Some of these nodal points are dreams, symptoms, and unconscious alliances.

We must therefore be attentive to the fact that the primary processes underpinning free association are in a state of constant interference, tension, or concordance with the primary processes supporting intersubjective relations. There exists a tension or concordance within speech that emerges in the group from the subject's unconscious, with its personal code and its subjectivity, and the act of addressing this speech to its recipients: the internal recipient (the other within) and the external recipients (the analyst and the other group members). There is also a tension or concordance between the speech of the subject and the speech of those who have preceded him.

The functioning of the group associative process is different and more complex than that which functions in the individual treatment.

Return to clinical work:
the associative processes and associative chains
in the group with Marc and the others

Analysis of three associative chains

The analysis of the first sequence of the group with Marc and the others has led us to distinguish three associative chains produced by the associative processes of the group. These three chains are organized by the unconscious and preconscious determinations of the psychic reality in the group and in the members of the group. The geometrical locus of these three associative chains is formed by the parts of psychic reality that were assembled, bound, and combined between Marc, Solange, and Anne-Marie, the principal artisans of the common and shared psychic reality in the group at that moment. They are ordered by the movements and objects of the transferences in the group. They express the relation of the group members to speech, to traumatic experience, to the choice of the name, and the point they all have in common is speech—that is to say, what speech can and wants to say or not say about a traumatic experience, the traumatic character of certain words, and nomination as decisive speech for the identity of each subject. Let us examine them one by one.

The first associative chain—around speech:
what speaking means

This series is inaugurated by Jacques' request to do a "round of first names" and his wish to know "who we are speaking to". This request and wish find expression in the transferences through a question about the identity of the psychoanalysts (Sylvie), Marc's concern about the "wild" interpretation, and his expectation of receiving verbal reparation. After being taken for Sophie, Solange speaks in the transference about how she has misunderstood the aim of the group: she had hoped she would learn "to speak properly" or gain access to "the words needed to speak" about her suffering. From the very first moments of the group, three questions are raised: Who is the other? What does speaking mean? What violence is contained in interpretation?

Marc's confession concerning a "marking" traumatic event condenses these questions. The alleged cause of the trauma is connected with an interpretation (wild words): but words are lacking to express the "marking" words; only the affect and its violence are transmitted. What was said remains unknown, enigmatic, and, for this reason, menacing. However, in the ambivalence towards transference objects, the psychoanalysts' words are endowed with the power of destroying and repairing.

These menacing words can only be something said during the last fifteen minutes: a decisive, ultimate utterance, associated with death. Here the associative process not only concerns the contents of speech; it also utilizes the procedures of speech: before being said in front of the whole group, and especially in front of those who possess the formidable power of destroying and repairing by speaking, the words must first be expressed outside the session, experimented with in their absence with a small group of similar others. They have to be exorcized of the menace of death that they convey and deposited in a speech-bearer before being re-expressed to a recipient who has finally been constituted to hear them—the group forming a chorus, container, prop, or witness. It is important at this point that the psychoanalysts, the recipients of Marc's discourse, are able to hear his confession in the movements of the transferences onto the group and onto Marc.

The elliptical character of Marc's confession has a twofold effect: first, it produces reactions of astonishment and paralyses the ability to think—in the analysts too—and, second, it makes the participants feel reserved about developing their associations. The structure of the unconscious phantasy that it mobilizes acquires greater complexity in a sort of polyphony to which several members of the group contribute.

With Marc, and then with Anne-Marie, an action is implemented through speech. Identified with the aggressor, Marc enacts, via speech, the direct transmission—and transference—of the violent affect towards the group as a whole. He enacts through traumatic repetition. As for Anne-Marie, she also carries out an action through speech, but she does so indirectly, by asking Solange to act as a bearer of her speech, to transport it for her, in her place. The effect of this speech-action manifests itself in a discovery that surprises Solange: namely, that someone else's speech, which she is conveying to others, speaks (for) her herself [*la parle elle-même*] and profoundly concerns her own history.

It can be seen very clearly here that what the others say opens up the path for Solange to the return of the repressed. The speech-bearer speaks in the place of another, for an other, but he also speaks for the Other who is in him: he finds in the words of the other a representation that was hitherto unavailable to him.

Alongside these representations of speech associated with life and death, another associative thread develops contrapuntally in the pleasure of playing with words and their polysemy (*repère, re-père, repaire, paire* . . .).

During these first sessions, speech was a central motif of the associative process. It was so for the participants: words from the past, heard and misheard, reappear in the here and now, in the thread of the associative discourse, words containing new understandings or misunderstandings, which have been effaced but are finally recognized, words of menace or salvation, words expressing expectations of reparation or devastating fears. It was also a central motif for Sophie and me in our recurrent questions about opportunities for offering or not offering an interpretation, or expecting the other to offer one. It was so for me, having come to this group with questions about the associative processes in groups and finding that these questions had a certain resonance with those that Jacques, Marc, and Solange were asking themselves.

The second associative chain: around the traumatic event

This series also begins with Jacques' wish to make a "round of first names". It inaugurates a recurrent question related to uncertainty about who is speaking, who is being addressed, and about each participant's identity. Marc, Jacques, and Boris develop and amplify this question by expressing the sense that they have of being disoriented, of losing their bearings, of being empty-headed, of being "beside themselves": they were feeling bizarre and angry.

These themes would overlap with Solange's associations when she discovered that the speech she wanted to master in order to "speak properly" was speech that could be used to express a "bunch of words" containing as yet unformulated sufferings, "sorrows" that were still unnameable. She would find out later which words she was lacking.

It is likely that Solange's "misunderstanding" right at the beginning of the first session put her in contact with her unconscious desire and conflict, that it reached and awoke in her a zone of suffering that she was unaware of, but from which she needed to protect herself. We can understand, then, the "disaffected" tone she adopts, barely hiding depressive feelings, when she says that she would have liked to be Sophie. But her voice immediately becomes livelier when she expresses her interest in the exchanges between Marc and Boris. Solange certainly identifies with them on account of the trait they have in common: that is, the sense of losing their bearings. But she identifies another trait in them that is important for her: they "speak to each other", not only in the sense in which one speaks to the other, but especially in the sense in which one speaks (for) the other [*l'un parle l'autre*] through identification. One is the speech-bearer for the other; each one finds in the other the words he is lacking at a time when he is without word-presentations, abandoned to the threat of the thing and to the anxiety of being invaded or emptied by it.

Admittedly, when Solange shows that she is sensitive to this function of speech-bearer, there is as yet nothing that allows us to understand the traumatic value that the maternal menace[1] has acquired in her phantasy—she herself does not know. But we had some reasons to suppose that, from this moment on, what she had told us about her identification with Sylvie and with the Marc–Boris relationship would determine the choice that Anne-Marie would make of Solange as her speech-bearer and the latter's readiness to let herself be chosen as such. We can see here how the apparatus of interpreting–signifying functions [*der Apparat zu deuten* (Freud, 1912–13)]. What Solange signifies, Anne-Marie interprets by entrusting her with this function that serves their common interests.

It will be recalled that these movements of identification in Solange provoked a depressive phase in her, immediately followed by the criticism she made of the "leaders", of their deficient, cold, and disappointing welcome. It was as though the disarray caused by the initial misunderstanding, by the awakening of her oedipal ambivalence, by her disappointment concerning our welcome required the representation of a cause and the designation of those responsible. This criticism should also be understood as a call for help from "real leaders". But Solange stopped herself there, and it was she who, having made herself temporarily the speech-bearer for several members of the group, refrained from pursuing this path, which was too dangerous for her owing to the intensity of her transferences and her anxiety that her criticisms might provoke revenge from us—the analysts—in the form of abandoning the group. It is striking that it is those group members who are apparently the least directly involved in the transference who begin, at this juncture, to be critical themselves. They, in turn, become speech-bearers for Solange, Sylvie, and Marc, who observe in silence what is going on.

We arrive here at a typical moment of group associative functioning, which I have described as the moment of chaos. The course of the associative events has not yet found a sufficiently structured organizer. It develops into a series of variations around several unconscious nuclei constituted of affects, anxieties, and unstable representations: the encounter with the unidentifiable unknown, the loss of limits, anger, and disappointment. Powerful transference movements mobilize these unconscious nuclei, and identifications are established.

When an associative path establishes a more precise connection between the unconscious nuclei and the transference onto the analysts—here the negative transference—the return of the repressed that is activated calls for other defensive measures against the emergence of unconscious contents. In the transference, it is the analysts who cause the sense of malaise in the group. The transference is resistance to gaining knowledge of the unconscious aspects of the sense of malaise, the anxiety, the difficulty of thinking, for each member and for the group. But the more the transference develops, the more it approaches the unconscious nuclei to which it prevents access; and the more it reveals their components, the more it organizes them.

This can be verified in the following sequence. The criticism about the welcome is suddenly transformed into a new, more precise representation, organized into a scene that is simultaneously both the representation of a cause, an origin, and correlative subjective locations: it is the psychoanalysts who are seen as obliging the participants to be present in the prolific and chaotic bedroom, teeming with children, in a situation of chaos redolent of a battle-field. The suddenness and rapidity of the associative utterances is a good indicator of the emergence of hitherto unconscious represen-tations.

This transferential representation of the parents' desire, their uninterrupted sexual relations, the origin of children, and the *rai-son d'être* of brothers and sisters, necessarily leads to a reactivation of the violence of the primal encounter with the sexual object, to the mobilization of a phantasy that can represent it, including the cause of their presence in the group. I have pointed out that the slip of the tongue (*sale/salle/chambre/champ de bataille*) condenses in a remarkable manner, as in a symptom, the different elements of the repressed contents that make their return. The closer they come to the preconscious, the more they disturb the participants' minds when the issue is to know which desires and which desiring subjects have determined the fact that they are now gathered together as a group. A first group organizer of the associations thus appears more clearly and throws light retroactively on the earlier associations that converge towards it.

At the beginning of the third session, Marc's "confession" forms part of this associative series and gives a new dimension to the phan-tasy of the primal scene, which has just established itself as the or-ganizer of the associations, transferences, and subjective locations in the group. Marc insistently emphasizes that this enigmatic "mark-ing" event is his name "itself", that it is his question; this mark rep-resents him for the group and, as can be seen from what follows, for his *re-père* (re-father) in the transference—that is to say, for me. But the organizing power of the unconscious phantasy induced by Marc's confession lies in the fact that it polarizes all the associations, transferences, identifications, and anxieties that occurred before this confession.

The model of the confession made initially outside the session, during the break, is used later on, as is the repeated reference to the last fifteen minutes. It is as if it were necessary to signify through this moment outside the session the time prior to the traumatic re-alization; or as if an initial space were necessary prior to speaking, a space representing the topography of the preconscious, the locus and function necessary for the assumption of its history by the I. Or again, it is as if it were necessary for that which could not be said directly to the parents, but which nonetheless concerned them, to be metabolized through the agency of brothers and sisters and be reinforced by it. But what is involved, if not an error? This is attested by the denomination of a confession: the subject is party to what happened, and what happened fulfils *too much* his wish that it should have happened as it did; the traumatic impact lies in the excess of excitation that causes the realization of his phantasy.

The scenario used by Marc to transmit the traumatic charge initially disorganizes the relative continuity of the associative process. But in fact it organizes it on a long-term basis. It serves as a model for Anne-Marie to introduce into the associative chain and into the transference network her own current traumatic event: this is kept at a distance both by being revealed outside the session to Solange and by the election of a speech-bearer who is given the task of speaking for her, in her name, to the group and to the analysts. Anne-Marie makes it possible, by the same token, for Solange to represent Sophie.

Here again the mention of the painful event is accompanied by a burden of guilt. It is worth noting, however, that Anne-Marie acquits herself not of a confession but of a "secret": this mother who has abandoned her daughter—albeit with her agreement—can only speak about her "error" by first depositing it in someone else. This other is chosen for a certain similitude that she has to her in this matter, to the point that the mother's delegate discovers and recognizes herself in the daughter menaced with cancer by the mother whose history she reports. The speech she conveys speaks of a current traumatic event (concerning someone else, here), which had happened to her elsewhere, in the past. This is how the bond of identification between the depositor and the recipient, analysed by Bleger (1967), is formed; and, from my point of view, it is a foundation stone of unconscious alliances.

The series relating to the traumatic event branches out into other adjacent series: a series concerning guilt and reparation; a series on times (now, in the past, repetition, the last fifteen minutes) and places (here, elsewhere, in the same or in another group; disorientation, being beside oneself, bedroom, battlefield, hospital, etc.) My intervention at the end of the third session punctuated this series and articulated it with the series concerning the traumatic event.

Third associative series: around the (first) name

This third series originates once again with Jacques' request (for "a round of first names"). Jacques is the first to speak after Sophie and me; he is the first to speak about his need for points of reference. After a pause, the series is set going again indirectly by Sylvie, who, questioning her hesitation about the identity of the psychoanalyst, asks Solange and Anne-Marie to give their first names, which they do right away.

However, at the beginning of the second session Solange feels the need to give her first name spontaneously, as if to underline Sylvie's exploit, but she does not manage to get the others to do the same: the "round of first names" is completed the following day. Sylvie, clearly attentive to first names, points out to Solange that the initial syllable of her first name is the same as Sophie's. By virtue of this trait, Solange can represent Sophie, be like her; but Sylvie, who is herself concerned by the initial letter of her own first name, does not include herself in this play of identifications; later on she says that her mother had wanted a boy rather than a girl and that her first name (changed here) was the feminization of the one that had been intended for the expected son.

When the time comes for each participant to say what has led them to this group, Marc says that he "registered because of my name". Here, once again, we must make two hypotheses:

1. Marc bases the "registration" [*"inscription"*] of his name on mine: it is likely that Sylvie's remark, identifying, for reasons best known to herself, Solange's first name in Sophie's, cleared the way for this formulation, the unconscious representation of which was already there at the moment when he had enrolled for this group. At that moment, in the transference and in the context of the associations, Marc's formulation signified, as closely as possible to its unconscious representation, his relation with his identificatory re-father (cf. his remark about my first name).

2. Marc's insistence on representing himself through the marking event probably signals the insistence of his first name as a signifier of his inscription as a subject, a signifier that may be thought of as being included in a scene that concerns his origin and his filiation: his transference "registering because of my name", his questioning about my first name), is an actualization of this.

Genealogy and structuring of the organizers
of the associative process

These three associative series are the result of the associative work of
the group members. This work draws on the intersubjective links and
on the links between the representations. Let us try to understand
how these different series are organized by one or several unconscious purposive ideas, their disposition, coherence, and effects.

I assume that a prevailing organizer defines the correlative locations on the basis of which the speech of each member and the
associative process at the group level are ordered. Solange, Marc,
Sylvie, and Jacques occupy decisive locations and fulfil particular
functions in this process: they situated themselves and were placed
by the others at the nodal point of the individual, intersubjective,
and group processes. These subject-bearers of phoric functions and
the unconscious psychic organizers of the group act as operators
of the group associative process (see chapter 8 on the intermediate functions and the phoric functions of speech-bearer, symptom-
bearer, and dream-bearer).

If we examine how the associative process organizes itself during
this sequence, we will be able to discern a genealogy of three primal
organizing phantasies, the specific nature and potential of which
are still buried in the unconscious of the subjects. The first is the
phantasy of the primal scene; the second the phantasy of a traumatic
scene; and the third the phantasy of seduction.

Before these organizers appear, a rather chaotic phase contributes elements that are precursors of the principal organizer: these
are sensations, emotions, affects, quite diverse expressions of anxiety
but whose common traits are denoted by the encounter with the
unknown, the loss of limits and identificatory reference-points.

The prolific "battle–bedroom" and the emergence of the phantasy of the primal scene

Already in the second session the associative process is organized
around a phantasy of the primal scene whose formula— *"Parents,
in a battle–bedroom, are making love/war. They are having too many children"*—comprises two complementary and antagonistic instinctual
poles: love–war. Around this phantasy are articulated representations
of violence and the affects associated with it during the whole pre-

liminary phase: the violence of the chaos of the founding stage of the group, anger about the loss of limits, the violence of procreative excess (after the violence of lack), the violence of the parents' omnipotence over the children regarding life/death issues, and envious violence towards other members of the group.

The phantasy of abandonment/exclusion

The first version of the phantasy of the primal scene is organized around the anxieties and representations of a sadistic scene in which persecutory violence dominates. A second version of this scene reveals the violence of rejection and abandonment. It is formulated as follows: "*Parents are abandoning/excluding children.*"

The phantasy of a traumatic scene

It is again through violence that the phantasy of menace/reparation interlocks with the phantasy of the primal scene. It is introduced with Marc's "confession" and the impact of his story on the group. A first formulation of this phantasy, closest to Marc's words, might be: "*A father is threatening/repairing a child, who finds his mark in this phantasy.*"

This unconscious phantasy reorganizes the associative process, the movements of the transferences, the subjective and intersubjective locations. By blurring the singularity of the scene of the event that he presents as real, Marc brings about the construction of the unconscious scene of this scene. By giving pride of place in his account to action and the instinctual charge of violence, he inscribes them in the earlier phantasies, which facilitated his account. The blow received elsewhere, passively, *in extremis*, by a wild analyst, is echoed by the blow given to the "leaders" who are not looking after their children adequately because they are busy elsewhere, in the "battle–bedroom", having other children. A locus of the primal scene is found, and in the half-open space of the slip of the tongue a repressed content kept in repression for and by several members of the group makes its return, causing the same disorganizing bewilderment as Marc's story had provoked. This scene of chaotic proliferation, in which violence and death are lurking, re-establishes the confusion of the first moments of the life of the group: here again, Marc's story, through the primacy it gives to the affective charge of the trauma evoked, indicates a cause and repeats the primal trauma—namely, of confusion.

This story has the effect of giving greater consistency to the organizing phantasy of the group. By enacting this violence towards the group and towards me (this was his unconscious aim), Marc is also signalling that this father, who was menacing in another time and another place, is still present in the group now, even though he might also be a father who can repair the damage caused to his son. This phantasy is thus laden with a great charge of anxiety, owing to the hate pervading it, which is simultaneously both masked and accentuated by the defensive demand for reparation.

From thereon this phantasy becomes the mover of the positive and negative transferences and the organizer of the associative processes; it is the *affective* binder of the identifications between the participants. I have pointed out how it reorganizes the earlier representations: it is above all the attractor of new representations, new phantasies, memories, new affects, and new subjective locations in the group. This organizing power of the phantasy resides in yet another characteristic: it is situated at the nodal point of the three associative chains connected with speech, the trauma, and the name. Marc's story says that *something that has been said* has *hurt* him, of which his *name* is the inscription.

Different versions of this phantasy scene, with multiple entrypoints and with permutative variations, are declined in the train of associations. The father–son relation announced by Jacques and Marc, in which Boris is caught up without realizing it, is taken up again by Solange with respect to the loss of "*re-pères*", but it is declined in a homologous relation (mother–daughter), and then inverted (daughter–mother).

A trait common to both Marc and Solange is identified unconsciously by Anne-Marie, through projective identification. She also shares with them the sense of having lost her bearings, of being menaced/menacing, and of needing to reassure herself about her capacity to be a reparative mother: it is to the double mother in Solange/Sophie that Anne-Marie appeals, feeling guilty for having been unable to protect her daughter from suffering—from this "fateful blow", as she would say later. Solange's discovery that she herself is the bearer of maternal speech that was once menacing for her as a daughter confirms, as it were, Anne-Marie's intuition. The emotion that grips them both after this confession and this discovery seals their identification in the phantasy, the terms of which are transformed as follows: *"A father/a mother is menacing/repairing a son/a daughter."*

The consolidation of the phantasy is now assured; its internal group structure underpins other dimensions of the psychic bonding of the group members and increases the coherence of its psychic reality: for example, identifications through symptoms are reinforced.

At the end of these four first sessions, all the configurations of this structure had been actualized in the associative series and in the transferences. Michèle's dream was to form a pivotal point in the genealogy of the organizers of the associative process.

The associative processes after Michele's dream

It will be recalled that the first session of the second day began with the telling of a dream that Michèle had had during the night: *"I had a surprising dream. I dreamt that I was making love in a very untidy bedroom with Marc's father, or perhaps it was mine. They both had greying hair."*

Several associative series were triggered by the incestuous phantasy underlying the dream. The first series is organized around the uncertainty concerning the father's identity, the common trait—the greying hair—between the two of them, and the recognition of the incestuous wish. The second takes up the thread of the first, starting with an element mentioned the day before: that is, *"the very untidy bedroom"*. There is a reference to disorderly love-making and incest. The third series revolves around the mention of catastrophes and accidents: a father's sudden and early death, a mother plunged into mourning, and a depression in adolescence, the disappearance of a friend in the mountains, an elder brother who died in early childhood, a mother's paralysis, a car accident. The fourth series revolves around the libidinal reinvestment following the evocation of these traumatic events and death; it is connected with the central motif of the dream with the phantasy of transgressing the prohibition against fraternal incest.

The dream takes up the main elements of the associations of the previous day; the dreamer works on them in her own dream. She dreams for herself, and she dreams for the group. The dream reworks the organizing phantasy of the trauma, which is still present and active; and the associations that it triggers lead one to suppose that it returns to the fore when the dangerous consequences of transgression emerge: accident, catastrophe, sudden death, and disappearance. The transference onto the analysts is underpinned by the conjunction of these two phantasies: they are asked to reassure the participants with regard to the limits of the barrier of incest.

All these paths bring us closer to the traumatic, violent, sexual, unconscious core of the principal phantasy organizing the psychic reality of this group. It is thus not surprising that the associations that develop after the telling of the dream encounter a defensive movement against the phantasy of sexual seduction of the son by the father. But at the same time, owing to Michèle's dream, a transformation occurs in the organizing phantasy of the group: the phantasy of the trauma and of the menace is henceforth associated with the phantasy of seduction and incest.

The transformations affecting the content of the associations are correlated with the resolution of certain transferences and the beginning of the appropriation by each subject of his singular phantasy. This was the case for Marc. The telling of the dream, the associative work, and the analysis of the transferences gave him access to the meaning of his symptom and to a process of transformation of his representation—confused and confusing—of the trauma. This was also the case for other participants.

Interdiscursivity and polyphony in the group associative process: the work of the preconscious

The genealogy of the organizers of the associative process as an indicator of interdiscursivity

Analysing the genealogy of the phantasies has led me to make several hypotheses concerning the organizers of the associative process in the group. The first is that the associative process is built on a double series of organizers: one is specific to the subject, while the other is shared and common to the whole group.

We cannot decide whether the individual organizers determine the group organizers, or whether the inverse is the case. Marc, like the others, comes to the group with his phantasy. His phantasy acquires an organizing power because its unconscious aspects can be shared with other members of the group: this is what is explored in the initial, whirlpool-like phase. Once it has become a group phantasy, capable of combining the psyches, the organizing phantasy becomes an attractor of phantasies that cause the scene, the version, and positions of the subjects to vary.

The second hypothesis concerns the fact that the associative process wavers between *the various versions of a phantasy*. I have noted two characteristics of these versions: the gaps between versions of one and the same phantasy reveal the organizing power of the basic phantasy and the richness of its dimensions, just as the diverse versions of a myth reveal its profound meaning, as Claude Lévi-Strauss has shown. At the same time, these versions may also be utilized as defensive formations against the emergence of the subject's position in his own secondary phantasy.

The third hypothesis concerns *the succession of the organizing phantasies*. A prevailing phantasy—and its versions—organizes the associative sequence, determining its contents and processes. But the associative sequence causes affective contents and new representations to emerge which attract, by contiguity, contrast, or continuity, another organizing phantasy. We are alerted to this by the transformations that occur during the associations. It is only by being attentive to the associative process and to the movements of the transferences that we can have access to the unconscious organizers. Violence, misunderstanding, disappointment, issues of nomination are signified, resignified, and reinterpreted through the avatars of the scene of phantasy that emerges in Marc's confession.

A fourth hypothesis contends that each group derives the specific characteristics of its psychic reality from an organizing phantasy that is proper to it and that tolerates a large variation in its structure. The genealogy of successive organizers gives access to the unconscious structure of the group and, through its variations, to its history and prehistory.

Interdiscursivity and polyphony

At the beginning of this chapter, I recalled that the plurality of discourses and the interdiscursivity of associative processes is a decisive characteristic of the group setting. A clinical analysis of the associative chains has just shown us how the course of the associations is organized, combined, and transformed under the influence of their three levels of individual, intersubjective, and group organization. The discourses interact, bind, separate, and differentiate themselves. What is said between the subjects also says something about each of them and to each of them. The analysis of the genealogy of the organizers of the associations has shown how interdiscursivity functions in diachrony.

The polyphony of the group associative chain is an effect of interdiscursivity. I have borrowed the notion of polyphony from the work of Bakhtine and Vorochilov on the structure of the literary work. (I have made use of the notion of polyphony in my work on the associative process, Kaës, 1994b, and more recently concerning dreams, Kaës, 2002a, 2002b: cf. chapter 9 herein.) Bakhtine contends that the polyphonic novel is elaborated at the crossroads of several structures, just as the word is a *polyphony* of several writings [*écritures*]: the writer's, his characters', the recipient's, and that of the historical, ethical, and cultural context. This polyphonic organization is characteristic of the very sphere of language, and Bakhtine extends the principle to any semiotic production: the logic that organizes it is that not of linear determination and identity but of the transgressive logic of the dream or revolution—that is to say, another law is in operation. Bakhtine does not confine his analysis to the status of poetic language in the polyphonic novel. He puts forward the idea of an *internal* audience, specific to each individual, "in whose atmosphere his deductions, motivations and appreciations are being constructed. . . ." His analysis of Dostoyevsky's novels shows how polyphony and internal dialogism function: for example, in *The Adolescent*, Bakhtine distinguishes the hero's own voice, that of his internal interlocutor, and the third narrating voice; then he identifies the common fund of words traversing and uniting this three-voiced structure, produced by the effects of concordance and discord. The question constantly emerges: Who is speaking? Who is thinking? Who is feeling? Who is dreaming? And these moments of uncertainty are resolved by the emergence of an I that, like a hero, accepts the polyphony and transcends it.

Two concepts run through the whole of Bakhtine's work: alterity and dialogism. We can turn them to our advantage by making the necessary transformations. The first claims that we are not psychic monads, but subjects whose desires and beliefs are related to those of other subjects, inscribed in a society: "I is hidden within the other and within Others", he writes. Language and, more rigorously, discourse, is the field of this encounter: "Discourse encounters the discourse of others along all the paths which lead towards its object, and it cannot fail to enter into a lively and intense interaction with it" (Bakhtine & Vorochilov, 1934–35, p. 92). Or again: "The speaker seeks to orient his discourse, and as far as the horizon which determines it, in relation to the horizon of others" (pp. 95–96). The concept of dialogism denotes the fact that each utterance presents relations with other utterances about the same object, quite independently of the fact that it may be a speaker's reply to his interlocutor's utterance. Accordingly, even the monological utterance has a dialogical dimension. Bakhtine calls the dialogical force of language pluridiscursivity. It struggles against the monological reification of the discourse. It is in this context that I have used the concept of polyphony in analysing the associative process, in order to emphasize the resonances and the transformation of the associative utterances through their assemblage.

Perspectives on the associative process and the work of the preconscious

Analysing associative processes was an opportunity to test the model of the group psychic apparatus and the hypotheses it comprises. The main question was that of gaining access, through the apparatus of language, to certain articulations between the formations, processes and topographies of the unconscious in the intrapsychic space, the intersubjective space, and the group space.

The analysis has taught us that associative processes are organized in groups from three sources of unconscious contents arising from repression, denial, or rejection. One of these sources is proper to each subject considered in the singularity of his structure and his history; the other arises from the relations between the group members in order to construct group ties. The third is important and must not be neglected: it is produced by the analysts in the group situation through their relations to the group. Each of these contents of the unconscious is bound in an original way and returns in the manifestations of the associative process. This analysis has allowed us to become acquainted with the effects of repression—or denial—and the modalities of the return of the repressed in the group and in the members of the group. It has brought us precious information concerning the mode of formation of the subject of the unconscious, the subject of speech, and the subject of the group.

I would like to open up a perspective that may be of interest to all psychoanalysts. It concerns what the analysis of the group associative process teaches us about the formation and work of the preconscious.

I have pointed out that, in the initial phase of a group, but also at other moments of the group process, the intensity and modalities of the instinctual encounter with the other, with more-than-an-other, temporarily imperil the activity of the preconscious, owing to the multiplicity of solicitations with which the ego of the members of a group is faced. The ego's capacity for binding representations and affects, for phantasying and thinking, is put to the test insofar as the internal and external stimulus barriers are deficient. Now the stimulus barrier function is a major function of the preconscious: the latter accomplishes it by utilizing the signifying predispositions and the word-presentations that are available to it. Studying the associative process, especially its group modalities, has led me to accord a position of importance to the activity of the preconscious and to define its formation and functioning when in contact with the preconscious psychic activity of the other.

These studies are precious because clinical practice, including individual treatment, regularly shows us that in a certain number of pathologies and psychic sufferings the preconscious activity of the subject is deficient or has not been able to constitute itself. This is the case for what are globally referred to as the borderline pathologies.

If we link these hindrances to the work of the preconscious to the preconscious activity of the other or a set of others, we are able to understand these pathologies better and to treat these subjects more satisfactorily. We must remember that the first word-presentations are initially contributed by the mother's speech in the primary group, by an other, or by more than one other. For each one of us this speech, its style, its intonation, its effects are linked to those first experiences, which helped us to name the things we perceived. In order for speech to be articulated and understood, a sufficiently common syntax and semantics are necessary; a shared interpretative instrument has to function. Freud (1912–13) calls the instrument that allows us to give meaning to the words and intentions of others an apparatus for signifying–interpreting [*der Apparat zu deuten*].

The work of the unconscious that a subject is in a position to carry out is based initially on the psychic activity of the mother, herself supported by her environment when she fulfils the alpha function (Bion), when she dreams about and for the infant (Winnicott), and when she constitutes herself as speech-bearer for the infant with regard to the internal and external stimulations facing him (Castoriadis-Aulagnier). Subsequently, in analysis or in a group situation, this work of the preconscious provides the conditions necessary for giving fresh impetus to the activity of symbolization in subjects who have been unable to have access to it.

It is in this way, and with this model, that I articulate the formation of the preconscious with intersubjectivity, and more particularly with the function of speech. The analysis of the group with Marc and the others has thrown light on this point by showing us how the group functions as an apparatus for transforming traumatic experience. We can observe how the preconscious of the participants functioned in the group, how the group associative process sustained it, and how reformulations after the event bore witness to this work—which, for these reasons, may be called a *work of intersubjectivity*.

NOTE

1. The mother had threatened her daughter, pointing out the dangers of cancer, to prevent her adolescent daughter from smoking.

8

Phoric functions:
speech-bearer, symptom-bearer, dream-bearer

The model of the group psychic apparatus and the praxis on which it is based has led me to pay particular attention to the psychic formations and processes that perform an articulating function between the group and the individual subject.

The analysis of associative processes has shown us the existence of nodal points and intermediate formations between the individual associative chains and the associative chain that is formed in the group. It has revealed the functions of certain persons who, in the group, embody and represent these nodal points: they are speech-bearers, symptom-bearers, dream-bearers, but there are also others who are bearers of ideals, figures of death or salvation, and so on.

We encounter such persons when they come for individual analysis and we analyse the dimensions related to the intrapsychic conflicts that these functions engender or in which they participate. Freud has given us an example of this with the analysis of Dora's treatment. The group psychoanalytic situation teaches us that the phoric functions that these individuals carry out have simultaneously and correlatively a subjective, intersubjective and group dimension. These three functions and their relations can thus be analysed.

In order to conceptualize these functions, I first turned to the category of the intermediary: we can find the premises of this category in Freud, Róheim, and Winnicott. This category, whose extension and meaning vary in each of these authors, was used by them for thinking about intrapsychic and intersubjective formations: the object and the transitional space are the prototype of it. I will confine my exposition to describing briefly this category in Freud's thought. (For further reading on the developments of this category in the thought of Freud, Róheim, and Winnicott, I refer the reader to my study: Kaës, 1985a.)

The category of the intermediary
in Freud's thought

The category of the intermediary traverses Freud's entire work, from its inception in 1895 up until 1939. Although Freud never makes it a specific concept, this category is a constant element of his thought, and it reappears each time the theory undergoes a major modification.

The intermediary and intrapsychic discontinuity

Freud makes use of the notion of intermediate formation when he is faced with the necessity of thinking about the link between two discontinuous orders of reality: between inside and outside, between conscious and unconscious, between latent dream thoughts and manifest dream thoughts, between the demands of the ego, the superego, and the id, between these and external reality, and between the individual and the group. In all of these cases the intermediate formations and processes perform specific functions of linking, mediation, and transformation.

The psychic apparatus thus has at its disposal in its internal organization agencies or systems specifically allotted to the work of the intermediary processes: the system preconscious and the agency of the ego, which Freud describes as a frontier-creature [*ein Grenzwesen*]. Instinct and phantasy, which Freud describes as creatures of mixed blood or mixed race, belong to this category, as do compromise formations, symptoms, and dreams. The dream is an intermediary between two states of the ego, the waking ego and the dream ego;

it is formed through intermediate thoughts that give access to its analysis. When he outlines his "social psychology", Freud attributes to the leader, as well as to the poet and to the historian [*der Dichter*], functions that also belong to the category of the intermediary. We have an example of the interlocking nature of intermediate formations if we consider the ego of the leader.

With these examples it seems that Freud assigned a central position to this category, while making a relatively limited use of it for certain formations, processes, and functions: a central position, if one considers that Freud describes either frontier-formations within intrapsychic space or formations that mark a limit between psychic reality and biological reality (like the instinctual drive) or social reality (like the leader); a precise and limited usage, if one accepts that it applies to original psychic formations destined to overcome the terms of a separation, a breach, a rupture, or a conflict, or to form a link between heterogeneous elements.

The intermediary and mediation
in Group Psychology *and* Totem and Taboo

As much as Freud's thought on the intermediary in the individual psychic apparatus draws on the clinical experience of psychoanalytic treatment, his views on this category in groups (and in culture) belong to the realm of speculation: although it was not possible for him to put them to the test in appropriate methodological settings, they nonetheless still have great heuristic value.

I will begin with the text of 1921, which is more explicit on this question than that of 1912–13. In *Group Psychology and the Analysis of the Ego* (1921c), the notion of intermediary is evoked in relation to the mysterious power of the hypnotist and his gaze. Freud notes the relation between this power and the dangerous and unbearable aspect of the gaze once the leader or the divinity are seen or can see their subjects. Freud (1921c, p. 125) gives as an example of this dangerous character the fact that Moses was called to act as intermediary between Jehovah and his people: "Even Moses had to act as intermediary [*Mittelsmann*][1] between his people and Jehovah, since the people could not support the sight of God; and when he returned from the presence of God his face shone—some of the *mana* had been transferred onto him, just as happens with the intermediary [*Mittler*] among primitive people."

Freud uses these two words [*der Mittelsmann, der Mittler*] in a sentence of five lines to characterize this primary function of mediator of confronting that which is unbearable and dangerous. The mediator functions as a sort of filtering screen, like a protective shield between the divine source of Omnipotence and those who are exposed to it.

Another specific trait of the intermediary is mentioned by Freud: Moses shares the characteristics of both entities of which he is the *Mittelsmann*: not only is he close to the people and has seen Jehovah, but he is delegated by the people and he receives from Jehovah a part of his power. He is thus installed in this position of intermediary on two counts: through delegation and through investment. The rays that emanate from Moses's face constitute a metaphorical figuration of the ambiguous character of this bond between the people and Jehovah—ambiguous because this bond is a saving and/or destructive power. The danger comes from the unbearable character of two elements that cannot face each other directly; it is this danger that puts Moses into the position of third party in this relationship. Moses is the one who brings together the two separated fragments of a whole united by an alliance. His position as a third party should thus also be taken into account from the point of view of setting up a process of symbolization. The person of Moses symbolizes partly God and partly his people: he cannot be reduced to either the one or the other—he is a hyphen between them.

Freud takes up and develops in this text several elements of an analysis outlined seven years earlier in *Totem and Taboo*. He is concerned with the taboo and the ambivalence of feelings:

A king's taboo is too strong for one of his subjects because the social difference between them is too great. But a minister may without any harm serve as an intermediary between them. If we translate this from the language of taboo into that of normal psychology, it means something like this. A subject, who dreads the great temptation presented to him by contact with the king, can perhaps tolerate dealings with an official whom he does not need to envy so much and whose position may even seem attainable to him. A minister, again, can mitigate his envy of the king by reflecting on the power which he himself wields [Freud, 1912–13, p. 33]

A few lines further on, Freud remarks that the violation of taboo prohibitions presents a disastrous social danger for society itself: in this context, the intermediary fulfils a social function of linking and compromise. Here, then, is an example of an intermediary function that can be understood from the point of view of intrapsychic processes and from the point of view of intersubjective group processes. The mediator [*der Vermittler*] is situated between the ego of the subjects and that which is awakened in them: by the divine or royal figure of the "archaic heritage" (of the archaic superego), of the relationship with the primal parent. The mediator breaks the hypnotic bond by introducing the social bond in the "group of two" (1921c, p. 127). He reduces the gap between the ego and ego ideals. Whether it is Moses or the Minister, the principal relation that binds these figures to the people or to the subjects is the ambivalent character of their relationship with a religious or political authority, a support of the Ideal, a metaphysical, metasocial, and metapsychic guardian. The central psychic process is the identification with intermediary persons: they can share a common trait with the object without destroying it and without being destroyed by it.

Phoric functions

These first outlines gave me precious indications concerning intermediate functions performed by certain subjects in the passages between the psychic spaces of each subject and common and shared psychic spaces: in a couple, a family, or an institution. I have called such functions *phoric*—from the Greek verb *phorein* [bear, carry], the root of which is found in metaphor [*metaphorein*: transport, displace]—for they include and transcend the link between two separate edges, the frontier between two discontinuous spaces. The persons who incarnate them are also in charge of these functions: they bear or carry them as much as they are borne or carried by them; they bear the trace of that which created them and of that on which they were founded.

The concept of phoric functions also acquires a more precise and more complex dimension insofar as it possesses a specific consistency simultaneously in the intrapsychic and intersubjective fields. Let us put these propositions to the test now by analysing three phoric functions: those of speech-bearer, symptom-bearer, and dream-bearer.

The functions of the speech-bearer

The concept of speech-bearer is a concept for dealing with the question of speech in intersubjective ensembles. Analysing the associative process has made me attentive to how speech is brought to the subject; how he is grasped by it; how he takes it up and burdens it with his own wishes and prohibitions; how he delegates it or offloads it.

In groups, we are dealing with two principal functions of the speech-bearer, which Castoriadis-Aulagnier (1975) recognizes the mother as having in the structuring of the psyche of the *infans*. I will remind you of them briefly.

The first lays stress on the maternal voice, in its physical, vibratory, sonoric, and musical dimensions, but also on the words that come through this voice. These words appear in the mother well before the birth of the newborn baby, but particularly at the moment when he comes into the world. They are words that accompany, comment on, and predict the supposed activities and thoughts of the *infans*. The first function of the speech-bearer is woven into activities of mimicry, the looks and smiles, the cries and tears, the smells, the contact, the props and supports of the mother and the baby. It is established at the moment of giving the baby a bath, at the moment of suckling and putting the baby to sleep, at the moment when the baby cries, when he has to be changed—in short, in all those moments that are moments of pleasure and unpleasure for the *infans*. It is through this type of experience that the mother brings the *infans to* speech, that she supports him *in* speech and constitutes him *through* speech, that she opens the door to speech for him. But it seems right to note that the child also supports the mother in the speech that she brings to him: he is an attractor of speech.

In this function of speech-bearer, the mother's presence and the speaking activity form an external stimulus barrier: they model the libidinal and narcissistic organization of the baby's body and, in a more general way, they participate in the structuring of the baby's psychic apparatus and thus of its unconscious and preconscious systems. A link can certainly be made here between the function of speech-bearer and the alpha function defined by Bion: the mother's speaking activity functions as the inductor of preconceptions that will subsequently be available for use by the child.

The second function of the speech-bearer exercised by the mother, or by the *infans'* substitute caretaker, consists in the fact that she bears the speech of an other: words that have been delegated to the mother by an other, generally the father, who, in our societies, embodies the paternal function, which she represents for an other, the *infans*. If the mother who fulfils this second function of the speech-bearer does not speak in her own name, if, being neither the cause nor the origin of it, she speaks in the name of an other, she is nonetheless the one who speaks and who interprets this speech. The mother performs this function when she articulates the rules, the laws, the prohibitions and the representations that correspond to them. At the same time as the words of interdiction establish in the child the reference to the law, they give him representations of it. These statements organize the child's relations to the mother's body, to the world, to fundamental differences: animate/inanimate; dead/alive; animal/human; man/woman; parents/children. The mother is the speech-bearer of an intersubjective order to which she herself is subject and which organizes her own subjectivity in her relation to that of her *infans*.

These two dimensions of the maternal function of the speech-bearer are distinct and articulated. They describe the function of "prosthesis" carried out for the *infans* by the maternal psyche. The mother speaks to the child and for the child: she accompanies his experiences with words, and she makes it possible for the child to gain access to his own speech.

For my own part, I would like to emphasize several points. The first is that the foetus, then the *infans*, also hears the father's voice and distinguishes it very early on from that of the mother. At least two voices are heard. The second is that the mother and the father not only put speech at the service of the *infans*, but they also satisfy the latter's demand to find signifying predispositions. By her activity of subject speech-bearer, the mother—but also the father—responds to this fundamental need of the human psyche: namely, of putting at the *infans*' disposition the means of representing his own experience for himself, of introducing him to the capacity of thinking and of thinking about himself. (Her phoric function might be called, drawing inspiration from Bion, that of a thought-bearer.) The mother—herself sustained by the paternal function—supports this capacity when the *infans* has to confront the experience of separation and "finding–creating" of transitional signifiers, as evidenced by the wooden reel game. She does not disillusion him about the fact that the words he uses are words that he thinks he has invented by creating them. The child will then be able to create significations that are his own and compare them with common significations, inasmuch as the mother is able to allow for the development in him of what I shall readily call *poetic illusion,* just as the poet has the illusion of recreating the world from words that are not entirely his own, but which he finds and recreates. She makes him a poet and narrator. The associative capacity of the *infans,* his associative style, will ultimately be marked by this way in which playing with words has been supported and tolerated by the mother conjointly with the specific effects of her own repression.

I will further add that the mother speaks (for) herself [*se parle*] through her function of speech-bearer: she speaks (for) herself in her first as well as her second function, when she speaks in the relationship of investment and delegation that she has received from the family grouping, and notably the father. The mother is the bearer of a speech to which she adheres. If she does not adhere to it, a catastrophic scission occurs in what the child hears, between what the mother says to him and what the mother's words to the child represent for her. Through her function of speech-bearer, the mother contributes her own instinctual investment to the psyche of the *infans,* and she also receives investment from the latter.

The necessity of the presence of an Other is not limited to the vital functions that she must provide to compensate for the *infans'* characteristic prematurity, just as a response to the "needs" of the psyche is also required. A major condition is necessary: the objects of experience and encounter that the mother proposes to the child and which she associates with words can only exercise their power of representability and figurability for the *infans* if they have been marked by the activity of the maternal psyche, which endows them with a *libidinal indicator* and thereby with a status of psychic object in conformity to the "needs" of the psyche. The materials and condition of representability and figurability are objects that have been shaped by the work of the maternal psyche. The imprint that the mother leaves on the object is a prior condition for these two metabolizations. Aulagnier acknowledges her debt to Lacan: the object can only be metabolized by the psychic activity of the *infans* if, and as long as, the mother's discourse has endowed it with a *meaning* to which her denomination bears witness. The meaning is swallowed with the object: by this formula Lacan was designating the primal introjection of the signifier and the inscription of the unary trait between the mother and the child.

The functions of the speech-bearer in groups: clinical studies

The first function described by Aulagnier can easily be identified in groups: a voice and a discourse that accompanies, comments, soothes, and gives meaning fulfil this function, not for *infans*, but for speaking subjects for whom words are lacking at that moment. Generally speaking, this function establishes links between experience and its designation, an association between words, a transformation of experience and use of speech. The formation of the apparatus for thinking thoughts described by Bion occurs in groups through this function of the speech-bearer and corresponds to what Corrao (1981) has called, by analogy, the gamma function.

The second function, *meta*phoric, describes an agency of delegation and representation of an order that is external to the group and whose discourse in the group sets out the laws, principles, and prohibitions. This metaphoric function introduces the reference to a third order in the dual unit that is striving to establish itself or to re-establish itself constantly between the group and its members.

I would like to point out that in the psychoanalytic situation, whether individual or group, this function is first, and foremost, one that the psychoanalyst fulfils when he announces the fundamental rule. He is not the master of this rule; he is himself subject to it and is its speech-bearer. He is the bearer of speech he has received, which constitutes him in his function as analyst and inscribes him within a symbolic order. The psychoanalyst is the bearer of speech permitting the lifting of repression, but on the condition of respecting a prohibition with regard to the direct satisfaction of archaic and oedipal wishes. It is in this register that interpretation is speech governed by the reality principle and not by the pleasure principle. Under these conditions, the announcement of the fundamental rule makes interpretation possible and, consequently, the constitution of a "space in which the I can come into being" as a separate, distinct subjectivity, bearing its own words.

I suggest that a third, *representative* function of the speech-bearer be taken into consideration. The speech-bearer is a vehicle of the speech of others, and he represents this speech to others. Through him the subjective locations of several members of the group are formed. Let us recall the function of speech-bearer that Solange is given and fulfils in the group: she constitutes this function by becoming the manifest and explicit speech-bearer for Anne-Marie, but also for Marc and several others. She represents them. This representative function is linked to the location occupied by the speech-bearer: in the nexus of the group, the speech-bearer is situated at the nodal points of three spaces: those of phantasy, of the associative discourse, and of the intersubjective structure of the group relations.

It is worth noting that in groups, the speech-bearer, though he speaks on behalf of someone else or several others and for a recipient, is not, however, always heard by them, just as the symptom-bearer is not spontaneously recognized as such. The speech-bearer also speaks of that which has been left on one side, and it is thus important that there is at least one listener; it is the psychoanalyst's function to lend his ear.

The relation of the speech-bearer to speech: the choice of Solange as speech-bearer

The choice of Solange as speech-bearer for Anne-Marie, Marc, and several others in the group is the result of several series of determinations. Some are specific to Solange, to the structure and history of her psyche; they are intrapsychic. Of those that are mobilized and actualized in this group, some are perceived and invested by Anne-Marie: these are intersubjective determinations. Others are defined by the organization of the phantasies, the transferences, and the associative process in the group: these are group determinations. Let us now examine their relations.

My hypothesis is that Solange *already has at her disposal* signs that will support the choice of her as speech-bearer. She finds that she is disposed to represent for an other, and for more than one other, a reparative imago, on behalf of Sophie, whose imago is too dangerous, rivalrous, superego-like for her: she knows this from preconscious knowledge when she wonders whether she is not somehow implicated in the fact of having been taken for Sophie. Solange says she is the bearer of a question about speech: she discovers that the ability to "speak well", which she would like to acquire, masks another, much more serious and important expectation: namely, of being able to speak about "her bundles" of suffering for which, precisely, she does not as yet have the necessary words. She is attentive to the exchanges between Marc and Boris "who talk to each other" in a language that is complementary and common. Solange identifies herself with one of the places in this intersubjective relationship in which other correlative places are available and can be occupied: it is precisely one of these places that Solange will occupy when Anne-Marie asks her to speak (for) her.

One can see here that Solange chooses to be chosen. The choice of Solange as speech-bearer is over-determined by traits that pertain to her history, to her identifications, to her unconscious conflict, to her phantasy. These traits are perceived and interpreted by the others in terms of their own "apparatus for interpreting". They thus constitute attachment points (points of purchase) for the identifications and movements of transference of Sylvie and Anne-Marie towards Solange.

But we must also take into consideration the fact that the choice of Solange as speech-bearer is over-determined by the organization of the associative network formed by the three principal series connected with *speech*, the *traumatic event,* and the (fore) *name.* These series are interwoven and develop; they are sustained by a few subjects in whom several associative threads are woven; they are oriented by the movements of the transferences, especially by the transferences onto the psychoanalysts and by the phantasies organizing them.

Solange situates herself, in fact, at the point at which the organizing phantasy of the group pivots and is condensed. She imagines herself in a location contrary to that of Anne-Marie (menacing mother) and homologous with that of Marc (menaced son). She is at the pivotal point of passive and active actions, at the meeting-point between the phantasy of menace and the phantasy of reparation. She places herself, and is placed, with her consent and without her realizing it, in the very place of her conflict between menacing/repairing, of her ambivalent identifications *vis-à-vis* the maternal imago. Her place in the phantasy is at the very locus of her symptom, and it is through traits common to several participants that the identifications with Solange occur. We have a remarkable example here of identification through the symptom.

We can see here that the speech-bearer fulfils his phoric function through the movement of his own desire and that he is called to the function by others who, together, prompt him to occupy this location and function. He speaks in the place of an other, but he also speaks for the other who is in him: thus he finds in the speech or words of the other a representation that had not been available to him hitherto.

The phoric function of the dream-bearer

The figure of the *dream-bearer* informs us about both the function of the dream-bearer and the function of the dream in groups—and in all intersubjective formations: in couples, families, and institutions. This figure appeared in our group with Michèle's dream and the function that she fulfilled in the group by dreaming and telling her dream. I have already analysed it at length, and I will return to it again in the course of the next chapter.

I just want to emphasize that dream-bearers dream for themselves, and that certain events from the previous day, the identifications and the transferences that mobilize them, determine the content of their dream. However, dream-bearers, like patients in analysis, dream *for someone* in the transference. It is thus not surprising that the destination—the recipient(s)—of the dream influences its content, and subsequently the telling of the dream and its effects inscribe it in intersubjectivity, upstream as well as downstream.

These "dreamers" of the group also dream *in the place of someone*, through projective or introjective identification. This function can obviously be codified in groups, families, and institutions and can mobilize, in addition to primary and secondary processes, tertiary processes that obey social and cultural logic and articulate dreams and myths (Dodds, 1959; Kaës, 2004). These dreamers become dream-bearers due to the effect of the internal necessity of establishing, by means of the dream, a psychic space that is larger than their own and whose limits are extended to those of an other, of more than one other, and to a whole group.

The symptom-bearer

Dora's analysis drew attention, at the outset of psychoanalysis, to the figure of the *symptom-bearer*. My reading of it contends that all the protagonists of the group around Dora contribute to nourishing the symptom by means of identifications in an unconscious alliance from which everyone derives benefit. Freud participates in this when he overlooks the fact that Dora's love for her mother forms the knot of Dora's symptoms and of his own symptoms (Kaës, 1985b; see also chapter 5 herein).

The analysis of the group also revealed the function of symptom-bearer carried out by Marc for the sake of other members of the group, but also for his own sake, access to the former barring access to the latter. Likewise, and with the same effects, Solange represents for Anne-Marie, but also for others, a nodal point of the symptoms. The symptom-bearer performs a phoric function and an intermediary function. He is also, for all these reasons, a locus of the return of the repressed in the psychic space of the group and in the internal spaces of each group member. When the symptom allows its foundations to show through, it is resolved, displaced, or transformed—the analysis of the group has furnished many examples of this. But it is rare for it to disappear, for what subsists of all these possibilities is also that which organizes the psychic reality of the group and its permanence. There are thus grounds for wondering if every group does not continuously secrete at least one symptom-bearer.

The ideal-bearer and other phoric functions

We can use the term "ideal-bearer" to refer to the subject whom Freud described as one representing and bearing, or embodying, the unrealized wishful dreams of others. As the heir or source of their narcissism, he is both His Majesty the Baby and the Ancestor. The ideal-bearer also embodies the figure of the leader who receives and represents the abandoned part of the formations of the ideal of each of us. This abandonment, which is necessary if identification with a common, powerful, and unifying object is to be established, is the basis of shared ideals. The ideal-bearer represents, embodies, the soul of the imaginary group body; he guarantees the permanence of linking and the existence of each individual.

The list of phoric functions and the figures they assume is unquestionably extensive, and a series of studies would be needed to describe each of them. We should mention the function of the *crypt-bearer* (or cryptophor) proposed by Abraham and Torok (1978), the *evil-bearer* whose prevalent figures are those of the scapegoat and the one who is possessed, or again the *memory-bearer* (historian, poet) or the *child-bearer*. It would be interesting to examine from this angle the figure of the *messenger*, whose place in the primal scene is clearly shown in Joseph Losey's 1970 film *The Go-Between*, while mythologies testify to its vital function in the representation of the bond between the divinity and men.

The double determination of phoric functions

One of the questions raised by phoric functions is that of distinguishing between what is specific to the subject in the function that he fulfils and what is assigned to him in this function by the group process.[2] The subject who fulfils a phoric function is affected by several sorts of determinations. He is called to this function by other subjects with whom he has ties and who, together, have a common interest in making this location and this function exist. But he also finds himself in this location through the movement of his own desire. We can make the hypothesis that the phoric locations determined by intersubjective links or by the organization of the group bring a powerful confirmation of the internal determinations that lead the subjects towards these functions. This is true of all the phoric functions.

The locations imposed by the group organization and the intersubjective determinations of phoric functions

The subjects who fulfil these functions occupy a certain place in the ensemble, often without realizing it, subject to a determination specific to the ensemble to which they belong and of which they are a constituting part. These locations and these functions are required in the organization of any linking situation: they are necessary for the intersubjective psychic process, but it should be noted that the subjects who fulfil them derive certain benefits from them and suffer certain disadvantages.

Belonging to a group—a couple, a family, an institution—requires a certain division of psychic work: a distribution of the psychic tasks is necessary for the maintenance and continuity of the ensemble. The subject who fulfils a phoric function participates in this division and distribution: thus the speech-bearer assumes or receives the task of speaking in the name of several others, in the place of an Other or of a set of others. He is their delegate and represents them. But his function depends on the ensemble.

The phoric location, the choice of the bearer, the function or functions that he carries out are determined by the structural necessities of the life of the group. The unconscious psychic organizers which govern the formation of the group psychic apparatus determine the distribution of the places and the tasks. In this sense, it is not only the subject-bearer who fulfils a phoric function: each one takes his place in the predisposed locations governed by the identificatory networks, phantasy scenarios, systems of object-relations, defensive systems or fundamental statements of the group. Everyone has their place in the ensemble and finds that the ensemble has assigned them a certain place. From this point of view, the leader fulfils his function owing to the necessity of the structure.

This point of view centred on the group needs to be compared with another point of view, which considers the role of the phoric functions in the formation and processes of intersubjectivity. A subject carries and transports—without realizing it—for an other, or for a set of others—without their realizing it—signs, affects, objects, good and bad, unconscious scenes, ideas and ideals. The subjects who are thus transported establish with the bearer unconscious links founded on their common interest in these transports of unconscious material.

Whether the determinations are of a group or intersubjective nature, in all cases what is carried and transported is psychic material subject to the effects of the unconscious, which are only observable in a group situation. All the phoric functions are situated at the nodal points of the common and shared unconscious phantasy, the associative discourses, and the transferences. They all form and inform the material of unconscious alliances, narcissistic contracts, negative pacts, shared denial: the "phoric" subjects hold their place and their functions in an unconscious alliance with those who assign these places and functions to them. The subject-bearers are, then, for whoever listens to them in the group and intersubjective process, excellent indicators or revealers[3] of the topography, economy, dynamics, and semiotics of these processes.

All phoric functions have their psychopathological side—their neurotic, perverse, or psychotic version. A psychotic version is the identification of the speech-bearer with what he says, or the messenger with what he announces.[4] A perverse version of the utilization of the messenger is the pleasure derived from making him say and repeat, eventually under coercion, what one rejects oneself.

The intrapsychic determinations of the bearer's phoric function

This group and intersubjective reading of the phoric function is not sufficient. It is not enough to say that what leads such and such a subject to fulfil a phoric function and to take the corresponding place in a group is determined and predisposed by the organization of the ensemble. This function and this place must be examined from another angle: the speech-bearer, dream-bearer, or symptom-bearer is led by the movement of his own unconscious wish to hold these functions and these locations. Certainly, they bear the speech, phantasies, conflicts, and symptoms of certain others, but they bear them along with their own, without realizing it. By fulfilling their functions as bearers and delegates, they fulfil their own purposes and they serve as a link, servant, and beneficiary to the grouping to which they must submit. The idea of a mandate from the group or a part of the group does not wholly define the functions that they exercise. The subject carries out phoric functions in the group by virtue of singular interests determined by his history and his structure. The problematic within which the internal necessity of the phoric function is inscribed is that of the subject of the unconscious inasmuch as he is subject of the group. It is also that of the person, in the sense of *persona*: the mask through which one speaks.

If we return to the example of the leader, we can see that in this respect he does not exist exclusively on the basis of the function he fulfils in the group; he becomes a leader owing to the intrapsychic determination that leads him to this position. The leader can only fulfil his function of ideal-bearer for the members of the group if he himself is intimately concerned with the function that he is asked to fulfil and for which he puts himself forward. This function and this place are not known to him in advance: he only knows them in the situation in which his capacity for bearing the ideal and of functioning in this intermediary position will be put to the test. This is why I have proposed this formulation: the subject who fulfils a phoric function chooses to be chosen. This is so for all the phoric functions.

A differential analysis might reveal the internal psychic necessities that lead this or that subject to fulfil one phoric function rather than another, but it is possible to outline a transversal problematic by showing that several sorts of determinations are operative in this choice. The psychic movements that orient the subject/bearer towards his phoric location and towards the functions attached to it receive their impetus from the particularities of the organization and functioning of his phantasies, his object-relations, his conflicts, his identifications, and his passive/active instinctual drive position. The subject/bearer finds the (*eu*phoric) opportunity here to satisfy his unconscious wishes to set up correlative defence mechanisms. Certain narcissistic desires are sustained by heroic identifications—for example, the grandiose Self of certain "family wage-earners"—or by the masochistic components of the drive for mastery, as a defence against accomplishing Ideals. Other determinations are orchestrated by issues related to the oedipal conflict or the fraternal complex: rivalry with the leader leads certain speech-bearers to throw themselves headlong towards the position of second-in-command (the lieutenant) or of the double, the shadow of the father, the mother, or an elder brother/sister. Other phantasy determinations and corresponding identifications are at work in the formation of the messenger (*go-between*) on the basis of his subjective position "between the two of them" in the phantasy of the primal scene. The function of the dream-bearer can be understood more clearly in the light of his internal necessity to include in his dream space, through the means of projective identifications, a more extensive psychic space than his own, or to extend this space to the dimensions of a whole group to make it into a more efficient dream container. This determination could also describe the activity of mediums in cults of magic possession.

Some characteristics common to all phoric functions

Certain general characteristics of phoric functions can be identified in the treatment of a subject destined to become a speech-bearer, dream-bearer, or symptom-bearer. However, they only manifest themselves in the complexity of their determinations in the group situation, for the latter solicits and governs them according to the demands of the group's own logic and interests. In psychoanalytic work in the group situation, it is not possible to treat the different levels of their organization independently. On the contrary: as with associative chains, we have to work on their nodal points and sift out that which belongs to the structure and history of those who become leader or second in command, hero or victim–emissary, speech-bearer, symptom-bearer, or dream-bearer, and that which pertains to the group structure and to the demands of its functioning. The main task of psychoanalysis in the group situation is precisely to carry out this unbinding between the ego and *Massenpsychologie.*

Plurifactorial determination is a characteristic common to all phoric functions. They are situated on the frontiers between the subjects, between the subjects and the grouping, at the point at which the intrapsychic topography, economy, and dynamics are articulated with group metapsychology, on the limits and at the passing points between unconscious and preconscious, drive and phantasy, affect and representation. Phoric functions are intermediary functions, and the figures that embody them are *passeurs.*[5] They have several characteristics in common.

Delegation, representation, and transmission

Phoric functions assume functions of delegation, representation,[6] and transmission. The speech-bearer speaks in the name of an other, in the place of an other: he is the delegate, the representative, the depositor, and the link in the chain of transmission. The process of delegation is a complex one that combines projection, projective identification, or deposit in an external psychic apparatus predisposed to receiving parts of the psyche (affects, emotions, instinctual charges, and representations), which an other (or more than one other) cannot or does not want to retain in himself and evacuates into, or safeguards in this other in order to spare them the fate that would be theirs if he were to keep them in his own psychic space. This delegation is thus an extratopographical extension of the subject's space. Examples of such processes can be observed in the function of the double in a sibship or in a couple, in the deposit in a child of an unacceptable or unrealizable part of the psyche of a parent or parents. Quite frequently the ensemble exerts a hold over these subject/bearers in order to keep them in these places and in these functions.

Capacity for containing

The subject/bearer's function is not only one of bearing and transporting, of transmitting and transferring speech, ideals, dreams, or symptoms. His function is also to contain these formations when they cannot be contained in the subjective space or in the group space. The speech-bearer harbours, contains, renders sayable and audible the speech of an other, just as the symptom-bearer is also the container of conflicts that have not been symbolized in any other way.

Semiotization and symbolization

The subject/bearer who takes on a phoric function is a bearer of signs: a semaphor. The speech-bearer carries out the semiotization of speech that has not been uttered or that has been hindered; the symptom-bearer gives consistency and visibility to latent or repressed intrapsychic conflicts. Both participate thereby in the process of symbolization, which finds support in these signs but can only be deployed if the link between these signs and what they signify or represent is established. It is the function of interpretation to create this link.

Other common or partly common characteristics

Other characteristics are common or partly common to phoric functions: for example, holding, handling, anaclisis, support. A differential analysis of phoric functions would show that some of them are characterized by a portage turned towards the outside while leaning on a point of support, whereas for others the portage is turned towards the inside, in the mode of ventral withdrawal. Some functions are strictly static (the same subject always bears the same things without transformation), whereas others are dynamic: they move and transform themselves, tracing a path, a trajectory. Some are transitory, others permanent. Some are unidirectional and irreversible; others are bi- or pluridirectional, reversible, and reciprocal. Some are organized *en abîme*[7]—*A* bears *B* which bears *C* which bears X and/or Y, and so on—whereas others are interlocking, like Russian dolls.

A remark concerning the reversal of the phoric function

I would like to draw attention to a remarkable trait that only concerns some phoric functions: they can turn into their contrary for intrapsychic and intersubjective reasons. This appears clearly with the speech-bearer who can change into a word-twister, a word-reverser, or the bearer of persecuting words. The control that can be exerted by the subject/bearer over the speech that he bears is connected with the grandiose phantasy of speaking (for) the other [*parler l'autre*] to the point of depriving him of his speech. Though he is a condition of thought, the speech-bearer can equally reverse himself into the position of one who impedes thinking. This reversal is observable in the ideal-bearer who can turn into a bearer of persecution.

An adjacent question merits our attention: it concerns the psychic consistency, for the subjects and for the group, or for any other linking configuration, of that which is not carried, transported, displaced, transmitted, transferred, contained, semiotized. It questions the fate of these leftovers, which are not carried towards meaning and which remain outside symbolization.

NOTES

1. The German word *Mittelsmann* denotes both a "middle-man" and a man-means [*homme-moyen*], in the sense in which one makes use of a means to do something—a man-instrument, as it were.

2. This position allows us to clarify the difference between the concept of phoric function and that which is proposed by systemic theory concerning the designated patient or the bearer of the family symptom. The concept of phoric function considers the subject not as an element of a system but as a subject of the unconscious. The part that is specific to the subject in the phoric function that he fulfils is recognized and combined with the way in which the group utilizes him for its own process and places the subject in this location.

3. I am in agreement here, though the problematic is altogether different, with the conception of Pichon-Rivière concerning the speech-bearer [*el portavoz*]: "The speech-bearer is the one who, in the group, at a certain moment, says something, and this something is the sign of a group process which, until this moment, has remained latent or implicit, as if hidden with-

in the totality of the group. As a sign, what the speech-bearer reveals must be decoded; that is, its implicit aspect has to be lifted. In this way it is decoded by the group—particularly by the coordinator—who indicates the signification of this (implicit) aspect. The speech-bearer is not aware of expressing something of the group signification which obtains at that particular moment, but rather he expresses or does something which he feels is peculiar to him" (Pichon-Rivière, 1970, p. 11.) There are a few notable differences between Pichon-Rivière's thinking about the *portavoz* and my conception of speech-bearer. Our researches have been carried out in different historical contexts, and we refer to different conceptual organizations. Aimed at demonstrating group phenomena, the orientation of Pichon-Rivière's thinking is marked by the first researches of social psychology, at a time when the group was essentially conceived, through the work of Kurt Lewin, as a dynamic totality in which each of the elements of the whole is dependent on the latter and some of them are "emergents" or "revealers" of the structure. Pichon-Rivière left in the background the question of the subject in the group. My work has been to think through the articulation between the subject in the group, the group, and the subject of the group with the categories of psychoanalysis. With regard to Pichon-Rivière's conception and my analysis of it, the reader can refer to Kaës (1993, 1994b).

4. This defence mechanism was described by Lévy-Bruhl in *La mentalité primitive* (1922), and his analysis is not only valid for primitive societies: "The method employed universally for protecting oneself against the misfortune announced is to get rid of the herald himself."

5. The word *passeurs* recalls Lacan's notion of the "pass".

6. Translator's note: the French word here is *représentance*: a general category including different types of representation (psychic representative, ideational representative, representative of the drive, etc.) and which implies the movement, the activity, of representation.

7. In France we refer to this organization *en abîme* of an image that bears its own identical reproduction in an infinite series as a "*Ripolin* effect" (a well-known brand of gloss paint) or a "*Vache qui rit* effect" (a familiar brand of cheese bearing an image of a laughing cow).

9

The common and shared dream space: dream polyphony

Some reasons for revisiting dream-theory

Though the dream is an eminently personal experience, can this experience be shared, conjunct, and common with that of other subjects? Raising this question in the field of psychoanalysis implies envisaging on new bases the notion of a dream space, the conditions of dream-formation, the dream itself, whom the dream is addressing and the effects of the dream narrative, and the nature of the relations between the subjects who share such a space.

In pre-Freudian times, but today, too, for the majority of humanity the dream is a group and, more precisely, a community affair. The dream has an eminent value for the dreamer in his relations with the group, for the group, and for relations with the great organizing principles of the world.[1]

With Freud, but already throughout the nineteenth century with the work of Hervey Saint Denis and Louis Ferdinand Maury, a revolution occurred that restored the personal space of the dream, established its meaning and function in psychic space, and developed the tools for becoming familiar with the processes that produce it. These discoveries were possible only under a certain number of conditions, some of which lay in the hypothesis of the unconscious and the definition of its object, others in the method of psychoanalysis employed in the analytic setting.

The epistemological closure of the psychic space of dreams

The conception of a dream space that is shared by, and is common to, several dreamers may seem *a priori* in contradiction with Freud's approach when he invariably asserts that the condition of possibility of the dream experience is that of withdrawing investment from the external world. Freud conceives of the dream space as closed for several reasons.

The first is due to psychic necessity: the momentary suspension of connections with the external world and the investment of the internal space through an inhibition of motor activity are the necessary (but insufficient) conditions for dreaming to occur, and with it the satisfaction of the narcissism of dreams (of the dreamer as hero of the dream) and of the narcissism of sleep (the ideal of inertia).

Psychic space is closed for a second reason, owing to epistemological necessity, in order to "circumscribe the unconscious alone" and to gain access to its internal logic. As soon as the perception–consciousness system is put aside and action is inhibited, the dream opens out onto the internal world, and investigation of the unconscious becomes possible. Once it had been received and interpreted as a "royal road to the unconscious", the dream then acquired the status of a model of paradigmatic intelligibility whose value was that of defining the consistency of psychic reality as it manifests itself in the internal space of a subject divided by the effects of the unconscious. This model would also make it possible to describe the primary processes governing this reality.

It was on this model that the method of the treatment was based, and psychic space is closed for a third reason, linked to the methodological setting that psychoanalysis employs and to the mode of access to dreams that this setting permits. From the very outset of Freud's discovery, the epistemological model of the dream was not only the model of the psychic apparatus, but also the model for the methodological setting of the treatment.

The epistemological congruence between the object of psychoanalysis, the theory of dreams, and the method was to produce a discovery resulting from the suspension of the variables obscuring access to it—namely, unconscious psychic reality, its formations and processes. Knowledge of the psychic space of dreams, and the discovery of the dream-work, of its internal logic and its unconscious contents then became possible.

The Freudian construction of a psychic space that is closed for these three reasons does not mean that this space is thought of as closed. But there are grounds for thinking that the fruitful framework Freud established both defines the limits of his investigation and produces, negatively as it were, something remaining to be known. We may suppose that what Freud thought about dreams does not describe all the dream experiences that psychoanalysis can speak of when it is founded on the *first* and paradigmatic setting of the individual treatment alone. It is these limits and these remainders that make it necessary to revisit once again our conception of dreams.

Revisions of the dream-theory

It is generally accepted today that Freud's view of dreams as the hallucinatory fulfilment of an unconscious wish is not the only way in which they can be envisaged. If we continue to understand the dream within the space of the intrapsychic reality in which it is necessarily produced by a single dreamer, the study of its internal conditions, its processes, its contents, and its meaning shows that the dream is also a creative experience (Meltzer, 1984), a reparative experience (Klein, 1930, 1933), and a transforming experience (Anzieu, 1985). It is also an experience that begins before the dream and continues after it.

A further reason for revisiting dream-theory lies in the shift of interest, within the field of psychoanalytic treatment, from the intrapsychic space of the dream towards its emergence and function in the transference–countertransference space. Several psychoanalysts have directed attention to the formation, consistency, and vicissitudes of the crossed dreams of the analyst and the analysand, to the interferences between their dreams about sessions (Neyraut, 1974), and to the status of the analyst's countertransference dreams.

A third reason for revisiting our work on dreams resides in the now established fact that other settings for psychoanalytic work, derived from the individual setting, have been created to meet the requirements of other modes of investigating and treating the effects

of the unconscious in the psyche. This was followed by new views on
the limits of intrapsychic space, now more open to its borders and
interferences with the psychic spaces of other subjects. This orientation introduced the dream into a different space, where it finds
another source of fomentation and develops specific effects.

My initial question—"How are we to think about dream experience when the relation of dreamers to their dreams is traversed by
the dreams of other dreamers?"—can today be submitted to psychoanalytic research on a sufficiently secure clinical basis. For my part,
I have worked on two ways of approaching dreams: initially, it was
dreams produced in a group situation and recounted in the group
that held my attention. I then derived from this approach some
useful propositions for revisiting the dream space of the analytic
situation and for questioning the so-called "individual" dream, as
it is recounted to us in this situation. This approach maintains the
conception of the dream as an intrapsychic formation necessarily
produced by a single dreamer, as an "egoistic" (Freud), individual
creation, but it accepts that the dream is profoundly woven in intersubjectivity. It explores its conditions, processes, contents, meaning,
and effects.

Three propositions concerning dreams

Three main propositions have organized my research into dreams
(see Kaës, 2002b). The first is that of a *common and shared psychic
space*. It is worth recalling that this space is originally structured by
the capacity for dreaming of the other—that is, of the mother—and
of more than one other—that is, the family group or the community—and, that this capacity is an essential factor in the dream-work
and in the development of its functions in the baby. The family
group is the first dream cradle of the newborn baby. The group itself
is "like a dream" (Anzieu, 1966): it is the container of the capacity
for reverie (Kaës, 1976), and the family functions against this primal
dream backcloth (Ruffiot, 1981).

The second proposition contends that, alongside the dream navel, which is rooted in the bodily mycelium, it is useful to assume *a
second navel of dream activity*, which has its roots in the intersubjective
mycelium. Taking up Freud's metaphor, I make the assumption that
these two navels rest on "the unknown" from which dreams well up.

From this point of view, the dream may be said to find its energetic substance in the bodily navel and its relational and narrative substance in the intersubjective navel.

The third proposition introduces the concept of *dream polyphony*. This concept describes how the dream is worked on by, and in, a multiplicity of spaces and times, images and voices. It integrates the idea of a plural, common, and shared dream space and of two dream navels. We have seen that in each dream, the raw material of the dream is formed by the day- and night-time residues of one's own dreams and those of a few others: dreams are formed in relation to each other and can be interpreted in terms of their relations of reciprocal support. The hypothesis of dream polyphony leads us into a "dream factory" where several dream spaces interpenetrate, where several dreamers make signs to each other and make themselves heard by several dreamers and several listeners, internal and external.

Dream polyphony in the group

In groups constituted as a methodological artefact for psychoanalytic work, the dream manifests itself with different characteristics from those prevailing in the individual treatment. Someone dreams in the group: he makes a narrative of it that he addresses to others, and the narrative arouses diverse psychic movements in the members of the group: it is spoken about, rejected, or passed over in silence. Usually an associative process is set in motion, an interdiscursive, polyphonic process, woven into the modalities and contents of the transferences, into the resistances and the repressions, but also into the hitherto unavailable representations towards which the associative work has cleared a path as far as the preconscious.

The dream fabric of the group

Before exploring in two examples the clinical manifestations of the dream, the status of the dreamer, and the vicissitudes of the dream in the group psychoanalytic situation, I want to come back to the idea that the psychic space of groups is itself already a dream space. The starting-point of this proposition was a study by Anzieu (1966) on the analogy between the group and the dream.

The group is "like" a dream (Anzieu, 1966)

This thesis comprises three main points: (1) The group is "like a dream": "human subjects go to groups in the same way as they enter the world of dreams in their sleep". (2) The group is the means and locus of the imaginary fulfilment of the unconscious wishes of its members. It is their infantile wishes and their wishes of "the day before" that are fulfilled in groups. Like the dream and the symptom, the group is the association of unconscious wishes that are seeking their path of imaginary fulfilment, and of defences against the anxiety that such fulfilments arouse in the participants' egos. (3) The phenomena that manifest themselves in groups are analogous to those of the dream. They resemble manifest contents and are derived from a limited number of latent contents; the primary processes, veiled by a façade of secondary processes, are determinant. The group, whether it carries out efficiently the task that it has assigned itself or whether it is paralysed, is subtended by an underlying phantasy.

From these propositions Anzieu derives the idea that the dream is the principle of intelligibility of the unconscious psychic phenomena that are revealed in groups. Consequently, the group, like the dream, is the royal road to the unconscious.

Several points of Anzieu's thesis have held my attention. In order for the group to be this "analogon" of the dream, a withdrawal of bodily investment by consciousness must take place in the members of the group; equally indispensable are a topographical and formal regression and an attenuation and dilation of the limits of the ego on the frontier between the overlapping individual and group envelopes. This momentary abandonment of internal limits in favour of the group space has the advantage that the group space becomes co-extensive, either partly or wholly, with the internal space of each member of the group. The group then functions in the isomorphic mode, as I have called it. Anzieu invites us to think that the group and the dream, in different forms, are spaces of the imaginary world of dreams, places of reverie and phantasies, but also of illusion and the illusory.

The essence of Anzieu's thesis was to show that the group is one of the places of the dream-fulfilment of unconscious wishes repressed in childhood or in the waking state. His intention was not to restore to the dreamer his subjectivity in the group. Now we have to take into consideration that this fulfilment and this manifestation occur in two interlocking psychic spaces: that of the individual subject and that of the group considered as the space of a psychic reality that is irreducible to that of its subjects considered in isolation. Still more precise is the idea that the members of a group communicate through their dream ego and that this is how the psychic material of the group is constituted.

Finally, and extending the field still further, we can consider that this dream fabric of the group is just one version of the dream foundations of intersubjective relations. Consequently, the analogy between the group and the dream implies common psychic processes that belong to the primary process: condensation, displacements, multiplication, diffraction, figuration, enactment, and dramatization. All these processes are ordered by an organizing principle of dream-thoughts (the purposive idea): they are the same organizing principles as those that govern group relations (unconscious organizers, notably internal groups).

The dream in the dream fabric of the group: clinical examples

A dream in the initial period of a group

During the nights preceding the beginning of a group, the dreams of the participants and the analysts often have as their theme a depiction of the confused relation of limits between the inside and the outside, the uncertain formation of the threatened group envelope, or anxiety about not being contained in the group. The transferential contents of these dreams are often very intense, as in this dream dreamt the day before the beginning of a group by Robert and recounted by him in the very first session: *"I had arrived for a rehearsal of a small orchestra; I was holding my violin in my hand and was rather anxious to know if I would manage to get my instrument in tune with those of the other musicians in the orchestra; there were a lot of dissonant notes and suddenly my bow no longer had any strings. The conductor was staring at me, and I could not help but lower my eyes."*

His telling of the dream aroused no associations, at least in the things that were said, just a few laughs (concerning the little violin held in his hand). Several participants said they had felt paralysed by the threatening idea that this dream prefigured a failure of the group, and the dreamer was treated aggressively, as if he had

attacked the conditions required for creating the group illusion
necessary for the formation of the group. The elaboration of the
dream could only be undertaken once the participants had understood that the dream had had this effect on them and that it
had brought into operation their defence mechanisms against the
danger of not being able get in tune with each other, just at the
precise moment when all their investments were directed towards
this project. The dreamer, for his part, recognized that by telling his
dream he had offloaded onto the group his own anxiety about not
being part of the group, which his dream portrayed as his anxiety
about having his "instrument" castrated, and his shame in front of
the others—anxiety that was easily identified by the dreamer and
by the group members. The dream acquired meaning and value in
his preliminary transference onto the psychoanalyst and the group,
the two recipients of the dream: he expected to be reassured by the
conductor about his potency and to receive support in face of the
reproving looks of the orchestra.

Robert's dream is a group dream[2]; it mobilizes the internal
groupality of the dreamer and all the participants. It is an internal
group threatened with discord. The content of the dream, as much
as its telling at a point when the group container was not as yet
constituted, brought out one of the specific anxieties that accompany the initial phase of psychic experience in groups—namely, the
tuning or adjustment of the psyches by means of a sufficiently common organizer, shared by the group members. This is why traumatic
dreams are frequent at the beginning of a group, but not all of them
are recounted in the first session.

If we turn our enquiry away from the content of the dream towards the effect of the dream narrative, it appears that the dreamer
has from the outset "enacted" a tension experienced as paradoxical
in the initial phase of the group experience: the paradox is one of
being and *not being* part of the group. At the same time the ego of the
participants has to assert itself as whole and undivided against the
regression towards the partial and the impersonal, and to constitute
itself as a perfectly adjusted element of a larger unit, as a member of
the unified "group body". The requirement of being simultaneously
both undivided and a member of a group mobilizes anxieties about
internal breaking up and dissonance (or splitting), resulting from
the conflict that divides the ego between its self-preservation and
the parts of itself that it will have to abandon (and which it experi-

ences as a castration) in order to fulfil its wish to be integrated with a united group. This demand is generally (and provisionally) resolved in the group illusion. It is this conflict that organizes Robert's dream, but his telling of the dream is received in a field that does not allow this paradoxical moment to be transformed into illusion.

The example of Robert's dream shows clearly that the dream was not transformable as long as the containing function of the group had not constituted itself; but it also shows that this dream could be elaborated subsequently in the group process and interpreted in the movement of the transferences.

Forming a group and being in a group arouse a fundamental tension between the demands of contributing to the group unit and maintaining the group's narcissism and the demands of the individual subject in his desire to serve his own purposes and to differentiate himself from others. The activity of dreaming forms part of this tension whose equilibrium is unstable. The dream and the narration of the dream, which is a personal production but one that can now be shared, follow this oscillation and mobilize this tension between the dreamer's narcissism and the group's narcissism. We have seen in this example that these narcissistic demands do not communicate, and it is this that threatens the group and each participant in this initial phase.

The articulation between the dreamer's dream space and that of the group: Michèle's dream

Michèle's dream, which I have already analysed at length, gives me an opportunity to return to the articulation between the dreamer's dream space and that of the group. I have shown that her dream is formed from waking residues that were in circulation the day before without being symbolized in the group. Michèle dreams for herself, but she also dreams in the dream space of the group. The telling of her dream gives rise to a defensive movement against the phantasy of sexual seduction of the son by the father, but it provides each group member, and the group as a whole, with figurative models of their unconscious conflicts and of their locations in the phantasy scenes that organize them.

Here it is worth while noting a particular feature of the telling of dreams in groups: the dream is used by others—certain others—in addition to the dreamer: it is put at their disposition; it has meaning for the others and in the group field, and it is likely that that which has meaning for some has no meaning for others. The polyphonic and interdiscursive structure of the dream transcends the specific meaning of the dream for the dreamer, and it is in the associative process that the associations emerge that make it possible to discover the meaning that the dream has for the dreamer—in other words, in what I call the work of intersubjectivity.

The functions of dreams in groups

Based on the analyses I have made, I want to propose an overall view of the main functions of dreams in groups:

1. *A function of the return of the repressed in a figurative form that is acceptable to the dreamer's preconscious.* This figuration is proposed to the group in the dream narrative. It thus also has a function in the group. The telling of the dream and the associations of the group members lead to the emergence of signifiers that were hitherto unavailable to other group members, but which they can now make use of.

2. *A containing function, which consists in the intersubjective treatment of unconscious thoughts and affects, of waking residues bearing significations that have remained unconscious and are charged with instinctual investments suppressed the day before.* The dream, like the group, is a shared psychic space in which effects of containing and transformation occur, both for the dreamer and for the group. In the group, the *gamma* function (Corrao) is a creation of the group members: it supports the containing function. It manifests itself through the search for and the carrying out of the alpha function of the other, of more than one other, of the group itself. When it is impossible to resort to the containing function of the group, the dreamer makes another attempt to find a container; he acts out (Pontalis, Masud Khan), he "dreams outside" (Racamier), or he brings a real external object (Friedman).

3. *A function of scripted and dramatic representation of the group psychic apparatus and of the subjective locations of each member in this space.* The privileged location of the dreamer in the group topography, dynamic, and economy, and thus in the dimensions of

the transferences, is that of the *dream-bearer*. I have tried to identify which internal necessities lead one subject rather than another, through the movement of his own desire, to fulfil a phoric function of dream-bearer. We can also examine the codification of the dream-bearer in groups, families, and institutions and try to understand how, alongside the primary and secondary processes, processes are mobilized that obey the specifically mythopoetic, social, and cultural logic and make dream-telling in groups into a major therapeutic instrument, known to us since antiquity.

4. *An evacuative function of the dream* (Bion, Bernard, Gaburri, Friedman) *consists in getting rid of wishes through dreams rather than elaborating the wishes that are seeking realization.* What Meltzer has theorized in analysis as the toilet–breast also applies to the group, which is invested and used as a toilet–breast. We can include in this category profuse dreams or avalanche-like dreams. They may or may not favour psychic elaboration in the group, the decisive factor being their utilization in the transferences.

We can verify that these five functions are those accomplished by Michèle's telling of her dream in the group: before her dream, Marc's symptom draws on the allegation of the reality of an event that "marks him"—of which he has received the "mark". The telling of the dream, the associative work, and the analysis of the transferences open the way to finding meaning in his symptom: access to the phantasy and thought of his incestuous relation with his father sets in train a process of transformation of his confused and confusing representation of his trauma. But also, one or another participant will be able to gain access to his own incestuous phantasy following the telling of the dream and the associations of the members of the group.

What does the work of dream-analysis in groups involve?

On this basis, we can be more specific about what the work of dream-analysis in groups involves. From my point of view, it consists essentially in bringing to light the common and shared dream space in which the formations of the unconscious of the subjects re-present themselves in their encounter with the other (with more than one other). It is not always useful to work on the dream-content, but in all cases it seems to me necessary to work on the fact that a narrative has been made of it.

The dream-address is constituted before the dream; it partakes in the dream-work and the dream narrative, and in this way the dream includes the other in its latent content. For this reason we need to be attentive to several things: to the way the dream is received, whether it is rejected or ignored, or whether it gives rise to associations. This is a very good indicator of the group process, of the situation of the transferences. It is worth observing how the dream narrative is used by the dreamer, in the transferences onto the therapists, onto the group members, and onto the group itself. In order not to lose his dream, the dreamer needs to find a listener, after having invented him in his dream. I do not think that we should ask the dreamer for his own associations, because that would be to transgress the group psychoanalytic situation, making it deviate towards a situation of individual pseudo-treatment in the group.

Particular attention should be paid to the topographical location and economic function of the dream-bearer in the group. The dreams of dream-bearers are traversed by the polyphony of the dream space. In the psychoanalytic situations I have analysed, the dream-bearers dream in the transference, for someone, or for several others; they also dream "in the place" of someone or several others. These dreamers become dream-bearers due to the internal necessity of establishing, through normal adhesive and projective identifications, a larger psychic space than their own, of depositing it in an extra-topographical container, that of an other, of more than one other, or of a whole group.

In groups, as in individual treatment, we need to bear in mind what Freud said about interpretation: it is infinite, since in the last analysis the irreducible dream navel remains in the shadows and forestalls an exhaustive interpretation of the dream. I have posited two dream navels, and this should make us even more wary, for now we know that the question as to who the true dreamer of the dream is remains an open one.

The common and shared dream space in the situation of individual psychoanalytic treatment: clinical studies

I have tried to establish that the concept of a dream space that is shared between and common to several dreamers accounts for the anchoring of the dream in an intersubjective matrix. This concept signifies that each dreamer dreams in the space of a plurality of dreamers, whose dreams traverse the dreams of each dreamer. The situation of the individual treatment furnishes us with important elements to back up the idea that certain dreams are formed at the crossroads of several common, conjoint, and shared dream spaces. Here are a few examples.

The two brothers and the maternal matrix of their dreams

When they were little, my patient and his younger brother used to share the same bed. They squabbled a great deal, sometimes violently; they were very sad about this and anxious to patch things up. When he mentioned this period in his life, the following memory came back to him: On certain evenings, before going to sleep, the two brothers would tell each other the dreams they had had the night before, with the idea of dreaming the same dreams the following night. From the night residues of their dreams they fabricated common day residues. A given word, emotion, or image had the function of triggering dreams in which they rediscovered the same characters or the same animals they had talked about before going to sleep. They often managed to fulfil their dreams, or perhaps, in telling them, they gave each other the impression that they had realized them. If the dream had succeeded in reconciling them, they did not squabble for the rest of the day—as if each of them had the task of guarding this dream and the objects that they had shared.

One evening, before going to sleep, they had talked about an adventure story called *L'Escadron blanc*, which they were very enthusiastic about. They had promised each other to go into the desert one day and chase antelopes, like the doe they surprised sometimes in the forest. The following night they both dreamed "almost the same" dream, which they told to each other in the morning: *A band of camel riders gets lost in the desert, and to survive they chase a group of antelopes.* "In my dream, I hope the camel riders will capture one of them—they have extremely powerful rifles—but that they won't kill it. My dream ends just as they are approaching the antelope. In my brother's dream, the camel riders are rescued by a patrol that has gone out looking for them."

The specificity of my patient's dream resides in that which has not yet been symbolized in his relationship with his brother. What remains obscure in this relationship, with its roots both in the early relations between baby and mother and in the fraternal complex, is brought onto the dream stage by the second dream navel. It is from this interpsychic navel, forming the maternal matrix of their dreams, that the material of their dreams emerges. What my patient's dream achieves is first and foremost the wish to dream the same dreams in a common and shared dream space with his brother.

The wish to meet each other in the same dream space seeks its path of realization in common dream objects. The common dream space reduplicates the shared bed; it brings to light the incestuous issues in the bond uniting my patient with his brother. Their strategy mobilizes inductions in the activity of the waking state so that the wish emerges, in each brother's dream, to be together in the dream.

The dreamer's associations lead him towards that which the common dream preserves—namely, the bond of homosexual narcissistic love that assures their joint defence against the hostile feelings they harbour towards each other, against brotherly rivalry, against murderous thoughts towards one another: they are displaced onto the antelopes, which are not killed. In chapter 4 of *Totem and Taboo* (1912–13), Freud refers to the study of William Robertson Smith when describing what constitutes the common substance that unites the members of a clan: the experience of kinship is constantly renewed through the common meal and ensures that each member is made of the same substance. I think that the common and shared dream is an expression of kinship. As in the common meal that cements kinship, the nocturnal fulfilment of the common wishful phantasy protects them against hostility throughout the following day.

Nevertheless each of the dreamers is in contact with "the spot where it [the navel] reaches down into the unknown", with this other part of the unconscious rooted in bodily experience. Their dreams are not identical; they have common and shared traits, but each one dreams his dream sustained by the same wish: namely, of joining his brother in the common, imaginary dream space. It is in this respect that his dream is "almost the same dream" as his brother's.

Dreams about the analyst, dreams about the analysand.

All analysts have dreamed about their patients, but rare are those who have been attentive to the effects of their dreams on their patients' dreams, and vice versa. Rare, too, are those who have accorded attention to their "session dreams".[3] Micheline Enriquez has noted what happens in the countertransference when such dreams occur in the analyst, the valuable help that she has derived from dreaming about her disharmonic patients "at times when they tested [her] to the limits of what was tolerable" (1984, p. 244). Her session dreams had the characteristics described by Michel Neyraut in analysands who have this type of dream: as with the analysand, the prohibition against contact is not respected, and personal space is infringed. Session dreams return the analyst to the status of a patient and give him an idea of his psychic conflicts, which are awakened or reawakened by the analytic situation and are involved in his commitment to psychoanalysis. They also preserve him "from the risks of acting out or disinvestment which are very tempting in trying treatments; and they bear witness to an effort and wish to gather up, to bind the process and the situation, in short to re-harmonise the treatment" (pp. 244–245).

The analysis of an analyst's session dream brings us further elements for exploring the shared dream space in the treatment. It was a dream reported to my colleague André Missenard (1987) by an analyst, Jennie, whom he had in supervision for the treatment of one of her patients. During a period when she was finding her analysands boring during the sessions, Jennie reported that during a session she had dozed off for a moment and had had the following dream: "*Gérard had his head resting against the hollow of my shoulder.*" This dream seemed to her to be oedipal in content and made her think about her patient's history. Social circumstances were such that Gérard's father had been away during many years of his childhood, so he had been alone with his mother; his father then came back, but he died soon afterward. The dominant material during this period of the treatment is illustrated by dreams of *a raging sea with terrifying waves, where he is on a steep path, in a situation of danger. He is in need of rescue.* The transference was positive and quite strong, but reserved. No doubt this was the reason for his incapacity to dream other phantasies than these representations of a terrifying sea.

Missenard makes the hypothesis that the analyst's dream corresponds to the insistence of threatening, pregenital maternal imagos through an oedipal enactment. "The expression of resistance belongs to the patient, and the figuration of the transference in his dream belongs to the analyst" (Missenard, 1987, p. 90). Such a dream constitutes in the analyst's psyche "an elaboration of the issues involved in the case in a way that is almost analogous in its effects to what would have been the same dream if the patient had had it (and dared to express it)" (p. 90), which confirms M. Enriquez's thesis. From this point of view, the analyst functions as a part of the patient's psyche, as in a relationship of transitional exchanges between a mother and her baby. Transformations subsequently occurred in the patient's social, professional, and love life. It is undoubtedly interesting to note that the analysand later dreamed that he was received by his analyst at a reception: there now appeared a session dream that was a group dream.

One might wonder whether for the analyst's dream to have had clinical and dynamic effects on the patient's development it was enough for the latter's unconscious wish to become representable in the analyst's thought. I readily concur with Missenard's commentary when he writes that "the dream translates the patient's unconscious wish which is embedded in the psyche of the dreamer who, literally, dreams for him the dream that he cannot have for himself", but he adds that "the analyst's dream expresses in this case the patient's oedipal wish, but also the analyst's countertransference" (Missenard, 1987, p. 91).

This point is of cardinal importance: in this example (as in several other dreams described in *La polyphonie du rêve.* Kaës, 2002b), we can consider that the analyst dreams about her patient, and no doubt for him, in his place. But it is no less certain that the psychoanalyst dreams for herself. I think that it is first and foremost because the analyst dreams for herself that the dream acquires in the transference–countertransference field its value of figurative representation for her patient. If the consistency of the common dream space is such, the analyst's work concerns the common psyche that has developed between them. This is precisely what Missenard is saying by proposing that "the psychoanalyst's dream concerns the unconscious psychic organisation which has developed between the two partners of the psychoanalysand/psychoanalyst couple: the dream is its symbolisation" (Missenard, 1987, p. 93).

In a common dream space, the dream is the co-creation of several dreamers. This space concerns not only sleep and dreams, but also waking activity, the dream narratives and their sharing, and the capacity to play with dreams, phantasies, and thoughts. The dream space partakes of the transitional area, of the foundational illusion of a continuity between psychic reality and external reality, which makes it possible to explore its fluctuations and limits without conflict.

The primal dream space: the psychic cradle of the newborn baby

The foetus dreams in the maternal womb; registrations of its cerebral activity suggest that this is the case, and furthermore that he dreams at the same time as his mother. These findings are precious to us, but we know nothing of his dreams, for he does not tell them. To suppose the existence of reminiscences raises once again the question of the earliest traces and of their transformation. In any case, we can imagine that this co-dreaming forms a common psychic space.

We know that the mother and the father and the family environment dream about the child. They dream about an imaginary, narcissistic, oedipal child; they dream of monsters or dead children; they dream of a divine or heroic child.

Freud was the first to speak about this prenatal dream space when he wrote (1914c) that "His Majesty the Baby" was dreamed about by the mother when he was in her womb, and already before then by the mother, the father, and the family group as a whole. The child is the bearer and hope of the "unfulfilled wishful dreams" of those who have gone before him and engendered him. It is in these "unfulfilled wishful dreams" that the child's narcissism, writes Freud, is grounded. We can imagine that what Bion was later to call the maternal function of reverie is already established in this prenatal dream space. The mother and the family as a whole dream about the imaginary baby; they include him (or her) in their dreams; they accord him a place. At this moment, his psyche is not separate from those who form his psychic cradle.

Thus, expecting a child inscribes the latter in the unconscious psychic organization of the parental couple and the family. It is in this organization that his own affective, mental, and relational development is able to develop, following the lines of force and structures partly pre-established by their common dreams. His first identifications, his first links, his ideals, his mechanisms of defence, his thinking will be grounded in this psychic cradle.

Numerous propositions plead in favour of the hypothesis either that the psyche opens onto the psyche of those closest to us, or that the latter includes common and shared psychic spaces with other dreamers. Donald Meltzer's research has led him to form the supposition of a primitive state of the psyche whose blurred contours and poorly defined frontiers create indistinct zones. References to such a notion are not lacking either in Margaret Mahler. For his part, Harold Searles has contended that there is a tendency in each individual to establish "symbiotic relations" that bear witness to the survival in each one of us of an original state of non-division and non-distinction between self and others. Bleger proposes an analogous idea with the concept of "syncretic link". The research work of these psychoanalysts permits us to describe either psychic spaces common to several subjects or parts that are common to the psyche of the subjects of an ensemble.

The effect of the mother's dreaming on her baby

To my knowledge little psychoanalytic research has so far been carried out into the existence and effects of these prenatal and postnatal common dream spaces. Mother–child consultations provide access to them, for it is often following a disturbance in this space that the parents (the mother in the majority of cases) seek help. Very frequently it is disturbances in the capacity for dreaming that are involved.

Kreisler (1984) reports the case of a four-month-old infant whom he followed in consultation for serious sleeping disturbances accompanied by agitation, screaming, and feeding difficulties. Apparently stillborn, the baby had been reanimated. During the anaesthetic his mother had suffered a severe shock and had almost died. The history prior to the child's birth was exceptionally marked by death and illness in the mother's family: she herself had had a miscarriage a year before, while her elder sister had lost a baby *in utero*. During the pregnancy, she had lost another sister who had had a violent death, and the following month a brother had had a sudden and serious illness. To avoid giving birth prematurely, she had to remain in bed during the last months of her pregnancy. The mother did not dream any more.

During the consultation, Kreisler challenged the views of the paediatrician and of the mother herself concerning the organic character of her baby's disturbances. He thereby opened up the possibility of exploring the connections between the current malaise and the events that had occurred during and before the pregnancy. At the following consultation, in which the mother and father took part, the baby's troubles had disappeared. The mother reported that when her sister had died, she had feared that she might have a miscarriage and had forced herself to control her grief. Then she spontaneously told the following dream: *"We were having a meal around the big family table; no one was absent. Jeanne (the dead sister) was conversing and laughing; no one seemed surprised, even though everyone knew very well that she was dead."*

Commenting on this consultation, Missenard (1985) points out how the mother's recovery of her capacity to dream was directly linked to the lifting of the repressive lock on her grief over her sister's death, and that this resulted from Kreisler's questioning of the organic diagnosis of the baby's illness. By suggesting to the mother that there was something behind the lock that she had closed, Kreisler posed as the part of herself that was repressed but which could become accessible. The dream re-established communication with the repressed and denied figure of death. Her baby no longer embodied the figure of the dead child. The mother literally *reanimated* her child and herself by virtue of her dream activity.

This said, a second question remains: what are the mechanisms and modalities of the mother's dreaming on the child's development? We need to bear in mind here that the infant's psyche does not yet have its own limits, that its functioning, essentially psychosomatic, is linked to the place that it occupies in the mother's psyche. Furthermore, the "direct and immediate" character of the primary identification between the mother and the infant, which takes place "earlier than any object-cathexis" (Freud, 1923b, p. 31), resides essentially in the role played by empathic projective identifications, where bonds are formed from the projection of oneself into the object and from the identification of parts of the object with parts of the self. Lastly, primary narcissism in the dual mother–child unit plays a determinant role in the common and shared dream space.

In the case treated by Kreisler, the split between the mother and the part of herself that was a bearer of child death-wishes, which her baby represented for her, made it impossible for the early bonds necessary for the formation of psychic life to be established in a reliable and symbolizing way. Research studies into the transmission of psychic life between generations have confirmed this proposition: what cannot be represented in the mother's psyche is displaced and borne by the child. In this psychotherapy, the restoration of the mother's dream space, through the dream that portrays the transcendence of the denial of the death of a loved one, re-establishes the child in a soothing internal psychic space.

The hypotheses advanced to account for this effect of maternal dreaming on the child's psyche have a more general character. For each of the members of the couple and the family, the brothers and sisters, and eventually other members of the family, the birth of a baby is the occasion for regressive movements that put each one in contact with the infantile parts of their own history, and notably with the family myths in which ancestral figures and the fate of children are represented. I assume that dreams are linked to this shared unconscious psychic organization and that the inscriptions that leave their trace in the child's psyche reappear in the dreams of his family members and later in his own.

What is striking here is that dreams appear to be the locus of unconscious primordial communication both in the mother's intra-psychic space and in the common and shared space that links her to her baby. This observation confirms one of the important functions of the maternal psyche—namely, that of protecting the baby against excitations and of constituting for him, thanks to alpha function, the elements of an apparatus for thinking thoughts (Bion). I would add that the mother's activity as speech-bearer by the mother and the function of the parental preconscious play a decisive role in the structuring of the baby's phantasy life, in the setting up of stimulus barriers, and in the construction of a language apparatus. All these functions contribute to defining the consistency of the common and shared psychic space.

Can the concepts of a common and shared dream space,
the dream navel, and dream polyphony
throw light on the general processes of dreams?

As we come to the end this chapter, we have come to the following conclusion: in the individual treatment setting, as in the group
setting, the dream space of each subject is traversed by the crossed
dreams of the other, of more than one other. The dream-formation,
well before it is addressed to an other, bears the mark of the encounter with the other, the other *of* the object and the other *in* the object,
because it occurs in a common dream space, a porous, strange, and
sometimes disturbing space. Beyond the desire of subjects wishing
to dream together, I have examined the work accomplished by the
dreamer in the common dream space and the functions fulfilled by
the subject who is a dream-bearer for other subjects. I have shown
how the "egoistic" space of the dream is re-appropriated through the
associative process.

Can the results that we have obtained throw light on the general
processes of dreams? How do they modify the way we listen to the
dream experience? And how does this listening lead us to think differently about the limits of psychic space? I indicated briefly at the
beginning of this chapter the three principal hypotheses around
which my researches into dreams are organized: they have been put
to the test of clinical experience in individual analysis and in groups.
Let us now examine what has become of them.

A common and shared dream space between several dreamers

I assumed first of all that the dream is elaborated by several
dreamers at the intersection of their intersubjective links and of
their identificatory and phantasy resonance with the dreams of
other dreamers. These dreams are linked together in the dream
fabric in which the group, the family, and the couple are woven.
This is also the case when, in analysis, dreams intersect and echo
each other.

In emphasizing the dream space that is common to and shared
between several dreamers, I am not losing sight of the fact that the
dream is the creation of a dreamer and that it is "egoistic". The capacity to dream, the dream-wish, the dream-work, the functions and

the meaning of the dream in dream experience are determined, in variable proportions, in each of these spaces. Certainly, personal figurative elements enter into the dream-work when it occurs in a group: the fact that the dreamer dreams for an other, with an other, in an other, does not detract from the fact that it is the dreamer who creates his dream. When certain elements of the dream are co-determined by the common and shared dream space, by the effect of the intersubjective situation, the dreamer's unconscious chooses one determined scene and not another; and this "choice" depends on his own history and on the presence of the other, as an internal object, in this scene. Nor have I lost sight of the fact that the wish to dream in the common dream space is a realization of the oldest wish of the human being.

Other dreams are organized predominantly with materials (scenes, affects, phantasies) mobilized in intersubjective relations, because there is an enigma to depict, traumatic experience to repair, anxieties to transform, a wish to rediscover, before or after separation, a common dream matrix. This is why I say that each dreamer dreams at the crossroads of several dream factories, in the space that binds together a plurality of dreamers whose dreams traverse the dreams of each one. There are thus good reasons for speaking of a dream *polytopy*.

The two dream navels

I have formulated a second hypothesis to the effect that the dream has two cradles, two navels. In order to back up this hypothesis, I have drawn on Freud's metaphor of the dream navel:

> There is often a passage in even the most thoroughly interpreted dream which has to be left obscure; this is because we become aware during the work of interpretation that at that point there is a tangle of dream-thoughts which cannot be unravelled and which moreover adds nothing to our knowledge of the content of the dream. This is the dream's navel, the spot where it reaches down into the unknown. The dream-thoughts to which we are led by interpretation cannot, from the nature of things, have any definite endings; they are bound to branch out in every direction into the intricate network of our world of thought. It is at some

point where this meshwork is particularly close that the dream-
work grows up, like a mushroom out of its mycelium. [Freud,
1900a, p. 525]

That which, in the dream-wish, grows up from the deepest levels of
the unconscious is rooted in bodily experience and passes in transit
through the dream navel: it is in this conduit, this place of passage
and transformation, that the tissue is formed in which exterior and
exterior, appropriation and subjection, active and passive are inter-
mingled.

I think that the first navel communicates with the second dream
navel. Certain elements of the dream refer predominantly to the
deep structure of the dreamer's internal world, and to figurative
schema that are internal groups. But the dreamer's unconscious
chooses elements of figuration and enactment that are determined
by his situation in his links with others. It is in this intersubjective
dream mycelium that dreams find their nourishment. It is a matter
of another germinative space in which the dream "reaches down
into the unknown".

In groups, the dreamer fabricates his dream with materials borrowed directly from the group; he dreams about what the group or
a participant (Michèle for Marc) has been unable to think about
[*l'impensé*]. This proposition may be extended to other figures of
linking, as we have seen in the examples of the mother–child couple, the dream of the two brothers, and the analyst's dream. What
is remarkable is that one and the same element serves to depict the
internal world and thoughts that have not yet been represented in
the group.

Dream polyphony

The third hypothesis has enabled me to describe how, from the
connections between the two dream navels and the formation of a
plural, common, and shared dream space, the dream organizes itself
as a combination of several voices or several voice-parts, of several
images and several scenes that form a whole.[4] The dream is a polyphony of several "writings" [*écritures*] of the dream; it has its source
in a series of utterances and enunciations constituted in childhood,

in waking life or in other dreams, in real and phantasized scenes that find a space of figuration in the dream, which are distorted by the dream-work. The interferences between the diversity of the sources, materials, and functions create the dream polyphony.

I have treated dream polyphony at two levels, one of which is its internal polyphonic organization. We can only have access to the polyphonic organization of the dream by inferring it from the dream narrative, the associations that it evokes, and the interdiscursivity specific to the associative chain. This narrative is composed of words, language, and speech addressed to an other or to more than one other. One dream, then another, dreamed by another dreamer, opens the way to the polyphony of the dream space.[5]

The dream is produced from the dreamer's internal productions and processes, through the characteristics of his internal characters, of the internal recipient or recipients, from daytime residues and from the traces or imprints of others inscribed in the dreamer's identifications. The intrapsychic determinants responsible for the polyphonic character of dreams are essentially related to the internal groupality and primary processes that govern them: condensation, displacement, diffraction, and the multiplication of a similar element. It is these same processes that govern the dream. In other words, the dream is traversed, well before it occurs, and after it has been dreamed, by heterogeneous discourses that form the material of the dream itself.

The other level is that of its polyphonic production. The hypothesis of dream polyphony leads us into a "factory of dreams" where the dreams of several dreamers are shot through by the utterances or perceptions of others, echo each other, and interpenetrate; where several dreamers make signs to each other and are heard by several dreamers, several listeners, internal and external, increasing proportionately the polysemy and richness of the dream experience.

The clinical examples have shown us that in each dream, several voices are at work: the day and night-time residues of the dreamer's own dreams and those of a few others. The raw material of the dream is to be found in this polyphonic material. The dream-work transforms them, half-effaced and half-readable, as in a palimpsest, amalgamated in a text that only becomes decipherable if we have a sufficiently precise hypothesis for decoding them and for restoring to the dream experience the procedures of poetic creation.[6]

To continue

If the dream is formed in the conditions that I have supposed, and if the dream experience can be represented in terms of the three dimensions that I have described, then the dream is indeed this "royal road to the unconscious" and the perspective that I am proposing should endorse this idea still further.

All these analyses portray in fact a relatively porous dream space joined up with three other spaces: the physical and bodily space, the intrapsychic space, and the intersubjective space. The unconscious is inscribed from the outset in all these dream spaces from the beginning of psychic life.

Psychic space and dream space are open from the beginning to the other, to more than one other. It is within this current of thought that I conceive of the hypothesis according to which the dream space is a personal space, but one that is traversed—and no doubt organized in part—by the existence of a shared and common dream space. The conception of a psychic space common to and shared between several subjects, and of a dream space partially open to the presence of the other in the dreamer's psyche, is to be set in tension, and not in opposition, with the propositions that stem from the classical approach to dreams in the analytic setting. Among these, two basic acquisitions are, first, that the dream is the hallucinatory fulfilment of a repressed unconscious wish and, second, that the closure of psychic space is necessary for dream-formation.

NOTES

1. For the Hebrews, the Egyptians, and the Latin people, dreams are dreamed by a dream-bearer; they are interpreted, as Dodds (1959) has demonstrated with respect to the Greeks of the classical period, according to a system of interpretation governed by a common and shared code. This is still the case today with the Pumé Indians from the Peruvian Andes, in the Candomblé culture of Bahia, or in Corsica, with mazzerism and the function devolved upon certain women to dream about forthcoming deaths in their village.

In this chapter, I have left aside other determinations and other approaches to dreams. Among these, we are greatly indebted to the founders of psychoanalytic anthropology of dreams (Róheim, G. Devereux). Although their object is different from ours, we also owe a lot to the work of sociologists and ethnologists on dreams. I am thinking in particular of the

sociological studies of R. Bastide, J. Duvignaud and C. Beradt, of the ethno-
logical research of R. Caillois, M. Perrin, B. Tedlock, and G. Orobitg-Canal.
I have not been able here to give an account of the work of G. W. Lawrence
(1998) who discovered a technique of group work called Social Dreaming.
According to this technique, the significance of a dream for the dreamer's
"internal world" remains in the background, while attention is focused on
the social context in which dreams appear and on their social significance.
(See the development of these researches in Neri, 2001, 2004.)

2. Some dreams that are reported to us during individual analysis or
during a group session represent several characters relating to each other,
all of whom form a little group, a larger assembly, or a crowd. I have
called these dreams "group dreams". They are a form of figuration of the
dreamer's dream ego; they are the scene of his characters and his internal
objects. I have made a thorough study of these dreams in *La Polyphonie du
rêve* (Kaës, 2002b).

3. Neyraut has described this type of dream in analysands; its particular-
ity is that it refers to the psychoanalytic situation. Owing to their complexity
and organization, these dreams are a good indicator of the integration of
the analytic process and of the evolution of the transference neurosis. They
bear witness to a "dramatisation of the neurosis around the psychoanalytic
situation", to an imaginary transgression of its rules. Its specificity is to convey the idea that a "symbolic bridge has been established between the conditions of the analysis and a determined infantile relationship" (Neyraut,
1974, p. 245).

4. The reference to the notion of polyphony in music theory indicates
an arrangement of several voices or several sounds. But in the context in
which I am employing the notion of polyphony, it must also include the
iconic material and visual forms of the dream. We must therefore speak of
dream poly-icony, or of polyptych, if we want to account for the numerous
folds of the dream in the scenes that are all linked together. Out of conven-
tion, we will accept that the more euphonic term "polyphony" assumes all
these dimensions.

5. This is also what emerges from the research studies of Gaburri and
Ambrosiano (2003) when they show that the dream constellation is produced by the dream re-dreamed by the group.

6. It is interesting to take the concept of polyphony into account from
another point of view: in literature, it challenges the belief in the author's
unicity; in dream-analysis it calls into question the dreamer's singularity. Indeed, if dreams, some more than others, are traversed by the wishful dreams
of an other, one may ask, who is dreaming in the dreamer? Which voices is
he the bearer of? And what is the subject of the dream?

10

Unconscious alliances

In order to form links from the very beginnings of psychic life and, later on, to form a couple, to live in a family, to form groups, and to live in a community with other human beings, we are invested and invest each other electively; we identify with each other unconsciously and then with a common object and trait. Our identifications unfold in various modalities: specular, narcissistic, adhesive, projective, and introjective, and they will be based on pre-existing harmonies, on the echopraxia, echolalia, and echomimetisms that accompany our first intersubjective experiences, prior to or on the fringes of speech; they will have aroused and encountered phantasy resonances, wish-fulfilments, and frustrations. To form links, these experiences and processes are necessary, as well as some others. But they are not enough: we still have to form and seal alliances between ourselves, some conscious, others unconscious, whose principal function is to maintain and strengthen (contract) our links, to fix their objectives and terms, and to make them last. Each one of us, unless we are autistic, needs the other in order to realize those unconscious wishes that are unrealizable without the other, and vice versa; the agreement that results generally remains unconscious, for reasons that I am going to explain.

Contracting an alliance is the act whereby two or several people unite in order to achieve a precise aim, which implies a common interest and mutual commitment. From the point of view of psychoanalysis, man's entering into alliances is based on specific processes and interests that are different from those that organize the alliances in which social anthropology, religion, political philosophy, or law are interested.

I have used the term "unconscious alliance" to refer to an intersubjective psychic formation constructed by the subjects of a link in order to strengthen in each of them, and to establish as the basis of their link, the narcissistic and object-investments that they need, and the processes, functions, and psychic structures that are necessary for them, which derive from repression, or from denial, rejection, and disavowal. The alliance is formed in such a way that the link acquires a decisive psychic value for each of its subjects. The psychic reality of the ensemble thus formed (the group, the family, the couple) depends on the alliances, contracts, and pacts that its subjects conclude and which their place in the ensemble obliges them to maintain.

Unconscious alliances organize intersubjective links and the unconscious of their subjects

Unconscious alliances are inscribed fundamentally in the psychic formation of intersubjective links or ties: the concept of intersubjectivity finds its material there, and the psychic reality of the link its consistency. Unconscious alliances produce their effects beyond the subjects, circumstances, and moment that made them necessary and shaped them; they are the agent and material of the transmission of psychic life between generations and contemporaries. The concept of unconscious alliance gives a precise content to this formula that I have used to represent the logic of linking: "not one without the other, or without the tie that unites them and contains them".

Unconscious alliances have another dimension, which concerns each subject involved in them. They require of them obligations and subjections; they distribute benefits to them and promise them pleasures: the benefits that the alliances bring are to be measured against the psychic costs that they impose on their subjects. But our attention must be directed at a still more important point: each of us is a subject of the unconscious under the sway of unconscious alliances. They produce a part of the unconscious and psychic reality of each subject.

Three major categories of alliances

I have distinguished two main categories of alliances. The first contributes to the structuring of the psyche: the oedipal pact concluded with the Father and between the Brothers, the contract of mutual renunciation of the direct satisfaction of destructive instinctual aims (Freud, 1912–13, 1927c, 1930a), and the narcissistic contract (Castoriadis-Aulagnier, 1975) form part of them. The second category comprises defensive alliances, in particular the negative pact (Kaës, 1989a), and their alienating and pathological derivatives, the community of denial and the perverse contract among them. A third category of alliance is formed by the offensive alliances that seal the agreement of a group to carry out an attack or an exploit, or to exert supremacy.

Whether they are structuring, offensive, or defensive, or whether they deviate into alienating and psychopathological impediments, unconscious alliances are the cement of the psychic material that binds us together in a couple, a family, a group, or an institution. Unconscious alliances are metapsychic organizations: they contribute to the structuring of the psyche in its narcissistic and object-based organization, in its modalities of wish-fulfilment, in its defensive or alienating formations. These are the propositions that I would like to develop in this chapter. (I am summarizing here, without going into the details of their description, the substance of several analyses of unconscious alliances: Kaës, 1989a, 1993.)

Structuring unconscious alliances

The fraternal pact and the contract with the Father

In *Totem and Taboo* (1912–13), Freud describes two forms of alliance at work in what he calls the scientific myth of the primal Horde: the first is the pact uniting the brothers in the repetitive murder of the archaic Father of the horde; the second is the totemic contract that links them to the symbolized Father and, from there, between themselves. Because it contains the symbolic guarantee of the alliance of the brothers with the father, this contract participates in the structuring function of unconscious alliances. The act of revolt transforms itself into a foundational act of an alliance, which is simultaneously a moment of meaning and a transcendence of the Oedipus complex. The contract involving a renunciation of the direct satisfaction of instinctual aims, the principle and effects of which Freud sets out in *The Future of an Illusion* (1927c) and in *Civilization and Its Discontents* (1930a), pursues the same aim and ensures the transmissibility of prohibitions and common ideals.

The pact between the brothers is based on a coalition, or a league: their alliance is offensive, the aim is to suppress

The pact between the brothers is based on a coalition, or a league: their aim is to get rid of the all-powerful, authoritarian Father who forcefully [*mächtig*] opposes the sons' need for power [*Machtbedürfnis*]. As the one who possesses all the women, the jealous Father prevents his sons from satisfying their directly sexual impulses by forcing them into abstinence. In *Group Psychology and the Analysis of the Ego* (1921c, p. 124) Freud notes that the consequence of this imposition of excessive power was that the brothers were forced "into the emotional ties with him [the father] and with one another which could arise out of their impulsions that were inhibited in their sexual aim. He forced them, so to speak, into group psychology." Driven out and separated from the Father, the sons were then able, Freud supposes, "to advance from identification with one another to homosexual object-love, and in this way win freedom to kill their father" (1921c, note 1).

In order to kill the tyrannical and persecuting Father, the brothers had to band together and form a league against him, for none of them could carry out the murder alone. No doubt several attempts had culminated in failure. After their first association and the rivalry that followed for possession of the women, the figure of the archaic Father reappeared in one of the brothers who had replaced him, and, under these conditions, he had to be got rid of. To be able to live together and to overcome repetition, the brothers had to invent the transition from a relationship based on power to one based on authority.

This transition was carried out under the influence of three organizing prohibitions: the brothers were obliged to institute the law against incest "by which they all alike renounced the women whom they had desired and who had been their chief motive for despatching their father" (1912–13, p. 144). This was the first prohibition of humanity. The second prohibition was maintained by the setting-up of the taboo, the aim of which was to protect the life of the totemic animal, a substitute for the dead father and an occasion for reconciliation with him: "the totemic system was, as it were, a covenant with their father" (p. 144), writes Freud, a system that ensured that the murderous act would not be committed again against him, in exchange for his protection and favours. The totemic covenant thus also protected the clan: "in guaranteeing one another's lives, the brothers were declaring that no one of them must be treated by another as their father was treated by them all jointly. . . . To the religiously based prohibition against killing the totem was now added the socially based prohibition against fratricide" (p. 146).

The prohibition against incest, the prohibition against killing the totemic animal, and the prohibition against fratricide are the three prohibitions laid down in the totemic covenant, which brings to a close the communal crime on which society is founded. The totemic covenant of the brothers guarantees henceforth the organization of the group structured by the fundamental prohibitions and the symbolic order that establishes the processes of civilization. Symbolic identifications are based on this covenant. From being offensive and destructive, their alliance has become structuring.

The model proposed by Freud in *Totem and Taboo* (1912–13) involves a change in the order of group ties: it consists in the shift of megalomanic investments and identifications with the unrestrained power attributed to the Father towards investments in the figure of the symbolic and symboligenic Father and the values of culture. This shift was the consequence of a crisis, a rupture, and a moment of transcendence that marked the transition from the ahistorical ties of the Horde to the intersubjective, historical, and symbolic ties of the patriarchal totemic group.

The contract of renunciation of the direct satisfaction of instinctual aims

Like the fraternal pact and the symbolic contract with the Father, the contract of renunciation of the direct satisfaction of instinctual aims fulfils a structuring function in the formation of the psyche.

In *Civilization and Its Discontents* (1930a) Freud inquires into the sources of human suffering, and particularly into that which pertains to the inadequacy of the regulations that adjust mutual relationships of human beings in the family, the State, and society. Freud wonders why the institutions we have created do not provide protection and benefits for each one of us. He proposes the following explanation: the cultural element on which institutions are based enters on the scene with the first attempt to regulate social relations. It is through the renunciation of the direct satisfaction of destructive impulses (cannibalism, murder of a fellow human being, incest) that the possibility emerges of establishing a contract that benefits the members of a community. Insofar as the latter is a lawful community, it protects us against violence, imposes Necessity, and makes love possible.

Without this transition from the law of the physically strongest to that of the community, "relationships would be subject to the arbitrary will of the individual" (Freud, 1930a, p. 95). The law on which the community is based stipulates that, in order to benefit from the protections of the community, we must in exchange renounce certain satisfactions. The achievements of culture are possible on this condition.

Instinctual renunciation and the establishment of a lawful community have a function and significance both in the individual psychic space *and* in the psychic space of social and institutional groupings. Freud describes the psychic basis of the legal foundation of the institution, the conditions of the legitimate affiliation of its subjects to a social ensemble, and the demands for psychic work imposed by culture on the instinctual economy, dynamics, and topography. What the pact of mutual renunciation of the direct satisfaction of instinctual aims establishes is non-immediateness: the detour imposed is the work of authority, and the work of authority is to bring into being thought and linking instead of physical struggle. The work of culture and its acquisitions are a conquest over murderous impulses and narcissism. Each time narcissism is seriously menaced, these conquests are endangered. (Freud had already conceptualized this between 1912 and 1914.)

The contract of renunciation directly involves the individual and collective components of the process of sublimation. Freud reaffirms here the similarity between the process of civilization and the libidinal development of the individual. The sublimation of instinctual aims is "an especially conspicuous feature of cultural development" (1930a, p. 97): both are obtained through constraint and renunciation.

Narcissistic contracts and pacts

Piera Castoriadis-Aulagnier introduced the notion of narcissistic contract to contend that each subject comes simultaneously into the world of psychic life, society, and the succession of generations as the bearer of a mission—namely, of ensuring the continuity of the grouping to which he belongs. In exchange, the ensemble must invest the new individual narcissistically. This contract assigns to each one a specific place in the group, a place that is signified to him by the community of voices, which, before each subject, has held a certain discourse in conformity with the myth of the group founder. This discourse includes ideals and values; it transmits the culture and the certitudes of society at large. Each subject must in one way or another make this discourse his own. Through it, he is linked to the founding ancestor.

Under these conditions, the concept of narcissistic contract accounts for the fact that the narcissistic investment that allows each individual to accomplish his own purposes, can only really be maintained to the extent that the chain of which the subject is a member and constituent part invests this subject narcissistically as the bearer of the continuity of the grouping. This is how the parents, first of all, make the child the bearer of the realization of their own "unfulfilled wishful dreams" (Freud, 1914c), and how they thereby guarantee his narcissistic foundations, just as it is through them that the desire of earlier generations had supported, positively or negatively, their coming into the world and their own narcissistic anchoring.

I have contributed some additional elements to the concept of the narcissistic contract. I have distinguished several modalities of

it. *The primal narcissistic contract,* based on investments of self-preservation, defines a contract of transgenerational filiation: it is in the
service of the totality and of the subject of this totality.

The secondary narcissistic contract, based on secondary narcissism, is
a contract of affiliation that redistributes the investments of the primal narcissistic contract and enters into conflict with it (in particular
when the subject establishes extrafamilial ties). These two sorts of
contracts are in the service of life.

The narcissistic pact is the result of an immutable assignation to
a location of perfect narcissistic coincidence. It is pathogenic and
in certain cases deadly. It belongs to the category of alienating alliances.

It seems to me that, in the intrapsychic space of the subject as
well as in the space of intersubjective links, the economic balance
between narcissism and the original tendency of the ego to relin-
quish its own substance and yield a portion of its libido to the benefit
of that which is outside,[1] is a central dimension of the narcissistic
contract.

Structuring alliances are complementary, interdependent, and
synergic. The contract of renunciation can only hold good if the
narcissistic contract fulfils its principal functions, and vice versa.

Defensive, offensive,
and alienating unconscious alliances

Offensive alliances

Offensive alliances are established on the basis of an organized coalition with a view to carrying out an attack on an other, or more than
one other, to exert ascendancy over him, to dominate or destroy
him: a football team, a group of commandos, a work group, or a
gang organize themselves on the basis of such alliances. J. P. Pinel
has proposed (2001) the notion of psychopathic alliance to account
for a general mode of acting violently, with destructive aims towards
an other, "by means of a more or less open and conscious coalition
between one or more of the actors and one or more silent accom-
plices against a victim who suffers the violent action". The psychopathic alliance is an offensive alienating alliance.

The negative pact

The negative pact (Kaës, 1989a) describes an unconscious agreement about the unconscious that is imposed or concluded mutually so that the link is organized and maintained with a view to maintaining the complementary interests of each subject and of their link. The price of the link is precisely one that is inconceivable for those whom it binds owing to the double-crossed economy that governs the relations of individual subjects and of the chain of which they are members.

The negative pact is a metadefence based on various defensive operations: repression and negation, but also denial, disavowal, rejection, or encystment. While it is necessary for forming the link, it creates in the latter that which cannot be signified or transformed, zones of silence, pockets of intoxication that maintain the subjects of a link in the position of being strangers to their own history and to the history of others. Let us now put these propositions to the test clinically in both the group and individual settings.

The negative pact in groups: clinical examples

As clinical experience has shown, the repression, denial, rejection, or splitting of dangerous representations are mobilized in the very first moments of the life of groups. The negative pact is simultaneously both the result of the mutually imposed operations of repression or denial and one of the processes of the combination or adjustment of the psyches of the group members. Generally speaking, the first measures of this process of adjustment establish the first unconscious alliances, and the combination of their unconscious contents forms the material of the unconscious psychic reality in the group.

We have seen this triple emergence of alliance, adjustment, and psychic reality in the group with Marc: Sylvie's question about the identity of the psychoanalyst was important for other participants, but the silence that followed the question was completely filled with the repression of this fleeting and dangerous movement of transference towards Sophie. This first outline of a negative pact was reinforced when Marc's "confession" evoked the danger facing the participants, although there was as yet no possibility of acknowledging and thinking about what constituted the danger. The unacceptable was repressed by everyone and deposited in the group. To complete the setting-up of the pact, Marc indicated an object capable of countering the danger: the very one who was a source of menace could (and must) repair the damage caused by the trauma. This demand for reparation came in place of the thought of the catastrophic change that the return of the repressed would represent.

The negative pact and catastrophic change:
the group of "skewered analysts"

Another clinical situation illustrates the constant relationship be-tween the defensive alliance and catastrophic change. It dates from the years when a small group of analysts assembled by Anzieu began to work in a setting where there was an alternation of sessions in small groups led by a pair of psychoanalysts and sessions in large groups with all the participants and the psychoanalysts together. This arrangement, called a "seminar", functioned for a week, with four daily sessions. Each evening, the psychoanalysts met among themselves to try to understand the unconscious dynamics of groups and of the seminar as a whole, including the dynamics of their own group.

The evening before the seminar began, Anzieu announced that he did not want to conduct the large-group sessions and hoped that two colleagues would carry out this function in his place. A rather lively discussion got underway in our team about this late, surpris-ing, and coercive decision: contrary to our usual ways of working, we were obliged to make a change in the arrangements without having reflected on the decision together. But we did not say anything about the source of our anxieties in relation to this decision: whether to take the place of the founder or to refuse his proposal and whether or not it was a good idea to form a "couple" in the group were among the pressing questions to which we urgently needed to find an answer. The conflicts dividing us were avoided for fear that the team might break apart. On the contrary, a tacit agreement was concluded to maintain its unity at the beginning of this seminar, and two of us, a colleague and myself, took on the task of conducting the large groups.

The tensions in our group were such that, under various pretexts, the sessions in which we analysed the ways our team functioned were suspended during the two following evenings. The negative pact that had been set up led us to abandon a part of our analytic function. Instead of working on what divided us, we passed over our disagreements in silence; we repressed the unconscious contents that caused us anxiety and left to one side the analysis of the functioning of our own group, of our intertransferences and the transference effects that followed in the participants. The suspension of our sessions was a case of acting out that rendered any kind of resolution or liberation impossible.

During the last session of the seminar, the participants came and sat down opposite us, in a line, mirroring our group: we were seated, close together, in a line, and were very embarrassed about having positioned ourselves in this specular and rigid way. There was a long period of silence, until one participant said to the other participants: "Well, here is a team of skewered analysts!" This depiction of the defensive soldering that had sealed our alliance unfroze our capacity to think as well as that of the participants, and we were then able to work with them on analysing other alliances concluded in the groups and in the seminar.

Some hypotheses concerning unconscious alliances in groups

After the seminar, in our group we attempted to work through this critical moment.[2] The analysis brought to light certain unconscious conflicts that kept us in the negative pact that was aimed at repressing or denying them. Anzieu's conscious wish was to extricate himself from the idealizing and persecutory transferences resulting from his position as founder of our team, and as heroic analyst of the large group capable of facing up to, containing, and reducing the most archaic anxieties. But his unconscious wish was to be substituted by a couple who might be equivalent to him, at the risk of seeing it fail in its impossible mission. Most of us, both men and women, sided with him, and we did not want to know anything about our ambivalence concerning the place that he had ambiguously left vacant, nor anything about the fraternal rivalry that his abdication had aroused in us. Our negative pact was based on our fear of losing a loved object, a protector, and the narcissistic confidence that we had acquired with him since the foundation of our group. The pact was aimed at renewing the ideal of a group united in the face of all opposition.

For my part, out of this experience I have developed several working hypotheses about the formation of the negative pact concluded between us and about its effects on the analytic process.

Analysing this experience has taught me that what each one of us had repressed or denied became the object of an unconscious alliance so that each of us was personally reassured, and reassured the others, that we knew nothing of our own wishes, our own affects (anger, abandonment, hate), or of the intolerable representations (forming a couple in front of the "father", being actors and spectators in a primal scene) with which we were confronted. We did not want to know or feel anything at all about these issues both as individual subjects and also to protect our relations with the others and our relationship with Anzieu. Our pact achieved the unconscious aim we all sought—namely, of forming a closely knit group, skewered by the shaft of the archaic paternal phallus. The negative pact was a solution for the anxieties raised in us by this catastrophic change; it took the place of our incapacity or refusal to think about what was involved in this change. It also took the place of a structuring alliance between brothers to usurp the place of the Father. But it was also the effect of the position taken by Anzieu in this conflict. We could neither attack him nor flee from him.

I also learnt that what was repressed and/or denied in the psychoanalysts was represented in the group of participants and organized it as a double of our own psychic space. The pact was embodied in the spatial arrangement of our group facing that of the participants, in the mirror that froze us in a disturbing symmetry, in a repetition blocked in space. It was the participants who recovered the capacity to speak, inventing the metaphor to pass from a formal signifier ("things are sticking together") to a phantasy (a collection of part-objects or pieces of objects run through with a skewer, just ready for eating) and to words of interpretation.

The pact formed in these conditions was associated with the inaugural trauma of the catastrophic change of setting that broke apart the stimulus barriers and the group structure that we normally used. In these conditions, I had some reasons to suppose that what had been denied or repressed by the analysts—who for the participants occupied an imaginary position here as founders of the seminar—had acquired for the latter the characteristics of the contents and qualities of the primal repressed. If my hypothesis is correct, the defensive unconscious alliance then becomes for everyone a powerful attractor of secondary repression. If this is the case, interesting perspectives are opened up with regard to the formation and transmission of the primal and of enigmatic (or archaic) signifiers by unconscious alliances in groups and in all configurations of linking.

On these bases and by integrating the contribution of other clinical analyses, I have arrived at a set of hypotheses of a more general character. I have tried to establish a point of view that shows that the group psychoanalytic situation gives access to knowledge of the individual structures of the formations of the unconscious in their articulations with the unconscious intersubjective structures of an ensemble. Unconscious alliances are situated at the nodal points of these structures. Considered from the point of view of the psychic topography, dynamics, and economy in the group, they are concluded so that the group and group ties are formed and are enduring, whatever their purposes or their quality may be: structuring, defensive, pathogenic, or alienating.

Clinical work teaches us that defensive unconscious alliances are formed in the initial period of the group process, when the members of a group meet each other for the first time. In order to come together as a group, the members of a group (or of any other linking configuration) must conclude, unwittingly, an unconscious agreement whereby they will have to repress, deny, reject, or efface certain representations. Unconscious alliances are not only constituted in order to keep representations unconscious according to the joint and mutually guaranteed interest of several subjects, thereby sealing their ties; the alliances themselves remain as unconscious as the ties that are created through them.

Unconscious alliances find their material, their energy, and their contents in these co-repressed, co-denied, or co-rejected representations. Current alliances are linked up with unconscious formations and processes already established in each of the subjects. The return of unconscious contents, when they are repressed contents, occurs through their effects in the group associative chain, in the transferences, in the shared symptoms, dreams, and phoric functions. When it is a matter of non-repressed (denied or foreclosed) archaic

Linking, alliances, and shared space

contents, the return of the unconscious contents occurs through acting out, splitting, collective delusions, primitive, bizarre objects, or enigmatic signifiers.

The analysis of unconscious alliances throws light on the archaeology of the group and on the archaeology of the subject.[3] They carry out specific functions in the formation of intrapsychic space, notably in its unconscious dimensions; and, at the same time, they support the formation and processes of intersubjective links that, in turn, reinforce intrapsychic formations and processes.

Every time an unconscious defensive alliance can be unravelled, it is the source of an important discovery for the subjects who were bound by it. From this point of view, it is quite remarkable that psychoanalysis itself was able to make several of its founding discoveries through the unravelling of such defensive alliances.

The negative pact and unconscious alliances in the individual treatment.

Two inaugural treatments in psychoanalysis

Freud found himself caught up in an unconscious defensive alliance with Fliess regarding the operation on Emma Eckstein's turbinate bones, as he was with Dora and the men in her life in her treatment. To get an idea of the unconscious issues at stake in these alliances, let us dwell for a moment on these two decisive moments in the invention of psychoanalysis. (I have developed this analysis: see Kaës, 1993, pp. 264–271.)

The bloody alliance between Freud and Fliess in the treatment of Emma Eckstein

The first was the negative pact drawn up between two men, Freud and Fliess, to operate on, penetrate, and finally injure the body of a woman in analysis with Freud, a female body they shared with each other in their bond of love. This pact was not only a massive resistance against the structuring alliance of the analytic situation: it attacked and destroyed it. It shows the power of misrecognition that this pact involved in order to preserve the unconscious interests of the bond between these two men and between them and the woman.

But this episode also indicates how each of them extricated himself from it.

Let us remind ourselves of the facts[4]: during their debates (their "congresses") on bisexuality, it became clear to Freud and Fliess that Emma should undergo an operation by Fliess on her turbinate bones, which, according to him, were the organic seat of her hysterical neurosis. The operation took place in Freud's presence. During the operation, Fliess "forgot" to remove a piece of iodoform gauze from the locus of his patient's operation. When Freud wrote to him about the pains Emma suffered following the operation, he denied reproaching him in any way for the conduct of the operation (letter of 8 March 1895, in Masson, 1985) and with this backing Fliess refused to recognize his surgical error. His own denial and the echo that it found in Fliess put Freud in the position of having to endorse this refusal to recognize the truth in order to preserve their friendship.

But that was not enough. To preserve this relationship, Freud was sacrificing precisely what he had just succeeded in binding by thought—namely, the link between the trauma and the phantasy—and he had just written to Fliess about this. In order to exonerate Fliess ("I did not want to reproach you for anything", letter of 20 April 1895), Freud went as far as to say, ambiguously, that "of course, she is beginning with the new production of hysterias, from this past period" (letter of 28 March 1895).

For these two men, for this "strong sex", which Emma makes fun of when she sees Freud coming back feeling faint at the sight of her blood, Emma is the figure of the hole that they want to explore and to fill with gauze and blood. Their pact is based on the denial of their wish and of their homosexual link; it is also the reason for Freud's refusal to acknowledge his own discovery of the phantasy of seduction. This pact shows what he is protecting himself against and what he is trying to preserve. Maintaining their relationship required them jointly to repress and/or deny that which in each of them could pose a threat to it.

The pact brings into play several defence mechanisms: the joint repression of the homosexual tie between Freud and Fliess; the refusal to give up the direct satisfaction of destructive instinctual aims (here the wild satisfaction of the epistemophilic impulse concerning Emma's body); and, finally, the disavowal of the knowledge Freud had acquired about seduction. This disavowal, which finds backing in Fliess's theory, is a veritable self-mutilation of thought, a necessary sacrifice in order to maintain the relationship with Fliess and to pave the way for the *passage à l'acte* on Emma's body, the locus of the intolerable representation. The consequence is the projection onto Emma of the jointly denied error and of the guilt for having satisfied a prohibited wish. But, more deeply, if Freud attributes the cause of the post-surgical difficulties to Emma's hysteria, it is less in order to make it responsible than to maintain what must be repressed in his relationship with Fliess and in his own thought.

The analysis of the group of "skewered" analysts has shown us that the aim of their pact was to deny their division. In this episode of the pact between Freud and Fliess we can see that their alliance contains the representation precisely of that which they want to keep unrepresented—namely, the hole of the feminine, their common phantasy about exploring it, about acting aggressively towards it and filling it up, and the homosexual interests of their relationship. That which is unrepresented in their pact is completely condensed and represented in Emma's body—a veritable link between Freud and Fliess. It is this infected body that appears in Freud's dream (known as the dream of Irma's injection), and which Freud was to recognize in the analysis of his dream. The return of the repressed part of the pact takes place for him by means of the *first* dream that inaugurates *The Interpretation of Dreams* (1900a) and the theory of gaining access to the unconscious by the royal road of dreams.

But this body is also present in the forms of denial that organize Freud and Fliess's mutual accusations of stealing each other's ideas. These accusations appear from this point of view as a displacement of what for them was intolerable about breaking and entering into Emma's body. They were to culminate in a breaking off of relations between them.

The pact is thus not only founded on neurotic repression. The mechanisms of the negative pact, which is based on denial, rejection, disavowal, and projection, will not be entirely eliminated; they will produce similar effects in other circumstances. Concerning the relationships between Carl Jung and Sabine Spielrein, and Sándor Ferenczi and Gisella Palos, Freud said in essence that it was not the men who were responsible in their affair, but the other (the women). Even though he urged Ferenczi not to pursue his relationship with the mother and the daughter, the exoneration served as a self-exoneration and projection of betrayal onto the other. The motive force of Freud's identification with Fliess, Jung, and Ferenczi, sustained by homosexual love and repressed through fraternal rivalry, is the same as the one that underlies all the paranoiac projections that Freud, in an attempt to free himself from them, would use to develop the theory of paranoia.

Founding psychoanalysis would involve placing at the heart of its debate the *proton pseudos* and the question of the subject in his relation to that which represents him: for Freud, this was Fliess as much as Emma. Founding psychoanalysis also required Freud to free himself from the alienating and pathogenic negative pact concluded with Fliess. This first extrication from what he was later to call the group psyche [*Massenpsyche*] required him to move beyond the non-differentiation of the common spaces between himself and Fliess, embodied by Emma's body and blood. This liberation, of which his dream was the motor, was necessary in order to gain access to the creative subjectivation both of his history and of his work.

Gaining access to the creative subjectivation both of Freud's history and his work[5]

The unconscious alliances in Dora's analysis

Dora's treatment was another decisive moment in the invention of psychoanalysis. It, too, was under the effect of an unconscious alliance, the untying of which opened the way to the invention of the analytic space. The account that Freud left us of Dora's analysis just after the treatment was broken off (1905e [1901]), and the notes that he added in 1923 after the analysis had been continued with Ruth Mack Brunswick, show us how Freud's countertransference formed an alliance with the resistance of his young patient and with the defences deployed against the analytic process by Dora's close relations. They also show us how Freud, by extricating himself from this defensive alliance, was able to pursue his discovery of the transference and countertransference.

I will not develop here the analysis that I have made of the issues that were at stake in this alliance. I would simply like to point out that it was formed after Dora's father had asked Freud to try to bring his daughter to reason. Freud listened to Dora with discernment when she told him that her father was having a love affair with Frau K and that Herr K had made advances to her. Freud gave credence to Dora when she spoke of this tacit arrangement between her father and Herr K, and he saw clearly how the two men had concluded the pact that allowed them to take advantage of Dora to satisfy their own amorous desires.

But while he recognized the existence and the motivating forces of this alliance, Freud went astray in his explanation. According to Freud, Dora only wanted to oblige her father to give up Frau K because she was in love, not with Frau K—this was his blind spot—but with her father. Freud was persuaded that her love for him was being used as a defence against her current feeling of love for Herr K.

One could say the same of Freud as he says of Dora: he is perceptive in one direction, with regard to the pact of which she is the object, but he goes astray in another—that is to say, with regard to the unconscious alliance that he concludes with her. He goes astray first of all in the explanation that he gives for Dora's behaviour: as she was in love with Herr K, she had accommodated herself for a certain time to the exchange and relations between the adults.

Freud was only able to recognize retrospectively, in his note of 1923, the failure of Dora's very short psychoanalysis. It was at this date that he attributed this failure to the homosexual tie between Dora and Frau K: "I failed to discover in time and to inform the patient that her homosexual (gynaecophilic) love for Frau K. was the strongest unconscious current in her mental life" (1905e [1901], p. 120). What organized Dora's object-relations, the homosexual desire for her mother with whom she identified secretly,[6] was also what organized her transference onto Freud. In the countertransference, Freud placed himself successively or simultaneously where he hoped Dora would be waiting for him: he smoked heavily like Herr K, for whom he presented himself unconsciously as a substitute, to the point that—and for other reasons as well—he failed to recognize either Dora's "gynaecophilic" wish or her own defence against this wish, that is to say, Dora's homosexual transference onto his own feminine part. Blind to this extent to Freud's countertransference, Dora's transference *in* Freud mobilized Freud's resistance to the highest point.

"The classical Oedipal theory protected Freud", notes Stroeken (1985). It can be seen how, once again, Freud's relation to his own theory was put to the service of misrecognition in the unconscious alliances that he formed with Fliess, Dora, and the men in Dora's life.

Unconscious alliances, countertransference, and mutual attachment to symptoms in psychoanalytic treatment

In these two examples, we are dealing with an alliance concluded for the realization of wishes that could not be satisfied without the assistance of the other and without the interest that the latter finds in contracting such an alliance with an other in order to satisfy his own wishes.

In both these cases, it is also a defensive alliance that is involved: the negative pact is the measure of the demand for psychic work, in this case repression and denial, required of Freud so that he does not have to recognize either his own repression or denial, which are in resonance with Fliess's and Dora's repression and denial. Correlatively, the repression and denial on the part of Fliess and Dora cannot be recognized as such by Freud to the extent that they serve his own interests of misrecognition. Likewise, Fliess, Dora, and the men in Dora's life are preserved from this knowledge to the extent that Freud's interests serve their own interests of misrecognition: each one reinforces and serves the interests of the other by serving his own.

The defensive alliances—more precisely the negative pact—which manifest themselves in these two treatments call into question the analyst's countertransference. The question of the countertransference does not only concern the theory of praxis, it also involves a basic epistemological problem, as Guillaumin (1994) has shown very clearly. The setting in which the analysand and the analyst evolve is always potentially subject to effects of swamping resulting from the intersubjective issues in which each of them, without realizing it, is deeply involved.[7] The structuring alliance based on the fundamental rule and on the psychoanalytic frame has the precise function of constituting a limit, a situation of containment, and a mode of figuration suited to the symbolization of the disturbing effects of these correlations of subjectivity. However, the setting can only deal with a difficulty if the conditions that produce it can be recognized and elaborated.

The alliance and the community of identifications
through shared symptoms

In Freud's alliance with Fliess, as in the one he formed with Dora, a community of identifications was established through the symptom. The production of common and shared symptoms is in the service of the necessity of linking—namely, to subject each individual subject to his symptom in relation to the function that it fulfils for himself and for an other, in and for the link. The symptom is thereby reinforced many times over.

If we only take into account the economic and dynamic function of the symptom for the subject who produces it, by inscribing him in his own particular history and in his own structure, we miss its value in the economy of intersubjective links. We miss the investment that it receives from an other, or from more than one other, in order to hold the relationship together, but at a price that remunerates the share of repression that belongs to each one in the alliance.

The analysis must then be directed at the intersubjective knot where the symptom has acquired, for the subject who makes himself the bearer of it, an inestimable part of his value. In such configurations, the symptom not only needs participation from *both* sides, as Freud saw clearly in Dora's analysis (1905e [1901], p. 40): from the side of somatic compliance and from the psychic side (unconscious thoughts). The account that Freud gives of Dora's analysis shows that a further contribution maintains the symptom, and that it comes from a third side: namely, from the intersubjective link.[8] This further contribution is to be sought in the alliances, contracts, and pacts that hold together the subjects of a link, through the symptom and the suffering of the one who, in their place, makes himself the body-bearer and the symptom-bearer, for himself and the others as well. This is his phoric function: the subject constitutes himself as such because he has already found he is predisposed to constituting himself as such, in order to serve both his own interest and the interest of those to whom he is bound either by an alliance in the service of realizing unconscious wishes or by a defensive alliance.

The stakes of unconscious alliances in the treatment

These two examples throw light on a tenacious type of resistance that narcissistic, perverse, or negative unconscious alliances, in which psychoanalysts and their patients can be caught up, set against the efforts of analysis. Certain treatments are suddenly broken off in order to save the situation for one or both of the partners in an alliance that keeps them subjected to each other, because the analysis and the undoing of alliances are more perilous for them than the alienation that is the price they pay for them. What patients (or analysts) keep out of the analysis is not only the place that they themselves occupy in the alliance, but also the place of the other. We are dealing with an intersubjective topography, economy, and dynamic that concerns two, three, or more subjects, where the overall effects are mutually reinforced because they are managed conjointly and in the same direction by all the allies.

The effects of this alliance generally manifest themselves in a self-destructive act, in a delusion, in a severe inhibition of thought or in perverse behaviour. When the patient breaks off the analysis, he is often trying to preserve the analyst from the effects that such an alliance could entail if it were reproduced with him. But this resistance to the transference protects the alliance itself, and the analyst can maintain it for reasons of his own.

Should we then, in face of this impasse, think that analysis is of no help for such subjects and that they are resistant to analysis? Faced with these difficulties, our inquiries are directed naturally towards that which, in the analyst, has proved to be inadequate for receiving the transference of these connections of links and investments soldered together in an alliance that has become unconscious. It is then possible to interpret or to reconstruct what is at stake for the analyst and the analysing subject. But there are also cases where an alternative to the classical psychoanalytic situation (joint therapy with a parent and their child, family psychoanalytic psychotherapy, psychoanalysis in the group situation; group psychoanalytic psychotherapy) makes it possible for the subject to have the experience, with a psychoanalyst, of that which links him to the other and to all the others as a whole. Another path of access to the analysis of the individual and intersubjective stakes of the alliance can be opened up in a transference/countertransference space that is more suited to receiving their investments.

The community of denial and the negating alliance

In its defensive function, the negative pact can be compared with two other formations: the community of denial briefly evoked by Fain (1981) and the negating alliance introduced by Couchoud (1986). They are both alienating alliances.

Fain has proposed the notion of *community of denial* to account for a mode of identification of the child with his mother when the latter does not manage to free herself from him and to designate an object of desire (the father) elsewhere than in the child; the denial of the existence of desire for the father is shared by both child and mother. In this case, the community of denial concerns the reality of the object of the desire of the other, and, consequently, it sustains a crossed projective identification: it thus maintains the state of non-separation between the mother and child. The notion introduced by Fain in this context possesses a greater extension and is applicable to all the modalities and all the determinations of communal denial.

The model of the *negating alliance* pertains to another situation. An example will allow us to understand how the two modalities of repression and denial are used to form this type of alliance. Based on the joint psychotherapy of a mother and her daughter, Couchoud has shown that their alliance is manifested in the hallucinatory over-investment by the daughter of representations that are non-repressed and conjointly denied by the mother's psyche. Both of them maintain in daily life the permanence of that which, in the mother, has not been elaborated or repressed, in such a way that everything that emerges is so devoid of meaning that it can only be attributed by the mother to her daughter's madness. The mother, who has been unable to repress the content of her own traumatic experiences, is preserved from delusion by virtue of the fact that she induces in her daughter what would have been her own delusion. Correlatively, the daughter entertains delusions so that the mother may continue to forget what for her is not repressable.

Such an alliance characterizes a situation where the link is used to keep out of secondary repression representations rejected by means of denial. The central notion is one of a failure to repress. This failure is the motive of the means employed to render impossible the unveiling of the non-repressed contents and to ensure the veiling of that which must be denied.

The perverse contract

Psychoanalysts were attentive very early on to the sway exerted by the perverse subject over his partners: the relation of the fetishist to his fetish only acquires its value from the power that the fetish has of fascinating the other and of arousing his subservience in the perversion. Some of them have been more sensitive to the alienating alliance which binds them together (Masud Khan, Pujet, Berenstein, and Eiguer). Among these, Jean Clavreul (1967) has emphasized the importance of the secret in the contract that binds the two partners of the perverse couple. It is the denunciation of the secret, the betrayal of the secret to third parties, the scandal, which constitutes the rupture:

> the potential rupture of such contracts has quite another meaning and quite another import than the failure of the love between normal or neurotic subjects. The fact that they are secret, that their terms and their practices are only known to the interested parties, does not mean at all that the third party is absent. On the contrary: it is this very absence of the third party, the fact that he is kept at a distance, which constitutes the key element of this strange contract. This third party, who is necessarily present for signing, or rather for countersigning the authenticity of a normal loving relationship, will have to be excluded here or, to be more precise, will have to be present, but in a position such that he is necessarily either blind, or an accomplice or powerless. [Clavreul, 1967, p. 98]

For her part, Castoriadis-Aulagnier (1967) has demonstrated the demands of the perverse enactment from which chance is banished in such a way that a strict coincidence occurs between a fragment of reality and the scene in which the perverse subject's phantasy is played out. The law that governs the contract and guarantees the coincidence is the law of pleasure [*jouissance*]:

> that which is demanded and which must be accepted by the partner relates, not to the mediation of love or to the allegation of love, but to pleasure taken as an object. Pleasure is the only guarantee of the existence of the object of desire (lack is denied), of the erasure of the gap between the object of the demand (the mediating object) and the object of desire (the metaphorical and lost object). [Castoriadis-Aulagnier, 1967, p. 122]

The "secret" in the face of third parties, the scene of the coincidence between the fragment of reality and the phantasy, constitutes the foundation of the contract. Pleasure is the law that governs it.

The metapsychological import and clinical interest of the notion of unconscious alliances

The main characteristic of the alliances in which we are interested is their unconscious character: this means that these alliances are formed in such a way that certain contents and certain objects, certain aims and stakes of the bond are unconscious to the subjects of this bond. Among these alliances, some are structuring, while others have an essentially defensive, pathogenic, or alienating function. It remains for us now to evaluate the metapsychological import of unconscious alliances and to outline the place that they could occupy in a psychoanalytic theory of linking and of the subject of linking. This is one of the aims of chapter 11.

From a clinical standpoint, the analysis of unconscious alliances has highlighted the interest of the group psychoanalytic setting: the subject is put to the test of experiencing unconscious alliances in which he has taken part and from which he has to extricate himself in order to become aware that these alliances have been, in part, constitutive of his subjectivity.

NOTES

1. This tendency was theorized by Pasche (1964) with the concept of anti-narcissism.

2. Anzieu, Missenard, Bejarano, and I have proposed and published different and complementary analyses of it.

3. It also throws light on other modalities of the negative pact that are more radical and identifiable in any kind of group, but particularly in groups with a strong alienating tendency, like sectarian groups. Developing the concept of the negative pact in the social field, Amati Sas (2005) has described a more automatic, perhaps impersonal defensive alliance, which affects subjects faced with certain situations of collective traumatic violence that are intolerable for psychic reality, but which become banal or acceptable owing to this defensive alliance. She calls this invisible alliance of familiarity with catastrophic circumstances "adaptation to any situation whatsoever", "as if" nothing was happening.

4. The documents of reference are principally Freud's letters to Fliess from 4 March 1895; 8 March 1895; 28 March 1895; 11 April 1895; 20 April 1895; 15 May 1895 (in Masson, 1985); and the study by M. Schur (1966) on "the waking residues of the dream of Irma's injection".

5. The relationship between Freud and Fliess is an example of the passionate transference that frequently featured in Freud's self-analysis. On this point, see the work of Anzieu (1959).

6. Stroeken (1985) has perceived remarkably well the nature of Dora's love for her mother: "her mother, the source of her desire, her disappointment and her fear of being abandoned by her". She was obviously seeking her mother even in her hostile identification with the father (Stroeken, 1985, p. 89).

7. The transference and the countertransference do not only consist in an unloading or discharge of the patient's or analyst's investments into the psyche of an other, in a topographical extension that would on the outside be the receptacle of that which is unrepresentable on the inside, or in the delegation to an other of the treatment of non-repressed representations. This perspective implies the notion that the spaces have become common and that intersubjective arrangements have been set up to manage the interfering psychic topographies, economies, and dynamics.

8. Further on in the same text Freud stresses the fact that "it is not necessary for the various meanings of a symptom to be compatible with one another . . . it quite regularly happens that a single symptom corresponds to several meanings *simultaneously; we may now add that it can express several meanings in succession*" (p. 53).

11

The subject of the unconscious, the subject of linking

Now that we are almost at the end of this book, I would like to return to the two questions that have organized it: does the psychoanalytic approach to groups concern psychoanalysts? and how can it contribute to the theory and practice of psychoanalysis?

If I have sufficiently established that the group is the locus of an original experience of the unconscious and certain forms of subjectivity, I would now like to try to answer these two questions by formulating them differently. The first is this: can the subject in whom psychoanalysis is interested, the subject of the unconscious, understand himself solely in terms of his intrapsychic determinations, or should we admit that he is formed conjointly in intersubjectivity? The second question, which emerges once it has been admitted that intersubjectivity describes a specific psychic reality, is this: how are we to think about the organization of this common and shared psychic space?

The intersubjective matrix of subjectivation

One of the questions of interest to psychoanalysts today is that of subjectivation. This term refers not only to the process of the formation of the subject, but more precisely to his transformation into an I [*Je*] who is capable of thinking about his place and his condition as the subject of the unconscious. My research into unconscious alliances, phoric functions, and the common and shared dream space has led me to think that subjectivation involves a double psychic process: one operates in each subject according to his internal determinants, while the other develops from intersubjective psychic space. The idea that I wish to put forward is that the I, the culmination of the process of subjectivation, can only gain access to its reflexive organization and to the appropriation of its own subjectivity in an intersubjective ensemble on which it is initially dependent and from which it will have to extricate itself, without, however, freeing itself radically.[1] The whole question is one of understanding how these two processes are interrelated and how subjectivation involves the notions of subject, subjection, and intersubjectivity.

The concept of subject

The concept of subject is a post-Freudian concept, but its premises were set out by Freud (in "Instincts and Their Vicissitudes", 1915c) when he represented the subject [*der Subjekt*] in terms of the twofold movement that constitutes him—that is to say, by the turning round of the active/passive instinctual polarities and by the reversal of the correlative positions of the object and the subject, of the ego and the other. Having been the passive object of the instinctual impulses of the other, the subject imposes on his own ego a passivity that transforms it into the object of his own impulses. It is worth noting that in this text, Freud suggests there is a link between the concept of subject, instinctual activity, and our links with others.

Lacan's critique of the confusion between the ego and the subject introduces another perspective: the subject is fundamentally a structurally divided subject who is subject to the formations and processes of the unconscious. In the Lacanian model, the subject is under the effect of—subject to—the primal *Spaltung* constitutive of the psyche, which Freud had already remarked on in 1895. The concept of subjectivation is not found in Lacan's work. To the extent that subjectivation implies a process of transformation and historicization, this concept does not find its place in Lacan's radical structuralism.

I think that both these conceptions are precious, but insufficient: the subject is not only subject to the reversal of the passive/active polarities of the instinct and to the reversal of the positions ego–others. He is not only divided from within; he is also divided in his relations with the other and with more than one other.

If we return briefly to the group clinical experience and focus our attention on Marc, we will see that his enigmatic confession signals quite precisely his position as subject, in the sense that Freud gave to this notion. Marc presents himself as a passive object of sadistic impulses that he attributes to the analyst of the earlier group; then he appropriates for himself the position of subject by reversing the polarities of these impulses onto himself, but also onto others: onto Jacques, for example. The movements of the transference reverse the correlative positions of the object and the subject, of the ego and the other.

Subjection

The concept of subject would not be sufficiently developed if we were not to introduce another notion, that of subjection. The Freudian subject who proceeds from instinctual reversals and from the reversals of positions, or the Lacanian subject who is constituted under the effect of the structural splitting [*die Spaltung*] of the psyche is a *subjected* subject. The subject of the unconscious is a subject subjected to the formations and processes of the unconscious; he is subject to an order, an agency, a law that constitutes him as subject. Linked to subjection is the notion of a correlative assignation of the subject and the object to locations governed by the demand for work of the instinct, by phantasy scenarios, and by the abandonment of the ego's identifications prior to adopting new ones in the service of the Ideal. Let me underscore the paradox of the subject: he is subjected and structured in this subjection. It is because he has been subjected that the process of subjectivation is possible—unless, that is, the subjection has become fixated in alienation.[2]

Subjection is not only an internal process. It also forms part of the mutual relations of the subject and the other. It will be recalled how the psychic combination of the members of the group occurred on the basis of a common and shared unconscious organizer: "A child is being threatened/repaired." This phantasy is an attractor of phantasy scenarios. Its effect is twofold: first, to construct the psychic consistency of the group; and second, to avoid singularizing the subjectivizing versions of each participant in his secondary phantasy.

Marc is subjected not only to his impulses and his unconscious phantasy; he is also subjected to the relations that he forms with the unconscious of the other members of the group. The psychic reality of the group that is organized around Marc's confession subjects everyone to the unconscious alliances that maintain the repression and the denial. This subjection in the negative pact saves Marc—but also the others—from having to recognize his unconscious phantasy and his position of subject. Subjected to his unconscious phantasy, Marc assigned himself first to the place of victim (passiveness suffered) and then, through a reversal of the instinctual polarities and the locations in the phantasy, into an executioner (active). In this situation of self-alienation, he remains split off from the unconscious stakes of his phantasy and stays alienated in the desire of the other, which I represent for him in the transference.

Access to secondary phantasy and the process of subjectivation: extrication from the "We" and the "One", and gaining access to the I

The intersubjective process and the internal work of the subject open the way to the process of subjectivation. They support him in his efforts to extricate himself from the alienating identifications and unconscious alliances that keep him in subjection. Clinical work teaches us in no uncertain manner that de-subjection entails complex and correlative movements of de-assignation in the intrapsychic and intersubjective locations, and that these movements necessarily involve the experience of separation, of disillusionment (of narcissistic collapse), of extrication from self-alienation in alienating unconscious alliances.

In the group, transformation is singularized from the moment when the organizing phantasy is integrated by the subjects as a constituent part of their subjectivity; that is to say, when the phantasy ceases to function only in the impersonal and anonymous mode that is characteristic of the primal unconscious.

To find his way towards subjectivation, Marc had to extricate himself from the position that he occupied in the phantasy: the group as a whole had kept him in it, with his unconscious consent and with the support of the negative pact that had bound them together. Marc had been the bearer of a shared symptom, supported on several sides, in his own economy and in that of the group. He had thus also been the bearer of the resistance to the work of analysis. He had to extricate himself from the transference that he had established onto me, onto my colleague, onto a participant, and onto the group. His transference onto Jacques made this possible: as if in a mirror, he placed him in his own role of son. He seduced and threatened him. As in his secondary phantasy, a double reversal occurred: first, a reversal of the wish to be seduced into the father's threat towards his son; and, second, a reversal of the threat suffered into a threat acted out in the transference towards a son who represents himself in his relationship to his father.

We have noted that this subjectivizing change in the relation to the phantasy entails a vacillation of the ego in its identifications: the ego's anxieties of being abandoned by its objects of identifications appear, linked to a correlative change in the ego and its links with its objects.

During the last sessions, someone reminded Marc of the way he had introduced himself to the group at the beginning: "*I am called* Marc", he had said. Marc had then identified himself with the "mark" of his subjection to an other, whom he had hitherto been unable to name. At the end of the psychoanalytic work with the group, Marc was able to recognize in his own name what, for him, was the mark of the traumatic violence of his phantasy of homosexual seduction by his father: "Elsewhere, in the past, a marking event had prohibited me from thinking of myself as the son of this father." He was then able to come to terms with the "I" that bears his name and name the father from whom he had received this name. He inscribed himself no longer in my name but in that of his father. This transformation was the culmination of the process of Marc's subjectivizing identifications through his work in this group.

It could be said, then, drawing on Freud's adage,[3] that where unconscious alliances were, and where they always are, the I can come into being, provided it extricates itself from the alienated subject in the identifications and unconscious alliances that keep it in subjection. It would thus be illusory to think that subjectivation occurs once and for all, that overcoming this condition of alienation leaves no traces. Psychic life oscillates between contrary movements in the process of "becoming I". The subject who is in the process of "becoming I" constantly reconstructs his history as he subjectivizes himself. It is in this respect that the work of historicization is a work that takes place in a succession of "deferred actions" [*après-coups*].

Subjectivation and intersubjectivity

Subjectivation is a process of transformation of the subject for which the I takes responsibility, and this process is affected by intersubjectivity—that is to say, the situation of the subjects of the unconscious in linking. One could also say that the condition of the process of subjectivation is intersubjectivity.

I have used the term "intersubjectivity" to refer to the dynamic structure of the psychic space between two or several subjects. This common, joint, shared, and differentiated space comprises specific processes, formations, and experience through which each subject constitutes himself, a part of which concerns his own unconscious. In this space, under certain conditions—in particular that of extricating himself from the alliances that keep him in subjection to the effects of the unconscious, but that also structure him—a process of subjectivation makes it possible to become an "I" who can think about his place within a "We".

We can complete the concept of intersubjectivity with the concept of *work of intersubjectivity*. I have used it several times in this book to indicate that intersubjectivity is to be envisaged from a dynamic standpoint: it imposes on the mind a demand for psychic work, owing precisely to the subject's necessary intersubjective situation. This demand for work on the mind duplicates that which is imposed on it by its necessary relation with bodily experience. It can be described in terms of the major prohibitions and obligations that the group imposes on its subjects in order to establish and maintain its own order. From this ensue some reformulations concerning the theory of anaclisis and the articulation between drive and intersubjectivity, the common and shared dream space, and the dream navels. It stamps the formation, systems, agencies, and processes of the psychic apparatus, and consequently the unconscious, with specific contents and modes of functioning. These obligations and these demands have as their correlate that the subject subscribes to them and, in certain cases, requires them in order to establish his own existence.

The concept of the work of intersubjectivity comprises the idea that each subject is represented and seeks to have himself represented in the object-relations, imagos, identifications, and unconscious phantasies of an other and of a set of others. Likewise, each subject forms links in psychic formations of this sort with the representatives of other subjects, with the objects of the objects that he harbours within himself. He binds them together.

If I call the work of intersubjectivity the psychic work of the unconscious of the other and of more-than-an-other in the psyche of the subject of the unconscious, this entails several consequences for our conception of the unconscious and of the subject of the unconscious. It is this that I would like to examine now.

The position of the subject of the unconscious
in intersubjectivity

The subject of the unconscious is a subject of linking

Among the concepts that have been developed to account for psychic reality in the group (the group psychic apparatus, phoric functions, the work of intersubjectivity, the common and shared dream space), the concept of unconscious alliances has opened up an effective path for analysing the process of the formation of the subject of the unconscious in intersubjectivity. By virtue of their structure, contents, and functions, unconscious alliances are the base and cement of the psychic reality that links us to one another: they form the material of the psychic reality that is characteristic of intersubjective links: a couple, a family, a group, or an institution. Unconscious alliances are effective at another level: they are one of the modes of production of the repressed unconscious and of the non-repressed unconscious required for forming links or ties. They fabricate a part of the unconscious of each subject: each one of us is the subject of such alliances. They are constitutive of the psychic reality of the individual subject, insofar as he is the subject of linking. (I have developed these propositions more fully in Kaës, 1993.)

Unconscious alliances are involved in the formation processes of the unconscious owing to the portion of the unconscious of the other (or of more than one other) that returns in the formation of the unconscious of the subject. Insofar as this is the case, we can speak of co-repression, co-disavowal, and co-denial. The field of psychoanalysis thus opens out onto all the configurations of the relations between one subject's denial and another's hallucination, between one subject's rejection and another's symptom. Formations of the unconscious are expelled, projected, exported by a subject or by a group of subjects into another psychic place: into the psyche of another or of several subjects, whether they are currently gathered together or whether they are linked intergenerationally.

In primary intersubjective ensembles (mother–child dyad, parental couple, family) and secondary ensembles (groups, institutions), formations of the unconscious are transmitted through the chain of generations and that of contemporaries, according to modalities fixed by alliances, pacts, and unconscious covenants. The formation of the superego and the functions of the Ideal also follow this inter-subjective determination.

Some of the alliances precede us. Unconscious alliances are at work in the formation processes of the unconscious and of the sub-jectivity of the subjects who have formed a union from the begin-ning—that is, before the arrival of the subject in the world. Each one of us comes into the world of psychic life within the web of the alliances that have been established before him, in which his place is marked out in advance. This place, which constitutes him in his subjectivity, can only be maintained insofar as he, in turn, subscribes to the terms of the alliance prescribed for him, but also for the en-semble. The history of his formation as I is simultaneously both that of his subjection to this place, and that of the gaps that the subject will have to experience and maintain with respect to this prescribed place.[4]

I have proposed that the subject of these alliances is the subject of the unconscious and that, correlatively, his alliance with the un-conscious of the other or of more than one other qualifies him as the subject of the unconscious. The subject of the unconscious is formed in the division between the fulfilment of his own purposes and his inscription in intersubjective ties. The subject of the uncon-scious is an "intersubject" ineluctably subjected to an intersubjective ensemble of subjects of the unconscious. This double status of the subject, and the demands for psychic work that are contradictorily associated with it owing to the fact that he is linked to intersubjective ensembles, divide him from within and form a compromise with the constitutive division of the unconscious.

One consequence of these propositions is that there exists for one part of each subject of the unconscious an ectopograpical or extratopographical locus, a *topos* that is inaccessible with the means of its *first* method—the practice of the individual treatment—and thus unthinkable with the categories of the metapsychology derived from it.

Some metapsychological reformulations concerning the theory of the unconscious

Our knowledge of the unconscious is not exhausted by the experience that individual psychoanalytic treatment makes possible. The metapsychology that has been developed needs to be revised when the practice of psychoanalysis is modified and when our knowledge of the psychic apparatus is transformed. The hypothesis of a psyche shared in intersubjectivity leads us to build models of intelligibility for this reality, its consistency, its structures, and its laws of transformation.

It is fitting therefore to conceptualize a third topography,[5] or a third metapsychology capable of accounting for the unconscious in intersubjectivity. The concepts of unconscious alliances, phoric functions, and polyphonic dream space have a double valency, subjective and intersubjective; they go some of the way towards furnishing an answer to the second question of how to conceptualize the organization of a common and shared psychic space.

The double metapsychological status of the concepts proposed

All the concepts to which I have just referred have a double metapsychological status. They are bifacial psychic configurations, organized on both sides. They do not belong exclusively to the individual subject, although he is party to, and a constituent part of, the ensemble, nor to the ensemble that would not exist without its subjects. We can describe them from the standpoint from which they produce and bind the unconscious material of intersubjective links, and we can understand them according to the terms of an *intersubjective* topography, economy, and dynamic. We can also describe them from the point of view of the *intrapsychic* organization of each individual subject: unconscious alliances are contracted and kept unconscious in order to realize the unconscious wishes of each subject; they are one of the modes of production of the repressed unconscious and of the non-repressed unconscious required of each of them in exchange for being part of the link.

These two points of view are dialogically related to each other: clinical work shows us that any modification in the alliances, contracts, or pacts that form the basis of the common and shared psychic reality of intersubjective links or ties calls into question the unconscious psychic structure of each subject. Reciprocally, any modification of the structure, economy, or dynamic of the subject—during a treatment, for example, or in adolescence, or during a divorce—is opposed by the forces that maintain the alliances concluded in the link of which the subject is a constitutive part.

Topographies of the unconscious

I can only outline this metapsychology here. A third topography needs to be developed to take account of the heterogeneous, ectopographical, and heterotopographical character of the unconscious. Other psychic loci serve as its depositaries and agents of production and transformation. The psychic spaces of linking are these other places of the unconscious, the processes and formations, economy and dynamics with which we are now more familiar.

Unconscious alliances, phoric functions, and common and shared dreams have a double topography: the alliances are situated at the nodal points of the repressed relations maintained by individual subjects and ensembles, at this point of conjunction, which is not that of a collective formation, but that of intersubjectivity. This plural topography encourages us to think that the unconscious is not entirely contained within the limits of individual psychic space. It cannot be totally localized in the first or the second topography of Freud's metapsychology. The psychic space of linking and that of ensembles are different spaces in the unconscious. The concepts of ectopography and polytopography could account for this metapsychology of the places of the psyche.

The composite dynamics of psychic conflicts

We need to build a new dynamic of the unconscious. Psychoanalytic work in the group situation modifies our conception of unconscious psychic conflict. Alongside the intrapsychic conflict of infantile psychosexual origin, there exists an unconscious conflict between the subject and the portion of his psyche that is in the possession of an other (or more than one other), or deposited in him (or them). Freud indicated one of the aspects of this in "On Narcissism: An Introduction" (1914c): the subject is divided between the demands imposed on him by the necessity of serving his own purposes and those that derive from his status and function as a member of an intersubjective chain, of which he is at one and the same time the servant, the link of transmission, the heir, and the actor.

From this point of view, the analysis of unconscious alliances has taught us that they are metadefences in the service of the repressing or denying function, and that in this sense they are measures for reduplicating the repression and denial, since they concern not only unconscious contents but the alliance itself: the latter remains unaware of the unconscious that it produces and maintains.

I have described how the major defensive operations constitutive of the unconscious in defensive alliances operate: defences through repression and denial, rejection, exportation, disavowal, depositing, or effacement. Either the same operations are carried out by all the subjects of a bond, or, alternatively, some repress while others deny. Clinically, the heterogeneous configuration is more effective for extricating oneself from alliances: when the return of the repressed occurs in certain subjects, it transforms the balance of the alliance by revealing its non-repressed/denied nuclei. This movement is one of the levers for getting out of a perverse contract or a mixed alliance such as the negating alliance. Unconscious alliances are the result of compromises concluded and maintained between several subjects. They are in the service of the production and maintenance of symptoms, subject to the interests of each individual: the alliance is their servant. Unconscious alliances do not only maintain the function of misrecognition that is attached to the symptom: the production of shared symptoms accomplishes, in addition, the aim of subjecting each subject to his symptom in relation to the function that he fulfils for an other, or for more than one other, in and for the link. The symptom is thus significantly reinforced and overdetermined, which increases the difficulty of unbinding it.

Elements of a crossed economy

A new economy needs to be elaborated. The pertinence of the economic point of view resides in the notion of psychic work. Our analysis of the combination and adjustment of psyches has taught us how linking mobilizes instinctual energy in each of the members and organizes itself with a view to mastering and transforming excitations, the accumulation of which can be pathogenic. The apparatus of the bond is a metapsychic tool for the management and transformation of the individual psyches, but it also a structure that forms and informs them.

An important aspect of the crossed psychic economy is the transfer of the individual economy towards the economy of linking, and vice versa. Displacements of energy occur from one pole of the group psychic apparatus to another, but the charges of investment are also distributed to several objects in the group, who are more or less correlated between themselves. Research into the process of diffraction has highlighted how the transfer and transmission [*die Übertragung*] of energetic charges onto all the components of the links takes place. This notion is useful to us for understanding the clinical experience of lateral transferences and countertransferences in the processes of the so-called individual treatment: the economic organization of the transferences in Dora's treatment, as in Emma's, could serve to illustrate these points.

NOTES

1. I wish to acknowledge my debt here to the major contributions of Castoriadis-Aulagnier (1984), who introduced us to the notion that the subject is a subject in a process of becoming, transformed by the process of historicization, through which he comes into being as I.

2. There is a strong link between subjection and *alienation*. Subjection does not have as its correlate alienation, but alienation is one of the vicissitudes of subjection. Alienation is the abandonment or the sacrifice of a part of the self in favour of the power of an internal or external other (agency,

person, idea, etc.). An example of self-alienation is the abandonment of the identifications of the ego in favour of the demands of the Ideal.

3. *"Wo Es war, soll Ich werden"*: in German *Ich* means I [*Je*] or ego [*Moi*]. I opt for the translation that stresses the notion of "becoming I" [*devenir Je*] for the I is different from the subject and the ego.

4. I should like to point out that the perspective opened up by Casto-riadis-Aulagnier concerning the narcissistic contract and the functions of speech-bearer inscribes the formation of the psychic apparatus within the confines of intrapsychic reality, language, and intersubjectivity: it overlaps and articulates them (see chapters 8 and 10 herein).

5. The necessity of constructing a third topography became clear to me as early as 1976 with the model of the group psychic apparatus. I have set out the perspectives and modalities of this in several texts (Kaës, 1993, 1999a) and more recently in my course at the IPA Congress, March 2004.

Epilogue

The epistemological debate initiated at the beginning of this book situated the principal concern of this work beyond "applied psychoanalysis".

With the group, we have changed vertex: we have passed from the "one by one" of individual analysis to the "several together" and the "one among others" of the group. This change has obliged us to conceptualize the organization of the psychic reality and forms of subjectivity that develop at the frontiers of the intrapsychic space and the intersubjective space.

In this process, the obstacles encountered have been of different orders.

New methodological settings have made it possible to treat, in a way that is different from speculation, the psychic experience of the unconscious to which they opened up a path of access. But it was necessary to constitute on sufficiently secure methodological bases a field of practice and research that conserves its psychoanalytic properties while evolving from the characteristics of the individual treatment.

This methodological difficulty was increased by a formidable epistemological problem: could the concepts built from the setting of individual analysis be "applied" without distortion to what proved to be a quite different and, in any case, specific psychic reality in these new psychoanalytic settings? This was a troubling question that would call into doubt certain assertions of the theory, if, that is, it turned out that the findings derived from psychoanalytic practice in the group situation brought to light new configurations of the processes and formations of the unconscious.

Only clinical experience, and the comparative clinical experience of diverse psychoanalytic practices centred on configurations of linking, has made it possible to qualify the consistency of the psychic reality of the intersubjective links in groups, families, couples, and institutions. This reality, its processes and its formations, are accessible only by means of such settings. One still has the task of specifying to which experiences of the unconscious the diverse settings of psychoanalysis give access; and, further, how and with which concepts and models we can conceptualize them.

Once this work had been embarked on, other questions emerged: do these experiences and concepts have an effect on our representation of psychic life, of the unconscious, and of the subject; and moreover, is the field of the theoretical and practical objects of psychoanalysis thereby modified?

It has thus been necessary to revisit on a different basis this old epistemological problem, which still remains to be resolved: if we introduce a methodological paradigm other than that of the individual treatment into the field of psychoanalytic practice while preserving its fundamental postulate, does this imply the need to reshape the metapsychology of the psychic apparatus and to reformulate the question of the subject of the unconscious? If we have built a new epistemological paradigm, should we not consequently ask ourselves once again what psychoanalysis accounts for and what it does not account for?

Throughout this research, I have had to accept the fact that in working on the frontiers between the subjective space and the intersubjective space we are faced with crossed or mixed forms of reality, with mixed formations, with "mixed blood", as the instinctual drive and phantasy were for Freud, on the frontiers of the bodily and the psychic. Crossing brings with it doubts about the stability of the territories of thought and the frameworks of practice. These doubts can lead to moments of solitude, disarray, and discouragement; but they are fruitful. The history of psychoanalysis attests to this fact, which gives us reason to have hope in its creativity, its revolutionary potential, and its capacity to heal.

In adopting this position, I wanted to inscribe the method of this research and its results within the framework of a contribution to the theory and general practice of psychoanalysis in the contemporary world.

REFERENCES AND BIBLIOGRAPHY

Abraham, N., & Torok, M. (1978). *L'écorce et le noyau*. Paris: Aubier-Flammarion.

Amati Sas, S. (2005). "La transsubjectivité entre cadre et ambiguité." Unpublished manuscript.

Anzieu, D. (1959). *L'auto-analyse de Freud*. Paris: PUF, 1959. [English: *Freud's Self-Analysis*, trans. P. Graham. Madison, CT: International Universities Press, 1986.]

Anzieu, D. (1966). Etude psychanalytique des groupes réels. *Les Temps Modernes, 242*: 56–73.

Anzieu, D. (1971). L'illusion groupale. *Nouvelle Revue de Psychanalyse, 4*: 73–93.

Anzieu, D. (1975). *Le groupe et l'inconscient*. Paris: Dunod.

Anzieu, D. (1985). *Le moi-peau*. Paris: Dunod. [English: *The Skin Ego: A Psychoanalytic Approach to the Self*, trans. C. Turner. London: Karnac, 1989.]

Aulagnier-Spairani, P., Clavreul, J., Perrier, F., Rosolato, G., & Valabraga, J.-P. (1967). *Le désir et la perversion*. Paris: Seuil.

Avron, O. (1996). *La pensée scénique. Group et psychodrame*. Ramonville St Agne: Érès.

Bakhtine, M., & Vorochilov, V. N. (1929). *Le marxism et la philosophie du language: Essai d'application de le méthode sociologique en linguistique*. Paris: Les Éditions de Minuit, 1977.

Bakhtine, M., & Vorochilov, V. N. (1934–35). Le discours du roman. In: *Ésthé-*

tique et théorie du roman. Paris: Gallimard, 1978. [English: Discourse in the novel. In: *The Dialogical Imagination: Four Essays*, ed. M. Holquist, trans. Caryl Emerson & M. Holquist. Austin, TX: University of Texas, 1981.]

Bakhtine, M., & Vorochilov, V. N. (1963). *La poétique de Dostoïevski*, Paris: Seuil, 1970. [English: *Problems of Dostoievsky's Poetics*. Ann Arbor, MI: Ardis, 1973.]

Baranger, M., & Baranger, W. (1964). *Problemas del campo psicoanálitico*. Buenos Aires: Kargieman.

Bejarano, A. (1972). Résistance et transfert dans les groupes. In: D. Anzieu, A. Bejarano, R. Kaës, A. Missenard, & J. B. Pontalis (Eds.), *Le travail psychanalytique dans les groupes*. Paris: Dunod, 1976.

Benson, R., & Pryor, D. (1973). Le compagnon imaginaire. *Nouvelle Revue de Psychanalyse, 13* (1976): 237–251.

Bion, W. R. (1950). The imaginary twin. In: *Second Thoughts*. London: Heinemann, 1967.

Bion, W. R. (1961). *Experiences in Groups*. London: Tavistock.

Bion, W. R. (1965) *Transformations*. London: Heinemann.

Bleger, J. (1966). Psicoanálisis del encuadre psicoanálitico. In: *Simbiosis y Ambigüedad*. Buenos Aires: Paidos. [English: Psycho-analysis of the psychoanalytic frame. *International Journal of Psychoanalysis, 48* (1967): 511–519.]

Bleger, J. (1967). *Simbiosis y ambigüedad*. Buenos Aires: Paidos.

Bleger, J. (1970). El grupo como institución y el grupo en las instituciones. In: *Temas de Psicología. Entrevistas y grupos* (pp. 89–104). Buenos Aires, Nueva Visión.

Burrow, T. (1927). The group method of analysis. *Psychoanalytic Review, 14*: 268–280.

Castoriadis-Aulagnier, P. (1967) *Le désir et la perversion*. Paris: Seuil.

Castoriadis-Aulagnier, P. (1975). *La violence de l'interprétation. Du pictogramme à l'énoncé*. Paris: Presses Universitaires de France. [English: *The Violence of Interpretation*, trans. A. Sheridan. London: Brunner-Routledge, 2001.]

Castoriadis-Aulagnier, P. (1984). *L'apprenti-historien et le maître-sorcier. Du discours identifiant au discours aliénant*. Paris: Presses Universitaires de France.

Clavreul, J. (1967). Le couple pervers. In: P. Aulagnier-Spairani, J. Clavreul, et al., *Le désir et la perversion*. Paris: Seuil.

Corrao, F. (1981). Struttura poliadica e funzione gamma. *Gruppo e Funzione Analitica, 2*: 25–32.

Couchoud, M.-Th. (1986). Du refoulement à la fonction dénégatrice. *Topique, 37*: 93–133.

Devereux, G. (1972). *Ethnopsychanalyse complémentariste*. Paris: Flammarion.

Diet, E. (1996). Le thanatophore. Travail de la mort et destructivité dans les institutions. In: R. Kaës, J.-P. Pinel, O. Kernberg, et al., *Souffrance et psychopathologie des liens institutionnels*. Paris: Dunod.

Dodds, E. (1959). *The Greeks and the Irrational.* Berkeley, CA: University of California Press.

Enriquez, M. (1984). *La souffrance et la haine.* Paris: Dunod, 2001.

Fain, M. (1981). Diachronie, structure, conflit oedipien. Quelques réflexions. *Revue française de psychanalyse, 45* (4): 985–997.

Fogelman-Soulié, F. (Ed.) (1991). *Les théories de la complexité, autour de l'œuvre d'H. Atlan. Cerisy Colloquium.* Paris: Seuil.

Foulkes, S. H. (1948). *Introduction to Group-Analytic Psychotherapy.* London: Heinemann.

Foulkes, S. H. (1964). *Therapeutic Group-Analysis.* London: George Allen & Unwin.

Freud, S. (1887–1904). *The Complete Letters of Sigmund Freud to Wilhelm Fliess, 1887–1904*, trans. and ed. J. M. Masson. Cambridge, MA/London: Harvard University Press, 1985.

Freud, S. (1897). Draft L (2 May 1897). In: *The Complete Letters of Sigmund Freud to Wilhelm Fliess, 1887–1904* (pp. 240–242), trans. and ed. J. M. Masson. Cambridge, MA/London: Harvard University Press, 1985.

Freud, S. (1895d) (with Breuer, J.). *Studies on Hysteria. S.E.*, 2.

Freud, S. (1900a). *The Interpretation of Dreams, S.E.*, 4–5.

Freud, S. (1901a). *On Dreams. S.E.*, 5.

Freud, S. (1905d). *Three Essays on the Theory of Sexuality. S.E.*, 7.

Freud, S. (1905e [1901]). Fragment of an analysis of a case of hysteria. *S.E.*, 7.

Freud, S. (1909d). Notes upon a case of obsessional neurosis. *S.E.*, 10.

Freud, S. (1911c [1910]). Psycho-analytic notes on an autobiographical account of a case of paranoia (dementia paranoides). *S.E.*, 12, 1–82.

Freud, S. (1912–13). *Totem and Taboo. S.E.*, 13.

Freud, S. (1914c). On narcissism: An introduction. *S.E.*, 14.

Freud, S. (1915c). *Instincts and Their Vicissitudes. S.E.*, 14.

Freud, S. (1919e). A child is being beaten. *S.E.*, 17.

Freud, S. (1921c). *Group Psychology and the Analysis of the Ego. S.E.*, 18.

Freud, S. (1923a). Two encyclopaedia articles. *S.E.*, 18.

Freud, S. (1923b). *The Ego and the Id. S.E.*, 19.

Freud, S. (1926e). *The Question of Lay Analysis. S.E.*, 20.

Freud, S. (1927c). *The Future of an Illusion. S.E.*, 21.

Freud, S. (1930a). *Civilization and Its Discontents. S.E.*, 21.

Freud, S. (1933a). *New Introductory Lectures on Psycho-Analysis. S.E.*, 22.

Freud, S. (1950 [1895]). Project for a scientific psychology. *S.E.*, 1.

Gaburri, E. (1999). Les constellations oniriques et le champ du groupe. *Funzione gamma, 1* (available at: http://www.funzionegamma.edu).

Gaburri, E., & Ambrosiano, L. (2003). *Ulalare con i lupi. Conformismo e rêverie.* Turin: Bollati Boringhieri.

Gallese, V., Eagle, M., & Migone, P. (2007). Intentional attunement: Mirror neurons and the neural underpinnings of interpersonal relations, *Journal of the American Psychoanalytic Association, 55*: 131–176.

Green, A. (1972). Notes sur les processus tertiaires. *Revue Française de Psychanalyse, 36* (3): 407–411.

Green, A. (1983) *Narcissisme de vie, narcissisme de mort.* Paris: Editions Minuit. [English: *Life Narcissism, Death Narcissism,* trans. Andrew Weller. London: Free Association Books, 2001.]

Guillaumin, J. (1979). *Le rêve et le Moi. Rupture, continuité, création dans la vie psychique.* Paris: Presses Universitaires de France.

Guillaumin, J. (1994). Les contrebandiers du transfert ou le contre-transfert et le débordement du cadre par la réalité extérieure. *Revue Française de Psychanalyse, 5*: 1481–1520.

Jaques, E. (1955). Social systems as a defence against persecutory and depressive anxiety. In: M. Klein, P. Heimann, & R. Money-Kyrle (Eds.), *New Directions in Psychoanalysis* (pp. 478–498). London: Tavistock, 1985.

Kaës, R. (1976). *L'appareil psychique groupal: Constructions du groupe.* Paris: Dunod (new edition, 2000).

Kaës, R. (1979). Introduction à l'analyse transitionelle. In: R. Kaës, A. Missenard, D. Anzieu, J. Bleger, & J. Guillaumin (Eds.), *Crise, rupture et dépassement. Analyse transitionelle en psychanalyse individuelle et groupale.* Paris: Dunod.

Kaës, R. (1980). *L'idéologie. Études Psychanalytiques. Mentalité de l'idéal et esprit de corps.* Paris: Dunod.

Kaës, R. (1982). L'intertransfert et l'interprétation dans le travail psychanalytique groupal. In: R. Kaës, A. Missenard, et al. (Eds.), *Le travail psychanalytique dans les groupes, 2: Les voies de l'élaboration* (pp. 103–177). Paris: Dunod.

Kaës, R. (1985a). La catégorie de l'intermédiaire chez Freud. Un concept pour la psychanalyse? *L'Évolution Psychiatrique, 50* (4): 893–926.

Kaës, R. (1985b). L'hystérique et le groupe. *L'Évolution Psychiatrique, 50* (1): 129–156.

Kaës, R. (1989a). Le pacte dénegatif. Éléments pour une métapsychologie des ensembles transsubjectifs. In: A. Missenard, G., Rosolato, et al., *Figures et modalités du négatif* (pp. 101–136). Paris: Dunod.

Kaës, R. (1989b). Ruptures catastrophiques et travail de la mémoire. In: J. Pujet, R. Kaës, et al., *Violence d'état et psychanalyse.* Paris: Dunod.

Kaës, R. (1992). Le complexe fraternal. Aspects de sa spécificité. *Topique, 50*: 263–300.

Kaës, R. (1993). *Le groupe et le sujet du groupe. Éléments pour une théorie psychanalytiques des groupes.* Paris: Dunod.

Kaës, R. (1994a). La matrice groupale de l'invention de la psychanalyse. Esquisse pour une analyse du premier cercle autour de Freud. In: R. Kaës (Ed.), *Les voies de la psyché. Hommage à Didier Anzieu* (pp. 373–392). Paris: Dunod.

Kaës, R. (1994b). *La parole et le lien: Les processus associatifs dans les groupes.* Paris: Dunod (new edition, 2005).

Kaës, R. (1998). L'intersubjectivité. Un fondement de la vie psychique. Repères dans la pensée de Piera Aulagnier. *Topique, 64*: 45–73.

Kaës, R. (1999a). La parole, le jeu, et le travail du Préconscient dans le psychodrame psychanalytique de groupe. In: R. Kaës, A. Missenard, et al., *Le psychodrame psychanalytique des groupes.* Paris: Dunod.

Kaës, R. (1999b). *Les théories psychanalytiques du groupe.* Paris: Presses Universitaires de France.

Kaës, R. (2000). Travail de la mort et théorisation. Le groupe autour de Freud entre 1910 et 1921. In: J. Guillaumin et al., *L'invention de la pulsion de mort.* Paris: Dunod.

Kaës, R. (2001). Psychoanalysis and institutions in France. In: R. Hinshelwood & M. Chiesa (Eds.), *Organisations, Anxieties and Defences: Towards a Psychoanalytic Social Psychology* (pp. 97–123). London/Philadephia: Wuhrr Publishers.

Kaës, R. (2002a). The polyphonic texture of intersubjectivity in the dream. In: C. Neri, M. Pines, & R. Friedman (Eds.), *Dreams in Group Psychotherapy* (pp. 67–78). London/Philadelphia: Jessica Kingsley.

Kaës, R. (2002b). *La polyphonie du rêve: L'espace onirique commun et partagé.* Paris: Dunod.

Kaës, R. (2003). Les processus et les formations archaïques dans les groupes. *Le Journal de la Psychanalyse de L'enfant, 32*: 51–74.

Kaës, R. (2004). Sogno o mito? Due forme et due destini dell'immaginario. In: S. Marinelli & F. N. Vasta (Eds.), *Mito Sogno Gruppo* (pp. 19–30). Rome: Borla.

Kaës, R. (2005). Les dépressions conjointes dans les espaces psychiques communs et partagés. In: C. Chabert, R. Kaës, J. Lanouzière, & A. Schiewind, *Figures de la dépression* (pp. 159–229). Paris: Dunod.

Kaës, R. (2006). La matrice groupale de la subjectivation. Les alliances inconscientes. In: F. Richard & S. Wainrib (Eds.), *La subjectivation.* Paris: Dunod.

Kaës, R., Faimberg, H., Enriquez, M., & Baranes, J. J. (1993). *La transmission de la vie psychique entre les générations.* Paris: Dunod.

Klein, M. (1930). The importance of symbol-formation in the development of the ego. *International Journal of Psychoanalysis, 11*: 24–39.

Klein, M. (1933). The early development of conscience in the child. In: *Psychoanalysis Today*. New York: Covici-Friede.

Kreisler, L. (1984). Bébés de mères endeuillées. *Revue du Centre Alfred Binet* (July).

Lacan, J. (1938). La famille. 1. Le complexe, facteur concret de la psychologie familiale. *Encyclopédie Française, 8*: 840–848.

Lacan, J. (1973). L'Étoudit. *Scilicet, 4:* 5–52.

Laing, R. D. (1969). *The Politics of the Family.* Toronto: CBC Publications.

Laplanche, J., & Pontalis, J.-B. (1964). Fantasme originaire, fantasmes des origines, origine du fantasme. *Les Temps Modernes, 215*: 1833–1868 (Paris: Editions Hachette, 1985).

Laplanche, J., & Pontalis, J.-B. (1973). *The Language of Psychoanalysis*, trans. Donald Nicholson Smith. London: Hogarth Press. [First published in French: *Vocabulaire de la psychanalyse*. Paris: Presses Universitaires de France, 1967.]

Lawrence, G. W. (Ed). (1998). *Social Dreaming.* London: Karnac.

Lévy-Bruhl, L. (1922). *La mentalité primitive.* Paris: PUF. [English: *Primitive Mentality*, trans. L. A. Clare. London: Allen & Unwin, 1923.]

Masson, J. M. (Trans., Ed.) (1985). *The Complete Letters of Sigmund Freud to Wilhelm Fliess, 1887–1904*. Cambridge, MA/London: Harvard University Press.

Missenard, A. (1972). Identification et processus groupal. In: D. Anzieu, A. Bejarano, et al., *Le travail psychanalytique dans les groupes. 1. Cadre et processus*. Paris: Dunod.

Missenard, A. (1985). Rêves de l'un, rêves de l'autre. *Psychiatries, 67* (4): 43–58.

Missenard, A. (1987). L'enveloppe du rêve et le fantasme de psyché commune. In: D. Anzieu et al., *Les enveloppes psychiques*. Paris: Dunod.

Meltzer, D. (1984). *Dream-Life. A Re-examination of the Psycho-Analytical Theory and Technique.* Strath Tay: Clunie Press.

Modell, A. (1984). *Psychoanalysis in a New Context.* New York: International Universities Press.

Morin, E. (1977). *La méthode, 1. La nature de la méthode.* Paris: Seuil.

Morin, E. (1990). *Introduction à la pensée complexe.* Paris: E.S.F. éditeur.

Napolitani, D. (1987). *Individualità e gruppalità.* Turin: Boringhieri.

Neri, C. (1997). *Il gruppo.* Rome: Borla.

Neri, C. (2001). Introducción al sueño social y relato de dos workshop que tuvieron lugar en Raissa y Clarice Town. *Clínica y Análisis Grupal, 32* (2): 41–52.

Neri, C. (2004) Social dreaming. Sogno e narrazione. In: S. Marinelli & F. N. Vasta (Eds.), *Mito Sogno Gruppo.* Rome: Borla.

Neyraut, M. (1974). *Le transfert. Étude psychanalytique.* Paris: Presses Universitaires de France.

Nicolis, G., & Prigogine, I. (1989). *Exploring Complexity: An Introduction.* Munich: R. Piper.

Pasche, F. (1964). L'antinarcissisme. *Revue Française de Psychanalyse, 29* (5–6): 503–518.

Pichon-Rivière, E. (1970). El concepto de Portavoz. *Temas de Psicologia Social, 2* (1978): 11–20.

Pichon-Rivière, E. (1971). *El proceso grupal. Del psicoanálisis a la psicología social, 1.* Buenos-Aires: Nueva Visión, 1980.

Pichon-Rivière, E. (1980) (with Quiroga, A. de). *Teoria del vinculo.* Buenos Aires: Nueva Visión.

Pinel, J. P. (2001). Enseigner et éduquer en institution spécialisée. Approche clinique des liens d'équipe. *Connexion, 75* (1): 141–152.

Pines, M. (Ed.) (1983). *The Evolution of Group Analysis.* London: Routledge & Kegan Paul.

Pines, M. (1985). *Bion and Group Therapy.* London: Routledge & Kegan Paul.

Pontalis, J.-B. (1963). Le petit groupe comme objet. *Les Temps Modernes, 211*: 1057–1069.

Pontalis, J.-B. (1972). Rêves dans un groupe. In: D. Anzieu, R. Kaës, et al., *Le travail psychanalytique dans les groupes, 1. Cadre et processus.* Paris: Dunod.

Pujet, J. (2002). Qué dificil es pensar. Incertitumbre y perpljidad. *Psicoanalisis APdeBA:* 129–146.

Pujet, J., Bernard, M., Chaves, G. G., & Romano, E. (1982). *El grupo y sus configuraciones.* Buenos Aires: Lugar Editorial.

Rouchy, J.-C. (1980). Processus archaïques et transfert en analyse de groupe. *Connexions, 31*: 36–60.

Rouchy, J.-C. (1998). *Le groupe, espace analytique. Clinique et théorie.* Ramonville St Agne: Érès.

Ruffiot, A. (1981). Le groupe-famille en analyse. L'appareil psychique familial. In: A. Ruffiot, A. Eiguer, et al., *La thérapie familiale psychanalytique.* Paris: Dunod.

Ruitenbeek, H. M. (1966). *Freud and America.* New York: Macmillan.

Schur, M. (1966). Some additional "day's residues" of "The specimen dream of psychoanalysis". In: R. Loewenstein (Ed.), *Psychoanalysis: A General Psychology. Essays in Honor of Heinz Hartmann* (pp. 45–85). New York: International Universities Press.

Springman, R. (1976). La fragmentation en tant que défense dans les grands groupes. *L'Evolution Psychiatrique, 41* (2): 327–338.

Stolorow, R. D., & Atwood, G. E. (1992). *Contexts of Being. The Intersubjective Foundations of Psychological Life.* Hillsdale, NJ: Analytic Press.

Stroeken, H. (1985). *Freud en zijn patiënten. Elfder Ure.* Amsterdam: Muntinga. [French: *En analyse avec Freud.* Paris: Payot, 1987.]

Widlöcher, D. (1986). *Métapsychologie du sens.* Paris: Presses Universitaires de France.

Winnicott, D. (1951). Transitional objects and transitional phenomena. In: *Collected Papers: Through Paediatrics to Psycho-Analysis.* London: Tavistock, 1958.

Yalom, I. O. (1970). *The Theory and Practice of Group Psychotherapy.* New York: Basic Books.

INDEX

Abraham, N., 35, 169
abstinence, rule of, 71, 83
adhesive identification, 61, 124, 190, 205
agglutinated nucleus, 25, 26
alienating alliance, 212, 227
alienation, 6–7, 20, 30, 123, 225, 233, 235, 242
Allen, W., 101
alliance(s) (*passim*):
    alienating, 212, 226, 227
    categories of, 207
    defensive, 61, 207, 214, 218, 221, 223, 224, 228, 241
        unconscious, 218
    negating, 226, 241
    unconscious: *see* unconscious alliance(s)
alpha function, 155, 162, 188, 198
alterity, 5, 14, 152
    internal, 14
    of the other, 14
Amati Sas, S., 228
Ambrosiano, L., 204
anaclisis, 35, 58, 123, 131, 175, 236

analytic listening, 10, 33, 51
anti-narcissism, 228
anxieties:
    depressive, 22, 129
    paranoid, 22
    primitive, 26
    psychotic, 24
Anzieu, C., xii
Anzieu, D., xv, 2, 31–34, 36, 40, 51, 95, 109, 114, 115, 118, 127, 181–184, 214–216, 228, 229
après-coup [deferred action], 236
archaic processes, 34
Aristotle, 14
Association Psychanalytique de France, 30
associative chain(s), 13, 34, 62, 76, 124, 135–138, 140, 144, 148, 151, 152, 157, 174, 202, 217
associative functioning, group, 142
associative process(es) (*passim*):
    group, 63, 70, 84, 90, 91, 135–155
        analysis of, 154
        interdiscursivity of, 151
        nodal points of, 136–138

257

attractors, 49, 98, 119, 126
Atwood, G. E., 14
Avron, O., 34, 35

Bakhtine, M., 48, 152, 153
Balint, M., 18
  Balint groups, 17
Baranes, J. J., 67
Baranger, M., 132
Baranger, W., 132
basic assumption(s), 24, 27, 48, 109,
    115
basic group(s), 24
Bastide, R., 204
"battle–bedroom", 75–77, 82, 87, 143,
    146, 147
behavioural interactionism, 14
Bejarano, A., 31, 33, 228
belonging, 20, 25, 34
  group identity of, 25
  notion of, 34
Benson, R., 103
Beradt, C., 204
Berenstein, I., 227
Bernard, M., 21, 189
Bion, W. R., xv, 2, 9, 17, 19–20, 24,
    26–29, 32, 34, 40, 48, 51, 101,
    103, 109, 115, 129, 132, 155,
    162–165, 189, 195, 198
bisexuality, 88, 219
Bleger, J., 25–26, 29, 57–58, 67, 144,
    196
body image, 94, 95, 100
Bohr, N., 52
borderline:
  pathologies, 10, 17, 24, 26, 42, 56,
    65, 154
  patients, 10, 56
    use of group setting for, 17
Buber, M., 14
Burrow, T., 9

Caillois, R., 204
Caillot, J.-P., 35
Canetti, E., 9
cannibalism, 5, 210
Castoriadis-Aulagnier, P., 5, 7, 45, 103,

115, 121, 123, 155, 162, 164,
    165, 207, 211, 227, 242, 243
castration:
  anxiety, 91
  symbolic, 88
catastrophic change, 214, 216
chaos theory, 49
Charcot, J.-M., 133
Chaves, G. G., 21
child-bearer, 170
classical treatment setting, 18
Clavreul, J., 227
clinical examples, 69–92, 117–120,
    123, 124, 129, 137–155,
    165–169, 185–199, 213–218,
    233–235
co-excitation:
  instinctual, 119
  internal, 60
  mutual, 60
collective delusions, 218
collective mind [*Massenpsyche*], 10
collective traumas, use of group
    setting for, 17
common dream space, 13, 192, 194,
    195, 199, 200, 203
community:
  of denial, 207, 226
  of identifications, 224
complementarity, principle of, 47, 48
complexes, 94, 95, 100
  oedipal and fraternal, 94, 95, 100
complexity, 47, 49–51, 139
  principle of, 47, 49, 50
  theory of, 49
compromise formation(s), 158
condensation, 32, 100, 103–107, 114,
    124, 185, 202
container, metapsychic, 115
containing, capacity for, 175
contextualism, 14
contract(s):
  narcissistic, 5, 7, 45, 121, 122, 171,
    207, 211, 212, 243
  perverse, 207, 227, 241
Copernican cosmology, 48
Corrao, F., 165, 188

Couchoud, M. -Th., 226
counteridentification(s), 124
countertransference(s), 55, 60,
    65–66, 79, 80, 87, 92, 193–194,
    221–223, 225, 229, 242
  dreams, 181
crypt-bearer (cryptophor), 169

death:
  -bearer, 35, 40
  instinct, 112
  see also Thanatos
Decherf, G., 35
Decobert, S., 29
defence(s):
  mechanisms, 26, 29, 44, 61, 90, 96,
    102, 116, 125, 129, 173, 186,
    196, 219
  primary, 24
defensive alliances, 61, 207, 218, 223,
    241
defensive organizers, 35
deferred action [*après-coup*], 236
delusions, collective, 218
denial(s), 35, 39, 90, 96, 122, 153, 198,
    206, 213, 219, 220, 223, 234,
    238, 241
  common, 61
  community of, 207, 226
  joint, 41
  shared, 171
depersonalization, 26, 120
deposit, 25, 26, 58, 125, 174
depository, 58
depressive anxieties, 22, 129
Derrida, J., 46
Devereux, G., 14, 52, 203
dialogical principle, 49
dialogism, 152, 153
Diatkine, R., 29
Diet, E., 40
diffraction, 32, 100, 104–107, 114, 124,
    185, 202, 242
  of transference, 64, 65
disavowal, 206, 213, 219, 220, 241
discourse(s), 153–155
  associative, 62, 136, 140, 166

plurality of, 59, 62, 136–138, 151
discretion, 71
displacement, 32, 75, 83, 100, 103, 106,
    114, 124, 185, 202, 220
  of transference, 87
Dodds, E., 124, 168, 203
Dora (Freud's case), 62, 64, 101, 157,
    168, 169, 218, 221–224, 229,
    242
"group-", 104–106
Dostoyevsky, F., 152
dramatization, 105, 107, 114, 124,
    185
dream(s) (*passim*):
  address, 190
  analysis, 189, 204
    in groups, 189–190
  common and shared, 240
  constellation, 204
  countertransference, 181
  ego, 158, 185, 204
  fabric, of group, 183–188
  formation, 101, 179, 199, 203
  functions of, in groups, 188–189
  intrapsychic space of, 181
  matrix, common, 40, 200
  model, 32, 109
  narcissism of, 180
  narrative, 179, 186, 188, 190, 202
  navel(s), 182, 183, 190, 192,
    199–201, 236
  polyphony, 179–204
    in group, 183–190
  psychic space of, 180, 181
  royal road to the unconscious, 180,
    184, 203
  space, 34, 124, 131, 173
    of analytic situation, 182
    common, 13, 192, 194, 195, 199,
      200, 203
    polyphonic, 239
    primal, 195–198
    shared, 34, 179–204, 232, 236,
      237
  theory, 179–181
  thoughts, 64, 104, 185, 200
  -work, 181, 182, 190, 199–202

dream-bearer(s), 13, 35, 40, 63, 126,
        146, 157–177, 188–191, 199,
        203
    phoric function of, 189
Durkheim, E., 9, 28
Duvignaud, J., 204

Eagle, M., xvi
echolalia, 205
echomimetisms, 205
echopraxia, 205
Eckstein, Emma (Freud's patient),
        104, 218–221
Ecole Freudienne de Paris, 30
Edelman, G., 98
ego (*passim*):
    adaptive function of, 28
    attacks on, 22
    ideal, 161
Eiguer, A., 35, 227
enactment, 185, 194, 201, 227
encystment, 213
enigmatic signifiers, 218
Enlightenment, 27
Enriquez, M., 67, 193, 194
epistemology of psychoanalysis, 10
Eros, 99
ethnopsychiatry, 125
evenly suspended listening, 52
evil-bearer, 169
Ezriel, H., 22

face-to-face setting, 53, 59, 62, 71
Faimberg, H., 67
Fain, M., 226
Ferenczi, S., 220, 221
fetish, 130, 227
fight–flight, 24
figurability through dramatization,
        107
Fliess, W., 104, 218–224, 229
Fogelman-Soulié, F., 49
Foulkes, S. H., xv, 2, 19–29, 32, 40, 51,
        109
Foulkesian group-analysis, 69
frame, 2, 54, 87, 223
    concept of, 25, 56–59
    frame of (metaframe), 59
    functions of, 58
    psychoanalytic, group as, 59–67
fraternal complex, 64, 102, 103, 173,
        192
fratricide, 209
free association, 57, 63, 135–137
French Revolution, 28
Freud, A., 104
Freud, M., 104
Freud, S. (*passim*):
    "A child is being beaten", 99
    Civilization and Its Discontents, 113,
            122, 207, 208, 210, 211
    *The Complete Letters of Sigmund Freud
            to Wilhelm Fliess*, 95
    On Dreams, 104
    The Ego and the Id, 101, 197
    and Fliess, treatment of Emma
            Eckstein, 218–221
    "Fragment of an analysis of a case of
            hysteria", 221, 222, 224
    The Future of an Illusion, 122, 207,
            208
    *Group Psychology and the Analysis
            of the Ego*, 3, 10, 11, 101, 121,
            159–161, 161, 208
    history and work of, creative
            subjectivation in, 221–228
    Instincts and Their Vicissitudes, 133,
            232
    The Interpretation of Dreams, 101, 108,
            110, 201, 220
    metapsychology of, 240
    "On narcissism", 11, 44, 195, 211,
            241
    *New Introductory Lectures on Psycho-
            Analysis*, 4
    "Notes upon a case of obsessional
            neurosis", 99
    "Project for a scientific psychology",
            98
    "Psycho-analytic notes on an
            autobiographical account of a
            case of paranoia", 99
    The Question of Lay Analysis, 52
    Studies on Hysteria, 64, 98

Three Essays on the Theory of Sexuality,
    108, 133
Totem and Taboo, 10, 52, 141, 154,
    159–161, 192, 207, 209
"Two encyclopaedia articles", 13, 38
Friedman, R., 188, 189
fundamental rule, 53–57, 71, 92, 135,
    165, 223

Gaburri, E., 189, 204
Gallese, V., xvi
gamma function, 165, 188
Gestalt school, 22
Goldstein, K., 22
Granjon, E., 35
Green, A., 102, 124
Grotstein, J., 59
group(s):
    agglutinated nucleus in, 25–26
    analysis, 22–24, 59
        Foulkesian, 69
    application of psychoanalysis to,
        17–36
    associative functioning, 142
    associative processes in, 135–155
        functioning of, 138
    basic, 24
    belonging, 25
    cohesion, 25
    concept of, 39
    dream polyphony in, 183–190
    dynamics, 9
    effects, 10, 30, 34, 70
        of unconscious, 10
    envelope, 34, 185
    field, 20, 109, 188
    formations, 24, 33, 116
    functions of dreams in, 188–189
    illusion, 33, 34, 127, 186, 187
    and individual, epistemological
        transcendence of the
        opposition between, 8–12
    interactionism, 22
    internal, 13, 21, 34, 64, 85, 86,
        93–108, 114, 117, 119, 124,
        127–129, 132, 149, 185, 186,
        201

    forms and processes of, 98–107
    primal, 98, 99, 100
    primary, 100–103
    secondary, 103
    as unconscious organizing
        schema of the group links and
        of the group as a whole, 113
    as intrapsychic formation, 13,
        93–108
    like a dream, 115
    as locus of its own psychic reality, 33
    matrix, 107, 109
    mentality, 24, 27, 109
        three positions of, 130–131
    metapsychic functions of, 4
    mind [*Gruppenpsyche*], 9, 10, 19, 26,
        29, 56, 93
    morphology, 60, 67, 106
    neuronal, 98
    as object of instinctual
        investments and unconscious
        representations, 112–113
    operative, 20–22
    phenomena, 17, 26, 39, 177
    position of subject within, 40
    practices, therapeutic, 19
    primary, 23, 35, 94, 107, 154
    processes, therapeutic, 35
    psyche [*Massenpsyche*], 39, 47, 109,
        221
    psychic, 98, 107
        primal, 99
        split, 98, 107
    psychic apparatus, 13, 34, 41, 42, 52,
        109–133, 153, 157, 171, 188,
        237, 242, 243
        model of, 112–116
    as psychic matrix, 23
    psychic organizer, 116
    psychic reality in/of, 34, 40, 69, 77,
        93, 138, 213, 237
        forms and processes of, 109–133
        logical levels in, 44–47
    psychic space of, 183
    in psychoanalysis, epistemological
        problem of, 37–52
    psychoanalysis extended to, 9

group(s) (*continued*):
  psychoanalytic investigations into,
    17–36
  psychoanalytic psychodrama in, 59
  psychoanalytic research into, 34–
    36
    French, 27–36
  psychoanalytic setting, 12, 33, 42,
    53, 66, 228
  as psychoanalytic situation, 53–68
  psychoanalytic theories of, first,
    26–27
  psychoanalytic thinking about, 18,
    35
  psychoanalytic work in, 69–92
  psychotherapy/therapy, 23
  relation of subject to, 40
  representations, 33
  scene, 114
  setting, 13, 17–19, 30, 36, 56, 94,
    106, 131, 151, 199
    countertransference in, 63–66
    transference in, 63–66
    use of, for patients suffering
      from neuroses, psychoses, or
      borderline states, 17
    use of, for collective traumas, 17
    use of, in supervision, 17
  situations, morphological
    characteristics of, 59
  small, 9, 24, 214
    psychic functioning of, 24
    as psychic object, 32
  soul [*Gruppenseele*], 10
  space, 14, 62, 64, 77, 92, 94, 119,
    126, 128, 129, 132, 153, 175,
    184
  as specific entity, 23, 26, 70
  as specific psychic reality, 39–40
  techniques, 28, 31
  therapeutic, 59
  therapeutic processes, 35
  therapeutic properties of, 23
  thinking, 13
    psychoanalytic, 35
  as totality, 22
  training, 59

  transference, 33
  unconscious phantasies of, 21, 23
  unconscious psychic organizing
    phantasy of, 85–86
  work, 24, 212
groupality:
  internal, 97, 98, 107, 186, 202
  intrapsychic, 70
  psychic, 13, 34, 93–108, 94, 95, 96,
    101, 102, 105, 107, 111
    processes of, 103–106
Gruppenpsyche [group mind], 9–11
Gruppenseele [group soul], 10
Guillaumin, J., 223

Haag, G., 35, 59
Hegel, F., 14
Heisenberg, W., 50
Henriet, J., xii
historicization, 232, 236, 242
hologrammic principle, 49
homeomorphic pole, 128
homosexual identifications, 74
homosexual link, 219
homosexual love, 221
  narcissistic, 192
  object-, 208
homosexual seduction, 235
homosexual tie, 219, 222
homosexual transference, 222
Husserl, E., 14

ideal-bearer, 13, 35, 40, 126, 157, 169,
    172, 176
identification(s) (*passim*):
  adhesive, 61, 124, 190, 205
  affective, 79
  common, 40
  community of, through shared
    symptoms, 224
  heroic, 173
  homosexual, 74
  hysterical, 100, 101
  introjective, 124, 168, 205
  narcissistic, 205
  network of, 94, 95, 100–101
  primary, 26, 197

projective, 25, 61, 124, 148, 168,
    173, 174, 190, 197, 205, 226
specular, 205
subjectivizing, 235
symbolic, 209
through symptoms, 149
urgent, 61, 72, 90, 119, 120, 127
ideological position, 130
Idol, 130
imaginary twin, 103
imagos, 95, 96, 97, 121, 194, 237
incest, 5, 83, 88, 149, 209, 210
barrier, 150
individual:
    and group, epistemological
        transcendence of the
        opposition between, 8–12
    as link in chain, 44
individual treatment:
    negative pact in, 218–221
    unconscious alliances in, 218–221
infantile sexuality, 3, 38, 39
instinctual drives, 39
institutional psychotherapy, 28
institutional setting, 67
interactional sociability, 25
interactionism, 14
    behavioural, 14
    group, 22
interdiscursivity, 53, 59, 62, 136–138,
    150–152, 202
intermediary [Mittelsmann], 159, 160,
    176
    category of, in Freud's thought,
        158–161
internal group(s), 93–108
    as unconscious organizing schema
        of the group links and of the
        group as a whole, 113
interpretation(s) (passim):
    "wild", 78, 80, 83–85, 138
interpsychic spaces, 51
intersubjective chain, 241
intersubjective links/linking, 1–6, 12,
    19, 35, 94, 131, 146, 170, 199,
    206, 212, 218, 224, 237, 239,
    240, 246

unconscious psychic reality of, 3
intersubjective reciprocity, 14
intersubjective relations, space of, 46
intersubjective space, 40, 126, 153,
    203, 245
    and subjective space, frontiers
        between, 246
intersubjectivity, 2, 13–15, 47, 112,
    168, 171, 182, 206, 231, 232,
    236–240, 243
    concept of, 6–8
    metapsychology of, 20
    subject in, 44
    theories of, 6
    work of, 89, 90, 155, 188, 236, 237
intertransference, 65, 66, 87
intertransferential analysis, 66
intrapsychic discontinuity, 158–159
intrapsychic formation, group as,
    93–108
intrapsychic reality, 181, 243
intrapsychic space, 9–10, 40, 46, 77,
    103, 110, 126, 129, 153, 159,
    182, 198, 203, 212, 218, 245
    of dreams, 181
introjection, 95, 97, 100
introjective identification, 124, 168,
    205
"Irma" (Freud's case), 104, 220
Isaacs, S., 22
isomorphic pole, 126–127, 130

Jaques, E., 122
jouissance, 227
Jung, C. G., 220, 221

Keplerian cosmology, 48
Kestemberg, E., 29
Khan, M., 188, 227
Kirshner, L. A., xiii–xvi
Klein, M., 9, 22, 24, 181
Kreisler, L., 196, 197, 198
Kurosawa, A., 70

Lacan, J., 6, 10, 17, 29, 30, 31, 98, 164,
    177, 232
Laing, R. D., 133

language, 3, 10, 26, 75, 99, 125, 152–
155, 160, 167, 198, 202, 243
Laplanche, J., xv, xvi, 100, 108
Lawrence, G. W., 204
Le Bon, G., 9, 28
Lebovici, S., 29
Lemoine, G., 29
Lemoine, P., 29
Levinas, E., 14
Lévi-Strauss, C., 151
Lévy-Bruhl, L., 177
Lewin, K., 9, 28, 29, 31, 39, 177
libido, oral organization of, 26
limitation, principle of, 55
link(s)/linking:
configuration, 1, 48, 49, 52, 127,
176, 217, 246
contractual forms of, 5
disturbances in, 19
economy of, 242
forms of, diversity of, 60
functions of, 158
intersubjective, 2, 5, 6
unconscious psychic reality of, 3
intrapsychic, 61
organization of, 50
psychoanalytic theory of, 4, 228
subject of, 2, 13, 228, 231–242
Losey, J., 170

Mack Brunswick, R., 221
Mahler, M., 196
Massenpsyche [collective mind], 10
Masson, J. M., 95, 219, 229
Maury, L. F., 179
mazzerism, 203
Mead, G. H., 14
mediation, 5, 158, 227
Meltzer, D., 103, 181, 189, 196
memory-bearer, 170
messenger (go-between), 170, 172,
173
metabolization, 137
metaframe, 59
metapsychic container, 115
Migone, P., xvi
mind, collective [*Massenpsyche*], 10

Missenard, A., xii, 60, 61, 193, 194,
195, 197, 228
Mittelsmann, 159, 160, 176
Modell, A., xv
Montaigne, M. de, 14
Moreno, J.-L., 9, 28, 29, 31
Morin, E., 49
multifactorial indetermination,
principle of, 47, 51
multiplication of identical element,
32, 104, 105, 114, 127
murder, 5
myth(s), 9, 117, 168, 198
mythopoetic position, 130, 131

Napolitani, D., 34, 96, 97
narcissism, 35, 41, 45, 103, 169, 187,
198, 210
child's, 11, 195
of dreams, 180
secondary, 212
of sleep, 180
narcissistic contract(s), 5, 7, 45, 121,
122, 171, 207, 211, 243
primal and secondary, 212
"narcissistic gang", 103
narcissistic identification(s), 205
narcissistic impulses, 112
narcissistic love, homosexual, 192
narcissistic pact, 130, 212
narcissistic suffering, 5
Narcissus, 99
negating alliance, 226, 241
negation, 100, 213
negative pact(s), 61, 171, 207, 213–
216, 223, 226, 228, 234, 235
in individual treatment, 218–221
Neri, C., 109, 132, 204
neuroses, patients suffering from, use
of group setting for, 17
Neyraut, M., 181, 193, 204
Nicolis, G., 49, 133
Northfield hospital, 24

"O", 129
object-relations, 4, 44, 94, 95, 98, 100,
102, 173, 222, 237

system of, 95, 100, 102, 171
oedipal conflict, 173
    nuclear, 26
Oedipus complex, 64, 102, 208
omnipotence, 30, 128, 130, 147
organizer(s):
    defensive, 35
    phantasy, 85, 117
    sociocultural, 34, 117
    unconscious, 33, 34, 97, 137, 151,
        185
Orobitg-Canal, G., 204

pact(s):
    between Brothers and with Father,
        122, 207–212, 216
    narcissistic, 130, 212
    negative, 207, 213–216, 218, 220,
        221, 223, 226, 228, 234, 235
Palos, G., 220
paranoid anxieties, 22
part-object(s), 24, 106, 216
    relations, 26
Pasche, F., 228
Perrin, M., 204
personality, psychotic part of, 58
perverse contract, 207, 227, 241
phantasy(ies):
    organizer, 85, 117
    primal, 95
    shared, 6, 13, 40, 101
    structural approach to, 99
    unconscious, 21–24, 237
        of group, 21, 23
phoric function(s), 13, 35, 40, 63, 90,
        124, 126, 146, 157–177, 217,
        224, 232, 237, 239, 240
    of dream-bearer, 189
    general characteristics of, 173–177
phoric location, 171, 173
Piccioli, E., xii
Pichon-Rivière, E., 2, 19–29, 34, 40, 51,
        96, 97, 109, 133, 176, 177
Pigott, C., 35
Pinel, J. P., 212
pleasure principle, 165
pluridiscursivity, 153

plurifocality, principle of, 47, 48
poetic illusion, 164
polyphonic principle, 47, 48
polyphony, 48, 49, 139, 150, 151, 152,
        153, 183, 190, 199, 201, 202,
        204
    dream, 201–202
polysemy, 73, 92, 140, 202
Pontalis, J.-B., xv, 31, 32, 33, 36, 100,
        108, 112, 188
portavoz, 51, 176, 177
possibility, principle of, 55
preconscious:
    collapse and disconnection of, 5
    work of, 5, 150, 153, 154, 155
Prigogine, I., 49, 133
primal Horde, scientific myth of, 207
primal phantasies, 95
primal repressed, 217
primal repression, 60
primal scene, 73, 77, 84, 87, 143, 170,
        216
    phantasy of, 73–77, 87, 143, 146,
        147, 173
primary defences, 24
primary group, 23, 35, 94, 107, 154
    links and matrix of, 41
primary identification, 197
primitive, bizarre objects, 218
principle:
    of limitation, 55
    of possibility, 55
Privat, P., 35
probability, subjective, 50
process(es):
    primal, 123–124
    primary, 24, 34, 64, 100, 103, 104,
        107, 114, 123–124, 137, 180,
        184, 185, 202
    secondary, 117, 123–124
    tertiary, 123–124
projection(s), 60, 221
projective identification, 25, 61, 124,
        148, 168, 173, 174, 190, 205,
        226
    empathic, 197
Pryor, D., 103

psyche(s):
  group combination of, 33–34
  three pillars of, 3–4
psychic apparatus:
  agencies of, 95, 96
  group, 13, 34, 41, 42, 52, 110–112,
    116, 120–121, 126, 129, 131,
    153, 157, 171, 188, 237, 242,
    243
    model of, 112–116
  individual, 42, 52, 111, 131, 159
psychic conflicts, composite dynamics
  of, 241–242
psychic cradle, primal dream space as,
  195–198
psychic groupality, 13, 34, 93–108, 94,
  95, 96, 101, 102, 105, 107, 111
psychic material, constancy and
  transversality of, principle of,
  47
psychic organizer(s):
  group, 116
  unconscious, 70, 95, 117, 118
psychic personalities, multiplicity/
  plurality of, 95, 101
psychic reality:
  common and shared, 89, 111, 117,
    138, 240
  group, 2, 13, 34, 40, 41, 53, 59, 61,
    69, 70, 77, 85, 90, 93, 95, 110,
    111, 116, 117, 120, 122, 131,
    132, 137, 138, 169, 213, 234,
    237
    logical levels in, 44–47
  unconscious, 2, 3, 38, 39, 40, 42, 93,
    95, 120, 181, 213
  transformation of, 42
psychic space(s), 2, 12, 44–48, 51, 58,
    70, 89, 111, 126–129, 136, 161,
    168, 169, 173, 174, 179–182,
    185, 188, 190, 195–199, 203,
    216, 232, 236
  common and shared, 6–8, 39, 45,
    46, 93, 198
  of group, 38, 41, 44, 94, 113, 122,
    126–129, 182–183, 198, 231,
    239

of dreams, 180, 181
family, 45
heterogeneity of, 112
individual, 14, 34, 40, 44, 210, 240
three, psychic formations in, 46–47
psychoanalysis:
  application of to group, 17–36
  clinical, in group situation, 69–92
  definition, 38
  epistemology of, 10
  extended to groups, 9
  theoretico–clinical objects of, 53
psychoanalytic process, efficacy of, 55
psychoanalytic setting, 56–59
psychoanalytic situation, group as,
  53–68
psychoanalytic training, 29
psychodrama, 28, 29, 31
  group, 125, 127
psychology of learning, 22
psychoses, patients suffering from, use
  of group setting for, 17
psychotherapy:
  individual, 2, 8–12, 15, 18, 19,
    24, 37, 38, 42, 43, 53, 54, 59,
    62–67, 70, 101, 135–138, 154,
    181, 183, 190, 191, 199, 239,
    242–246
  institutional, 28
psychotic anxieties, 24
psychotic part of the personality, 58
psychotic patients, 10
Pujet, J., 21, 50, 227

Quiroga, A. de, 21

Racamier, P.-C., 188
Rat Man (Freud's case), 99
reality principle, 124, 165
reciprocity, intersubjective, 14
recursive retroactive loop of effects on
  causes, 49
regression, 5, 24, 102, 184, 186
rejection(s), 18, 30, 39, 90, 96, 103,
    114, 122–127, 147, 153, 206,
    213, 220, 238, 241
  shared, 61

reparation, 88, 91, 124, 138, 140, 144,
    147, 167
  demand for, 78, 87, 90, 148, 214
representation(s), group, 33
repressed:
  primal, 217
  return of, 41, 63, 88, 90, 91, 140,
    142, 153, 169, 188, 214, 220,
    241
repression(s), 3, 5, 6, 26, 27, 35, 61,
    72, 90, 96, 116, 120, 122, 147,
    153, 164, 165, 183, 206, 213,
    217–220, 223–226, 234, 241
  primal, 60
  secondary, 217, 226
resistance(s), 10, 22, 30, 33, 55, 64, 66,
    82, 83, 89, 118, 137, 142, 183,
    194, 218, 221–225, 235
reverie, 182, 184, 195
reversal into opposite, 32, 124
Rickman, J., 22
Rimbaud, A., 14
Robertson Smith, W., 192
Rogers, C., 29
Róheim, G., 115, 158, 203
Romano, E., 21
Rosenfeld, H., 102
Rouchy, J.-C., 34, 35, 106
Ruffiot, A., 182
Ruitenbeek, H. M., 9
rule of abstinence, 71, 83

Sacerdoti, C., xii
Saint Denis, H., 179
Sandler, J., 59
Sautet, C., 83
scapegoat, 126, 169
Schaltstücke ["connecting pieces"], 64
Schreber (Freud's case), 99
Schur, M., 229
Searles, H., 196
secondary narcissism, 212
self-alienation, 7, 122, 123, 234
semiotization, 175
setting, 2–4, 10–12, 26, 33, 37–38, 42,
    52–57, 62, 107, 127, 132, 135,
    181, 216, 223, 228, 245

analytic, 43, 180, 203
  classical treatment, 18
  concept of, 56–59
  face-to-face, 53, 59, 62, 71
  group, 13, 17–19, 30, 36, 56, 63, 66,
    94, 106, 131, 151, 199
  institutional, 67
  psychoanalytic, 56–59
    group as, 59–67
  spatio-temporal, 63
signifier(s):
  enigmatic, 218
  "last quarter of an hour", 84–85
situation:
  concept of, 56–59
  psychoanalytic, group as, 59–67
sleep, narcissism of, 180
slip of the tongue, 75, 76, 143, 147
small group, as psychic object, 32
sociability:
  interactional, 25
  syncretic, 25
social psychology, 8, 11, 21, 25, 29, 31,
    159, 177
  psychoanalytic, 21
Social Security system, 19
sociocultural organizers, 34, 117
sociometry, 31
space(s):
  group, 14, 38, 46, 48, 62, 64, 77, 89,
    92, 94, 119, 126, 128–129, 132,
    153, 169, 175, 184, 187
  interpsychic, 51
  of intersubjective relations, 46
  intrapsychic, 9, 10, 40, 46, 77, 103,
    110, 126, 129, 153, 159, 182,
    198, 203, 212, 218, 245
  transpsychic, 46
Spaltung [splitting], 41, 232, 233
speaking, meaning of, 138
specular identification(s), 205
speech-bearer(s), 7, 13, 21, 27, 35,
    40, 51, 63, 81, 82, 88–91, 126,
    139–146, 155, 157–177, 198,
    243
  functions of, in groups, 165–168
  maternal function of, 162–165

Spielrein, S., 220
splitting, 35, 39, 61, 90, 96, 186, 213,
      218, 233
   of transference, 64
Springman, R., 108
stimulus barrier, intersubjective
      mechanisms of, 5
Stolorow, R. D., 14
Stroeken, H., 222, 229
structuralism, radical, 232
subject:
   -bearer(s), 146, 171
   concept of, 232–233
   subjected, 233
subjection, 201, 232–238, 242
   concept of, 233
subjectivation, 6, 35, 50, 70, 88–89,
      129, 221, 231–236
   concept of, 232
   intersubjective matrix of, 231–237
subjective probability, 50
subjective space and intersubjective
      space, frontiers between,
      246
subjectivity(ies), 5, 7, 38, 44, 66, 90,
      112, 126, 137, 163, 165, 184,
      223, 228, 231–234, 238, 245
   correlations of, 7
   intersubjective bases of, 5
sublimation, 5, 211
superego, 101, 158, 161, 166, 238
   archaic, 161
symbolic identifications, 209
symbolic representation, 32
symbolization, 5, 6, 60, 122, 155, 160,
      175, 176, 223
symbolized Father, 208
symptom(s), 39, 46, 55, 61, 64, 87, 114,
      137, 158, 169, 172, 175
   -bearer, 13, 35, 40, 63, 126, 146,
      157–177, 224
   formation of, 35, 41, 124
   identifications through, 149
   joint, 13
   mutual attachment to, 223
   shared, 84, 217, 224, 241
syncretic sociability, 25

Tarde, G., 9, 28
Tedlock, B., 204
thanatophor, 40
   see also death-bearer
Thanatos, 99
thinking:
   complex, three fundamental
      propositions of, 49
   group, 13
"third topography", concept of, 40,
      239, 240, 243
toilet–breast, 112, 189
Torok, M., 35, 169
totemic contract, 208
transference(s) (passim):
   central, 33
   common and shared, 51
   connection of, 106
   diffraction of, 65, 106
   diachronic, 64
   displacement of, 87
   group, 33
   homosexual, 222
   horizontal (group), 21
   idealizing and persecutory, 215
   lateral, 23, 33, 64, 242
   negative, 142, 148
   objects, 33, 107, 57, 65, 139
   positive and negative, 148
   splitting of, 64
   vertical (individual), 21
transferential field, 21, 27
   –countertransferential field, 1, 57
transformation(s), 53, 100, 152–153,
      158, 188, 195, 201, 232–236,
      239, 240
   laws of, 96
   medium of, associative process as,
      137
   process of, 12, 110
   failure of, 5
transgenerational chain, 44
transitional analysis, 58
transitional space, 158
transpsychic space, 46
transsubjectivity, 15
transversality, principle of, 48

traumatic experience, 91, 138, 155,
200
traumatic violence, collective, 228

uncertainty, principle of, 47, 50
unconscious (*Ucs.*) (*passim*):
concept of, 2, 26, 39, 42, 110, 237
dynamic of, 241
effects of, 13, 17, 31, 34, 39, 56, 69,
135–137, 171, 180, 181, 236
group, 10
hypothesis of, 39, 93, 179
knowledge of, 3, 8, 38, 42–43, 48,
51, 57, 135–136, 239
as aim of psychoanalytic work, 42
infinitude of, 43–44
non-repressed, 35, 39, 237, 240
return of, 35
primal, 39, 60, 98, 234
as primal internal group, 98–99
psychic experience of, 245
repressed, 35, 39, 203, 237, 240
subject of, 1, 2, 8, 10, 13, 20, 27,
35, 41, 44, 67, 94, 107, 112,
115, 116, 154, 172, 176, 207,
231–242, 232, 246
theory of, 239–242
topographies of, 240
unconscious alliance(s), 1, 6–8, 13, 34,
40, 41, 45, 65, 66, 72, 90, 107,
115, 116, 120, 123, 125, 132,
137, 144, 169, 171, 232–241

concept of, 205–229
defensive, 61, 122, 217
in Dora's analysis, 221–223
in individual treatment, 218–221
narcissistic, 224
negative, 224
offensive, 207, 212
perverse, 224
structuring, 207–212
unconscious organizers, 33, 34, 97,
137, 151, 185
unconscious phantasies, *see*
phantasy(ies), unconscious
unconscious wish(es), 6, 24, 32, 115,
172, 173, 181, 194, 203, 205,
215, 224, 240
dream-fulfilment of, 184
utopian position, 130

Vorochilov, V. N., 152, 153

Wallon, H., 25
war, traumatic neuroses engendered
by, 19
Weber, M., 9
Weller, A., xii
whirlpool/chaos, 128, 129, 151
Widlöcher, D., 62
Winnicott, D., 7, 58, 155, 158
word-presentation(s), 59, 62, 79, 90,
141, 154
work group, 24, 212